OVERCOMING

THE LEGACY OF

OVEREATING

How to change
your negative eating habits

Updated Edition

Nan Kathryn Fuchs, PH.D.
Foreword by Hyla Cass, M.D.

Originally Published as
My Mother Made Me Do It

Lowell House
Los Angeles

Contemporary Books
Chicago

About the Author:

Nan Kathryn Fuchs, Ph.D., is the author of *The Nutrition Detective: A Woman's Guide to Treating Your Health Problems Through the Foods You Eat* She is the Nutrition Editor of *Women's Health Letter*, and has a private nutritional counseling practice in Sebastopol, California.

Library of Congress Cataloging-in-Publication Data
Fuchs, Nan Kathryn.
    My mother made me do it : how your mother influenced your eating
patterns—and how you can change them
Nan Kathryn Fuchs.
        p.   cm.
    ISBN 0-929923-10-3
    ISBN 0-929923-27-8 ppbk.
    ISBN 1-56565-453-6 update
        1. Eating Disorders—Psychological aspects. 2. Mothers and daughters.
    3. Food habits—Psychological aspects. 4. Nutrition.
    I. Title.
    RC552.E18F83   1989 89-15764
    616.83 ' 25—dc20

Requests for such permission should be addressed to:
Lowell House
1875 Century Park East
Los Angeles, CA 90067

Text Design: Laurie Young

Manufactured in the United States of America
10 9 8 7 6 5 4 3 2 1

ACKNOWLEDGMENTS

I am deeply grateful to my friend and editor, Janice Gallagher, who pursued me until I agreed to write another book and who was instrumental in its shaping; and to Tricia Hoffman, whose quiet love, total support, and cooking allowed me to work long hours and still eat properly. To Susan Amerikaner, who led me to Laura Eldridge and Tricia Hadden; to each woman I interviewed; and to those in my practice who contributed to this book by teaching me more about eating disorders through their openness and sharing, my sincere thanks.

No book is written by a single author. This one is greatly enhanced by the unselfish cooperation of a number of people whose loving honesty and support were accompanied by an expert analytical eye. My appreciation to all the other health professionals who read early manuscripts, granted me interviews, and contributed to the final product: Kathleen Martin, Ph.D.; Fred Wilkey, Ed.D.; Carolyn Katzin, M.S., Guy E. Abraham, M.D.; Jim Rouff, M.S., R.D.; Stuart Z. Epstein, M.D.; Iris Black, M.A., M.F.C.T.; Valerie McIlroy; Sheila Horowitz, M.F.C.C.; and Melvyn Werbach, M.D.

Thanks to Jack and Ersie Kinney, who taught me not to be afraid of computers and who helped me tame my beast into a willing assistant; to my brother, Hal Fuchs, who lived through much of the early days with me and also knows the meaning of being a food packrat and compulsive overeater; and most especially to my mother, Jeanette Fuchs Allen, who gave me the best of everything she knew and has always been willing to learn more.

AUTHOR'S NOTE

Because we are not biochemically identical, we have different nutritional needs; therefore, it is important that you consult with a physician before making any major dietary changes as a result of reading any information in this book. A physician can diagnose physiological imbalances and monitor your progress.

Although this book deals with eating disorders, anorexia nervosa—self-starvation—is deliberately not included. Anorexia is an eating disorder often accompanied by such strong denial that it is best dealt with in private or group therapy, and the physiological damage that can result from anorexia should be initially assessed and treated by a medical doctor.

While this book was originally written for women, it pertains to men as well. When you see the word "woman," think of it as a person of either gender, and know that the influence a woman has on the eating patterns of her daughters applies equally to some degree on the eating patterns her sons develop.

All of the stories in this book contain inaccuracies. They were told to me by children who saw their mothers through the eyes of a child, not through the eyes of an adult. In all cases, mothers remembered the same incidents differently than did their children. Both sides of the stories are true, for it is what we believe, not necessarily what happened, that affects our choices and our lives.

To all mothers whose children remembered significant and insignificant events imperfectly, I apologize for any pain caused by these inaccuracies. It was never our intention to hurt you. You were wonderful mothers who did the best you knew how, and we were wonderful children, even if we didn't know it at the time.

This book is dedicated to all mothers and children.

A final note: the case histories included in this book are based on research and personal interviews. The names of individuals have been changed to respect their privacy, unless they have given their express permission to be identified.

CONTENTS

FOREWORD

Much of the work I do with patients is to educate them about the role of diet in emotional and physical health. I have given many of them Nan Fuchs's earlier book, *The Nutrition Detective*. Now she has gone to another level, presenting us with a sensitively written and solidly based explanation of the origin and treatment of eating disorders, from both psychological and physiological perspectives.

In my own psychiatric practice, I incorporate many of these same principles: family dynamics; the intrapsychic meaning of an eating disorder; and physical aspects, which can include hypoglycemia, food sensitivity, or other imbalances.

Food is the earliest and most consistent tangible "connector" between mother and child. It becomes associated in our mind with love. All the pain and conflicts around love and relationships can be, and have been, played out in the feeding arena. Many an unhappy woman has sat in my office, defensively, painfully, and with resignation, echoing the phrase, "My mother made me do it," and I have agreed—up to a point.

"Yes, your mother had an enormous impact on shaping your personality and habits. However, she also took care of you in the best way she knew how. Now, as an adult, you can begin to nurture yourself in the way you would like. You have the power to do for yourself what your mother couldn't do for you."

This process of reparenting oneself involves insight, forgiveness—of both mother and self—and techniques to uncover what one needs and how to get it. All of these components are found in Nan's current book.

Recent scientific research has proven that there is a powerful mind–body connection. Our thoughts, both conscious and unconscious, can make us either sick or well. Conversely, a physical imbalance can cause a variety of mental and emotional problems.

Nan Fuchs speaks about the physiological and psychological reasons why so many women have eating disorders. This book is about food and eating habits, yes, but it also covers the much larger area of relationships where love is the currency and food its symbol. She elaborates on how mothers have unwittingly passed on to their daughters confusing and harmful messages about the role of food and feeding, bestowing food as reward and withholding it as punishment.

Nan is quick to point out that mothers are not at fault but rather are themselves victims of their own childhood experiences. She goes on to offer practical solutions to break this harmful intergenerational chain so we do not automatically and unconsciously pass these problems on to our daughters. She shows us, too, how to heal our own inner child, still very much alive within the adult.

Examples from her practice illustrate the sensitivity with which she both listens and gives not only advice, but love, to her patients. The specific exercises she includes in each chapter enable the reader to follow her own self-help program, handing back responsibility for self-care while giving gentle support and guidance. This is the best of good parenting.

Overcoming the Legacy of Overeating is more than an excellent compendium of factual information on eating disorders. It is a wise, loving, and inspiring heart-to-heart talk with the reader. If love heals, then this book will do it.

Hyla Cass, M.D.

WHY A NUTRITIONIST?
AND WHY *THIS* NUTRITIONIST?

As I began to write a book on eating problems, I asked myself, "Why me? Why isn't a psychotherapist writing this book? A number of therapists have written books on this specialized subject, but none, I realized, has been able to combine the emotional aspects with the nutritional. Many of my patients with eating disorders were already in therapy when they came to me for advice. They came looking for the missing link that would enable them to break out of the cycles of bingeing or overeating and guilt.

This book is based in part on my practice and on the way I work with people who have eating disorders, combining the understanding of these eating patterns with an individual's nutritional needs. Many eating disorders are cultural. They originate in childhood and are patterned after the habits of our mothers, aunts, grandmothers, or other women who raised us. Out of these diverse experiences comes an unhappiness that is the result of using food for a dozen different reasons other than its original purpose—to nourish. The pattern of weight gain, guilt, low self-esteem, and health problems begins to be passed down in many of our families from mother to daughter.

I have noticed that an extremely large number of women I counsel come from families where the mothers did not teach the daughters to cook because of a lack of knowledge, time, or interest. As adults, the daughters feel overwhelmed by the realization that they lack the fundamental skills they need in order to feed themselves, and they rely heavily on fast foods, restaurant meals, and frozen dinners—all of which are often too high in sugars, fats, and sodium. Unless they learn how to cook, these women are likely to teach their own daughters to rely on such foods as well. As a nutritionist I eliminate many misconceptions and myths surrounding food, and I guide these women to books that will help them learn basic skills for cooking healthful, tasty meals.

Like the people I interviewed and those I work with in my practice, I grew up with an overeating problem. My story also weaves its way through this book. What surprised me most as I gathered material was how much I saw myself in other women's anecdotes. It's likely that you, too, will see yourself here and there in the scenarios in this book.

If you have children, your story doesn't stop with you. You risk passing your eating problems on to them, continuing a pattern that may have been in your family for generations. Your struggles and your unhappiness can be passed on more easily than can skills such as tying shoelaces or buttoning blouses, for children watch us closely and mimic our actions. With awareness, love, and dedication, you can break these habits and free yourself, your children, and generations to come.

I know. I became a nutritionist to solve my own health problems, which had resulted from years of overeating and abusing food. I grew up with allergies, food cravings, and low blood sugar. Even after I began to unravel my health problems and eliminate some of my symptoms, I did not become the vital, healthy woman I am today until I broke free from overeating. Bingeing always created some health problems in me. I'm certain that if I had chosen to have children, I would have passed my overeating on to them unless I was able to first change it in myself.

Probably the biggest reason I turned to food was my feeling that there was a lack of love in my life. I had no friends, and I had never felt close to my mother. I felt unloved and unlovable. Eventually, I was given a number of opportunities to look at myself differently, both through my own eyes and through those of others, and I discovered that I was filled with a love I had never been able to express.

Part of that love I give to my patients. In addition to talking about nutrition, we also talk about their loving themselves and how they can get to that place inside of them. I am not a psychologist, but I find that when I sit quietly with my patients and share my love with them we can discuss food in a nonthreatening, nonjudgmental way.

For example, nothing I had said in my months of work with Eva had enabled her to stay away from sugar long enough to feel good. Her years of drinking alcohol had caused her to have low-blood-sugar moodiness and fatigue, and her use of antibiotics for several months to eliminate a series of colds had given her a vaginal yeast infection that would not go away. This overgrowth of yeast, *Candida albicans,* was being fed by the sugars in both her food and the alcohol. As long as Eva drank and ate desserts, I knew she wouldn't feel good. After months of encouraging, supporting, cajoling, and prodding her, I was ready to admit defeat.

One day, Eva was walking out the door, her head down and her feet stumbling. I could tell from her expression and body language that she felt all we had done in that session was repeat information from past sessions rather than finding the magic formula she was seeking. I felt frustrated.

"When you love yourself as much as I love you," I told her, looking into her eyes, "you'll take care of yourself and stop eating sugar."

In that moment, something happened. Eva heard me, and she felt the love. Tears started to pool in the corners of her eyes, and she turned to give me a tight hug. "Thank you," she said. Then she left.

After Eva had been able to avoid sugar and alcohol for several months, I asked her what the turning point had been for her. "I could love myself," she said, remembering how her mother had always focused her love and attention on Eva's younger, prettier sister. "When you told me you loved me, I finally got the permission I was waiting for."

Love is transforming, and when it is accompanied by information—such as understanding the physiological reasons for bingeing and what you can do to correct them—the transformation can be dramatic.

This book takes an important step in solving the problems of overeating by looking at them from several points of view. It contains some information you may already know, as well as nutritional information so new that even your doctor may not be using it—for example, the fact that the nutritional answer for people who feel powerless to stop eating starches and sweets is to restore the body's biochemical balance.

It has not been my objective to cover every issue surrounding negative eating patterns, but rather to discuss some of the most common areas I've seen. If this book helps you gain a different perspective on your eating problem than you have gained through therapy or nutritional counseling alone, it will have played an important role in your journey to freedom. And because I have seen so many people with eating disorders who have come from homes where their parents also ate inappropriately, I believe this book can help you to free yourself and your children from the guilt, shame, and unhappiness that come from overeating.

In a lot of families with problems, denial is the major way of dealing with pain. Children are told that problems they see aren't there—"Your mother does *not* have a drinking problem. She's in bed because she doesn't feel well today." As a result, they grow up not trusting what they see or hear. Many people turn to food as one way of supporting the denial they have learned in their homes. This book is one tool you can use to move beyond the denial you learned as a child and look honestly at the issues in your life.

Overcoming the Legacy of Overeating can be the book that helps you to integrate your emotional work with a therapist or 12-step program with a nutritional program. Since there are few nutritionist-therapists available to put the two components together, you will have to make some of the connections and design a program that includes both aspects. By working the steps at the end of each chapter you will have an emotional/physiological solution to your overeating.

My preference is for any person with an eating disorder to have group or individual psychotherapy to work out the emotional aspects of eating on a deeper level than is possible through any book. For those who are unable to afford therapy or to find a therapist knowledgeable about eating problems, Overeaters Anonymous is one free organization designed to provide emotional support around food issues. It can help you face your issues of denial in a caring atmosphere. The love and support you find when you talk with other people and realize you are not alone can give you more than any book. The combination of support and information is ideal.

Many people find that therapy and/or the support from a group like Overeaters Anonymous is enough. Others find that even with the best emotional support, something is missing. Like these women, you may find that your solution comes from a number of sources: you can combine seeking outside support with understanding how and why your particular eating patterns began, dispelling the myths you were taught about certain foods, learning how to balance your body's biochemistry, and practicing good nutrition. Like many of my patients, you will find the program in this book to be very compatible with a Twelve-Step program like Overeaters Anonymous.

Begin by becoming aware of what you need to do, whether or not you are able to do it at this time. Sit with your awareness for a few days. This awareness is your first step. It is allowing you to be conscious of both the emotional and physiological parts of your condition. When you can, take an action step and begin your program. Remember that being aware is not enough; it must be followed by action. Take the steps given at the end of each chapter, or devise others to more specifically fit your particular needs, and work them every day. This is how you change negative eating patterns.

There have been books on eating disorders written by therapists from the point of view of psychological imbalances alone; still others have been written by perceptive women who have shared their answers to their own problems. This book is a new model for working with eating disorders. It contains more than one approach. The combination of understanding good nutrition, being aware of biochemical imbalances, and addressing the emotional origins of your overeating provides you with enough information and insight to select the solutions, both emotional and physical, that apply specifically to you. Until nutritionists and psychotherapists begin working closely together, it is up to you to combine the two.

Because most psychotherapists know little about the effects of nutrients on eating disorders, this book is one that had to be written by a nutritionist. I hope the perspective provided here will bring you closer to your healing and give you the ability to break the chain of overeating that exists in your family. You deserve it—and so do your children.

INTRODUCTION

Overcoming overeating is not just a matter of discipline. If it was, all well-disciplined overeaters would stop bingeing. Overeating is not just an emotional problem you can stop by better understanding yourself. What then is the problem, and why does it persist? Seven years have passed since the first publication of this book, originally entitled *My Mother Made Me Do It*, and people still binge and stuff themselves to the point of discomfort. Dozens of books on eating disorders have found their way into bookstores and still people overeat. Why is this?

I believe most people overeat because they have not found a way to change their negative eating habits. They have not addressed both the *emotional* reasons for overeating and the *physiological* reasons. Herbert Benson, M.D., Deepak Chopra, M.D., and others, have shown us that the combination of mind and body is needed to provide us with permanent solutions.

But the majority of health care professionals, especially those working with eating disorders, still work with either one issue or the other. They have been trained in the workings of the body or of the mind and rarely consider the importance of the other—or they don't know how to integrate the two. Often, books and seminars touting solutions to overeating are given by people who have found their particular answer. But their answer isn't the answer for everyone. Only a combined body–mind approach, tailored to a person's individual needs, can result in a permanent solution.

Frequently there are biochemical reasons for overeating a particular food. Bingeing on chocolate, for instance, is often a sign of a magnesium deficiency. Chocolate happens to contain more magnesium than any other food, and a chocolate craving can be your body's way of giving you the information that you need more magnesium. All the willpower in the world won't take away your craving for chocolate until you increase whole grains and beans—sources of high magnesium—or add more magnesium to your nutritional supplements.

Similarly, if you eat candy and cookies as a reward for getting through a difficult day at work or with the kids, you need to understand where this pattern began and find other satisfactory rewards, not just take a magnesium tablet. Bingeing on sweets in general—not just chocolate—is not the sign of a magnesium deficiency. Physiologically, it can be due to low blood sugar, an overgrowth of a yeast called *candida*, or your body's sensitivity to refined sugar.

Your bingeing may have begun after incidents of childhood sexual abuse in which case just regulating your blood sugar may not be enough to overcome your overeating. In fact, many people who overeat have been sexually abused—both men and women. Often they stuff their feelings and memories of being abused by eating or use food to separate themselves from their bodies and feelings. While this is certainly an emotional response, the foods they choose to eat may contribute to physiological imbalances. So, once again, the whole person needs to be addressed. It is never enough to look at only one side of this two-sided coin.

Overeating may be a response to depression, either temporary or long-term. If you have few pleasures in life, eating too much of a food that tastes good may be one of the only enjoyments in your life. There may be biochemical reasons for your depression, especially if you have suffered from it for many years. Although many people look at depression as being purely emotional, or treatable only with pharmaceuticals, nutritional solutions have been well documented in scientific studies. Here, again, we need to look to the mind–body solution to change your eating patterns.

The emotional aspect of overeating frequently begins in childhood. Since mothers are the people who usually buy, prepare, and serve food to us from infancy, many of our emotional patterns go back to the relationships we had and have with our mothers. It is not their *fault* that we overeat, but they may be at the core of our conscious or subconscious reasons for doing so. In fact, many eating patterns are passed down from generation to generation. We tend to eat the kinds of foods our mothers prepared. We don't eat breakfast when our mother's skipped this meal. We punish and reward ourselves with foods as they did. For this reason, most of the chapters on overeating and the emotions address the mother/child issues. Unknowingly, our mothers passed along to us a legacy of overeating, and unless we break this pattern we are likely to pass it along to our children, as well.

If you overeat and have tried other methods to control or conquer this problem, you have not looked at both the emotional and biochemical components. Until you do, you may be forced by either your body or your mind to continue your struggle. This book will help you design a program specifically for your needs. Each chapter highlights a reason for overeating and ends with steps to take to move beyond this obstacle. *You must work these steps daily for at least three weeks to initiate a new pattern, otherwise you will only have a good understanding of your problem, not the solution you seek.* The solution to your condition is based on action, not understanding. This book is designed to give you the tools. The action is up to you.

Overeating is a negative eating pattern. Just as you took steps to form this pattern, you must take steps to change it. Old patterns are easy to continue. They are familiar even when they're uncomfortable. It takes time to get used to an unfamiliar action, but eventually it, too, becomes familiar. The people who have taken action to bring balance both to the emotional and biochemical sides of their overeating pattern have stopped their struggle and obsession with food. I did. You can, too.

A note about gender: This book was originally written for women who overeat and for their daughters who often adopt similar eating patterns. But we are aware that women are not the only people who overeat, nor are daughters the only children who take on their mother's patterns. We would like to encourage men to use this information to overcome their legacy of overeating. Please do not be put off by the frequency with which we refer to mothers and daughters, and the infrequency with which we address men and sons. This book is for everyone.

PART ONE

Generations of Pain

The deep bond between mother and child surrounding food begins in infancy, where food and love are intertwined. Our knowledge of food comes from our primary role model—our mother. No matter what we're taught about food in school, most of our knowledge of food and the majority of our eating patterns originate at home. Women are usually the caretakers within the family structure, and mothers often become role models for their children. They traditionally do the shopping and cooking, and when they're too busy to cook they put TV dinners in the microwave to feed themselves and their families. To understand our eating patterns, and those we unconsciously pass on to our children as their role models, we need first to examine the relationship between how and what we eat and the women in our family, from mother to daughter to granddaughter.

Some of the stories you read in this book may resonate strongly with you and remind you vividly of your own past. Because you will be looking at a number of emotional issues, you may want to take a closer look at the ones you identify with most before moving on to the next by selecting a chapter heading that speaks to you rather than reading straight through the book. Later chapters will discuss in greater depth the issues brought up in Part One. They present a number of solutions to problems touched upon in this section.

Because overeating is a legacy passed down from generation to generation, many of the Taking Action steps to take at the end of each chapter contain information for breaking that pattern both in yourself and in your children. *It is very important that you make the time to work them every day for three weeks.* By doing so, you can break your own overeating pattern. You can also help your children avoid the unhappiness and struggles you have had. What a gift you can give yourself and your family!

You will notice that some eating problems appear throughout the book in various forms. For example, if we associate food with love, we may eat when we feel unloved, or we may eat to avoid expressing our feelings when we don't feel loved enough, or secure enough to do so. This overlapping occurs in may people's lives. In fact, many of us overeat for multiple reasons.

The rest of Part One introduces you to a variety of self-help tools, including affirmations, one of the most successful methods for retraining your mind and emotions. Meditation is also included, not as a religious or spiritual practice, but as a method that teaches you how to listen to your body. A short, daily practice of meditation can help you identify your emotions and choose the kinds and amounts of food you need to give you greater health and vitality and help you to achieve your proper weight. This section concludes with information on the importance of gradually incorporating physical exercise into your program to help you decrease your appetite and give you a feeling of well-being and accomplishment.

1

FROM MOTHER TO CHILD TO GRANDCHILD:

How it Began and How it Can End

The pain of guilt that comes from overeating is like no other pain. It is with you whenever you eat—one, two, three, or more times every day—and it never leaves. It is a pain so deep and hurtful that it rules many peoples' lives. Some women feel so desperately unhappy and out of control around the issues of food that they decide against marrying and having a family in order to avoid passing their unhappiness on to their children. Others do marry, have families, and pass on their eating patterns to their children, especially to their daughters.

ELIMINATING BLAME

My own unhappy childhood led me to a decision in my twenties that dramatically changed the course of my life. Fearing that any child of mine would be as unhappy as I had been, I decided never to have children. I blamed my mother for not seeing my pain and making it all better. This decision was an admission of my own failure to create happiness in my life, along with a feeling of frustration at not knowing how to prevent the same despondency in another person.

This is my story and yours. Like many of you, I have been a compulsive overeater most of my life. As a child and young adult I was unhappy, unable to give or receive love, and I was overweight. Like many women, I blamed my mother for my unhappiness. At the time, I didn't even know why. As I examined my past, I realized she was instrumental in my having learned many of my attitudes about food. We share some of the same eating patterns, and I picked up some of my eating disorders from watching her. And yet she was never to blame.

If you have ever blamed your mother or anyone else for your unhappiness, it's time to stop, as difficult as it may be to do so. Most mothers did the very best they could and were completely unaware of what they were doing to themselves or of how much their actions influenced their children.

Lee and her mother, Helen, are one such link in a long chain of anger and blame. Meals were anxious, unpleasant times for Lee as a child, times when her parents would bombard her with questions for which Lee never had the right answers: "I remember my mother as being very critical. I felt under attack most of the time, especially at meals. I didn't feel safe. I never knew when I was going to be criticized or what I was being criticized for."

Lee grew up afraid to talk about her little fears and joys. She and her mother were never close. For a long time Lee was angry about this, blaming her mother for her own critical nature and for her emotional distance from the people she loved the most.

"No wonder I grew up afraid to talk about my feelings," she said. "My mother didn't encourage it. I eat to cover up feelings I can't express. It's not my fault; my mother is responsible for the way I am today. She made me do it."

Lee's mother, Helen, is an assertive, capable woman whose own mother was too busy playing cards, shopping, and talking with friends to stay home and fix meals. In fact, she was proud to be more than "just" a mother, and she had maids who cooked for the family. She and Lee were never close, and Helen resented her mother for not creating a homey atmosphere or teaching her how to cook.

"I remember sitting at the kitchen table, eating dinner alone," Helen said. "The maid was in the kitchen, staring out the window. She didn't talk to me. I always rushed through my meal and ran upstairs to my room and turned on the radio—I needed something to connect to, and there was no one there at home. My mother was too busy with her friends to spend time with me, so I spent a lot of time alone."

"Did you turn to foods as your friend?" I asked her.

"No, I enjoy food, but nothing more. I turned to my girlfriends at an early age when I felt alone or anxious. My mother had a sensual relationship with food. She used it to soothe herself. I didn't want to be like her, so I went in the opposite direction. I think a lot of my unhappiness as a child came from the way she treated me."

Both Lee and Helen blamed their mothers for their early childhood unhappiness, and Lee also blamed Helen for her overeating. Beneath this blame is an undercurrent of anger, and as long as the anger and resentment are present, it is difficult for both Helen and Lee to understand that their mothers did the best they could. Both have responded to the lack of communication in their homes, although they responded differently. No one was wrong. No one was to blame.

It took me many years to stop blaming my mother for the unhappiness I felt as a child. I realize now that she was an unintentional participant in a chain of overeating that began generations ago in our family. After talking with her recently, I finally saw where some of my habits began and understood the reasons for many of them. They were valid reasons at one time, but they are valid no longer. By understanding them I was able to free myself from patterns of overeating. You can, too.

THE (ROLE-) MODEL MOTHER

"Your daughter may grow up bingeing like you do unless you find a way to change," I said to Susan, startling her. She had come to me for nutritional counseling to help her lose weight, not to talk about her slender eight-year-old. "You were thin when you were a child, too, weren't you?" I asked, remembering some of the stories she had told me about her past.

Susan nodded yes solemnly, listening closely.

"Unless you change your pattern of overeating, you may pass on to her much of your unhappiness about being overweight and teach her to eat for the same reasons you eat. You may be teaching her about healthy foods and giving her moderate portions, but she's more likely to do what you do, not what you say."

I surprise my patients when I talk to them about their children. It rarely occurs to them that they are passing along their eating patterns and the resulting unhappiness to their children. Even when they blame their mothers for the women they have become, they do not see the connection between the way they eat and what they were taught at home. And when they do they often do not have enough understanding about why this pattern originated to break free.

Looking back, I realize that much of my unhappiness was expressed through food and resulted from overeating. I saw I had learned many of my eating habits from my role model, my mother, and I used food as she did for some of the same reasons: feeling unappreciated and unloved, and continuing the family habit of eating constantly, which was a cultural pattern. As I understood her *reasons* for always having more than enough food in the house and for cooking so many rich foods that made me heavy and even more unhappy—another family habit, combined with my mother's trying to fatten up my underweight father—I was able to forgive her and change my patterns. The more I opened myself to love—my own and others'—the easier my journey became. Understanding, forgiveness, and the creation of new habits and patterns were my keys to eating normally.

The implications are tremendous. You have more power than you ever dreamed. You have the power to create happiness and greater health in your own life and the ability to be a role model for your descendants. You can end the unhappiness you experienced as a child and still feel today.

ALL CHILDREN ARE DEAF—
BUT NOT BLIND

When you tell your child he or she does not have to stuff themself with food, it is not enough. All children are deaf. This includes your child who doesn't hear what you say, but sees what you do—and mimics you. If you eat quickly, your child probably eats quickly even when you tell her to slow down. If you eat until you're uncomfortably stuffed, so does she. If you grab a handful of cookies in the morning as you rush off to work instead of sitting down to breakfast, even though you prepare a good meal for her and tell her how important it is to eat well in the morning, don't be surprised to see her follow your lead when she's in a hurry.

Julie recalls, "My mother was always telling me to chew my food well and slow down. She reminded me that you eat less when you eat more slowly, and both of us ate too much. But we rushed through every meal. I almost swallowed my food whole."

Because they often finished before the rest of the family, Julie and her mother would have second, or even third, helpings. They were both overweight, and Julie was unhappy at her failure to control her overeating.

"Why did you eat so quickly?" I asked her.

"Out of habit, I guess. I remember one day when I tried hard to slow down. I chewed each mouthful until my food was almost lique-fied, but when I finished, I realized that my mother had had a second portion, and I didn't want to miss out. So I took another helping and wolfed it down."

"What made you continue eating quickly when you wanted to lose weight so badly?" I wondered.

"My mother kept eating fast. If it was such a bad habit, I figured she would have changed."

Your child does not understand that there's anything wrong with her actions when they are the same as yours. In her eyes, mother is the authority, if not the *infallible* authority. No matter what you say, she learns from your actions, not your words. If you are concerned about your daughter's eating habits, there may be little you can do to help her unless you change your own.

Even if they don't understand your actions, children see what you're doing. Whether or not they talk about it, they are aware of discrepancies between what you say and what you do. If you are in pain over issues surrounding food, chances are that your child sees your pain. When she sees your pain but you tell her nothing is wrong, she learns denial and becomes confused.

As you have insights about your own eating habits, share some of your observations with her. Include her in your healing instead of pretending your problems don't exist. Don't shut her out and make believe everything's all right. Whatever's not all right with you may not be all right with her as well. When you pretend, you teach her that pretending is acceptable. Your struggle is not a private one, and neither is your daughter's. This is a family issue with which everyone in the family can help, even the children.

YOUR MOTHER DIDN'T MAKE YOU DO IT

As a child I used food for a number of reasons: It was at times my friend, my mother, my reward, a way of "stuffing" my feelings. Food was frequently more than nourishment, and I misused it most of my life. Until a dozen years ago, I had spent the majority of my life overweight enough to feel uncomfortable and unattractive. My extra weight contributed to my unhappiness.

After I ate fatty meals of cheeseburgers, french fries, and milk shakes, I felt guilty. When I binged on chocolate and overate ice cream, I felt guilty. But accompanying the guilt was some small feeling of satisfaction, of soothing, that I received only through food. It was a trade-off—my heaviness and sluggishness for a little pleasure.

I believed my mother was to blame for all my childhood unhappiness without knowing why. There was no one else around I could accuse for my pain. And yet it was not until recently that I came to see my mother as a composite of the role models in her own family when she was a child: her mother and, to a greater extent, her grandmother. So, even though in a way "my mother made me do it," she was not to blame. My unhappiness and my resulting eating disorders were not her fault.

For a number of reasons, you may be afraid of becoming like your mother. The love-hate relationship many women have with their mothers is common. The more you see aspects of your mother in yourself, especially when they are negative qualities, the more you want to become her opposite. This fear, and the accompanying struggle to separate yourself from your mother, is often a source of deep unhappiness and anger. We are more likely to clearly see our mother's weaknesses, which we want to avoid, than her strengths, to which we give little significance. Yet we tend to be a composite of both.

Your mother and grandmother may have grown up in an age when people didn't talk about or examine their feelings like we do or have as much knowledge of nutrition and biochemical imbalances. Some of their attitudes surrounding food were cultural, and they never thought about them. In our struggles we all do the best we can at any given moment. You have the advantage of having more information available to you than your mother did. That's all.

As children, we are often helpless to understand what we're doing and to change, and it is the child within us who resorts to blaming others. You are not helpless any more; you are powerful. This book will help you regain and use your power to become a person who is more at ease with food, more at ease with your body, and infinitely more aware of the role food has played in your family and in your own life. By removing any blame you've placed on others, you open yourself up to receive more love. And love truly heals.

Take the time now to heal the hurt child inside you by beginning to understand how and why your mother may have misused food and where her attitudes came from, so you can stop blaming her. Become aware of the anger you have been storing, so that your anger and hurt can eventually be replaced by forgiveness. Forgiveness does not condone your action, as Stephen Levine says in his beautiful book, *Healing into Life and Death*. Instead, its purpose is to touch you with mercy and loving kindness. It allows you to move on rather than remaining stuck in your anger or resentment. Look at your own attitudes toward food that began when you were a little girl, and see how many of them have become a part of your present life, even when they don't work for you.

How it Began and How it Can End

Begin by reading this book, incorporating the suggestions on affirmations, meditation, and exercise. Then work the Taking Action exercises as they appear. These exercises begin in Part Two, "In the Beginning—and the End—Was Food." Some are designed to help you get more in touch with feelings you may not have looked at or worked through. Some may have questions for you to answer or suggestions for you to follow, such as writing a letter to your mother that is for your eyes only, or writing down an imaginary dialogue between you and your mother to help clear out old feelings of anger and resentment. They can help you to understand how, where, and why your eating disorder began. Other exercises will teach you how to choose the foods you need in the proper amounts. Still others will help you to help your daughter along with yourself.

You may initially skip the Taking Action exercises, but be aware that until you work them or take other action to change old negative eating patterns, it is unlikely you will have the success at overcoming your overeating that you're seeking. Awareness is the first step, but it is not the only step.

A notebook may be an important tool to help you organize these exercises and any notes you want to keep. You might write down passages from this book that are particularly meaningful to you so that you can reflect on them at a later date. Your notebook can also be a place where you collect recipes and menus to use in planning meals differently. It can become your own personal guide to changing patterns that no longer work.

Part Two of this book introduces you to the causes of a variety of overeating problems. It traces the association of food with love that we learned as infants, and it explores the many other meanings food takes on as we grow—for example, as a means of gaining attention and approval or as a method of communicating.

Part Three, "Emotional Answers to Emotional Problems," talks about the emotional effects the causes of overeating have on us. Each chapter contains anecdotes from the lives of people who have overcome and are continuing to work through their issues concerning a particular aspect of overeating. These anecdotes show you a variety of reasons why we overeat or eat inappropriately. Some people, like me, were never hungry and ate out of habit. Others saw food as a reward, as a substitute for expressing feelings, as a way of showing love, or as a way of getting approval. There are a variety of emotional reasons for overeating—a number of scenarios that are played out daily in homes throughout the country—and a number of solutions.

It is not enough to pay attention to whether or not you are hungry if you eat to keep from feeling emotional pain. You must understand where this pattern began, understand that it is no longer a valid response, and then find other ways of handling your pain and anger. It is not enough to put smaller portions of food on your plate and retrain yourself to eat less if eating large amounts was one way to please your mother and you try to please people who offer you food. First you have to see how and why you use food to make yourself feel valued, and then you must find value in yourself outside of food and reestablish new patterns before you will be free to eat, and serve, smaller amounts.

There is no one reason for overeating or one path to take to change any pattern. If the only solution lay in self-love and self-acceptance, people with biochemical imbalances could gain control over food through therapy. Part Four, "Physiological Answers to Physiological Problems," addresses some of the physical reasons we crave foods or overeat. It explores a number of biochemical imbalances and tells you how to identify and correct them. This section contains invaluable information for many of you who feel powerless over food. When you understand that it is not necessarily your will but a chemical imbalance that contributes to your behavior, and when you know what to do when you crave chocolate, sweets, bread, or other foods, you may find yourself finally able to change your overeating pattern.

Part Four also includes chapters on food cravings that will help you determine whether your overeating comes from food sensitivities or nutrient deficiencies (for example, a chocolate craving may be linked to a magnesium deficiency). This section explains why you may binge on sweets when your blood sugar is a little low, and it shows you how to eat to get the results you are looking for even when laboratory blood tests show you are not clinically hypoglycemic. It includes a new chapter on the biochemical aspects of depression, and how your eating patterns may be affecting your moods.

The chapters in Parts Three and Four all contain scenarios described by people I have counseled and interviewed. By looking at a number of different family scenes and recognizing yourself in one or more of them, you can better understand the core emotional reasons for your overeating patterns, and you can examine yourself to see whether there may also be a physiological reason for why you eat as you do.

As you read the scenarios in this book, you may see yourself clearly in one of them, or you may see parts of your life scattered throughout several. I believe you will find something of value to begin your journey of healing in these stories, which are designed to help you find your way out of the daily pain you experience surrounding food.

Use the questions and suggestions at the end of each section to explore your past and present and to change your future. Talk with your children and share this information with them. Bring them into this process of change you are entering, because they are already part of your pattern. Silence and denial did not help me, they have not helped you, and they will not help your children. They can only reinforce your patterns.

Part Five, "Your New Program," leads you further away from your problem by offering a number of practical solutions. These solutions are applicable to all of us, no matter how or why we have misused food in the past. This section begins by addressing the myth of good and bad foods. Often, we avoid a particular food because we erroneously believe it is bad for us. As you will see, few foods are truly bad; in most cases there are foods that are simply "better" than others. With a clearer understanding of how particular foods affect you, you are now ready to design an individual eating plan that will help you remain physically and emotionally free from food cravings and negative eating patterns.

For cultural reasons, we tend to eat differently during holidays and celebrations. Part Five contains a chapter on how to eat during these times without feeling like an outsider or slipping into old familiar patterns of overeating, while still enjoying ethnic dishes and being part of a familiar celebration that is unlikely to change. As I've said, many of our patterns began at home. It is unreasonable to expect your family to understand or support you. Be grateful if they do, but be understanding of them if they don't.

It is difficult to make dramatic changes in your life by yourself. Part Five concludes with a number of suggestions you can use to support yourself, including having the support of friends and of a peer group such as that found in Overeaters Anonymous or other Twelve-Step programs. Because individual therapy provides specific insights and support you cannot find in any book, this book concludes with suggestions for finding both a nutritionist and a therapist, should you decide to pursue this path.

EATING PATTERNS ARE LIFE PATTERNS

Your eating patterns affect more than your weight and health. They are often repetitions of other negative patterns in your life. The way you act around food is likely to be the way you act in other areas of your life. If you don't make time to prepare the healthful foods you need and instead find yourself having to grab empty calories, you may not make time to prepare a report for work or clean the house. If you make excuses and rationalize about an eating habit you don't like, you are likely to make excuses for other things. Do you start diets or eating programs, only to drop them before they're finished? You are likely to lack follow-through with projects at work, school, or around your home.

Susan never managed to find time to plan meals or to stock her kitchen with healthy staples so she could fix a proper meal at the end of a busy day. Whenever she was in a hurry, she'd pick something up for dinner at a fast-food restaurant. Lately, this had begun to happen often, and even though Susan knew the fatty foods she was eating were not good for her or her daughter, she continued to procrastinate. Planning ahead had never been her forte.

Susan also put off cleaning her house unless she had to. Like shopping for groceries, cleaning was not a priority. She would often get by with a minimum of each. Eventually, Susan woke up: "I realized that if I cleaned my house it was like giving myself a present. I didn't have to live in that garbage anymore. One day I told my daughter, 'We're going to clean this bedroom.' She asked me, 'Why? Is someone coming over?' I understood just how far my procrastinating had gone. Look what I was teaching my daughter! We were living in garbage, and we were eating garbage!"

The degree of success you experience in your life may well be reflected in the success you have surrounding your issues with food. As you take action by removing the barriers and eating more healthfully, and as you gain understanding and control over food, the rest of your life will shift. When you realize you are worth taking the necessary time to prepare food ahead of time so there is something healthful for you to eat when you come home after a busy day, you are more likely to take time for a lunch break on even the busiest of days. You are more likely to take care of yourself in other ways— finding time to exercise, to practice relaxation exercises, to meditate, to do something you enjoy rather than spending all of your time working.

When you make time for yourself, you are teaching your children to do the same thing. When you love yourself enough to look at your eating patterns and try to understand where they came from, and why, in order to move beyond them, you're teaching your children to love themselves, too. When you concentrate on becoming a happier person you're telling them, "Happiness is important. It's worth spending time on yourself so you can be happy. I'm worthwhile, and so are you." And because you're saying this with actions, your "deaf" children will "hear" your message clearly.

Eating is one of the most often repeated patterns in your life. Most of us eat three or more times every day. When you feel overstuffed, sick, bloated, angry, depressed or guilty over the kinds of food or the amount you've eaten, you are reinforcing your unhappiness and dissatisfaction. When you eat appropriate amounts of healthy food most of the time, you are reinforcing your feeling that you are taking care of yourself. Your eating patterns permeate your life and color other activities. When you change some of your eating patterns, other habits change as well.

It is not selfish to take care of yourself. This is an important lesson both for you and to teach your children. Taking care of yourself is modeling healthy behavior. It is one of the most important things you can do for yourself and your family. When you take care of yourself, you are not being a burden to others. You are showing your capabilities and demonstrating them to those around you. Take care of yourself so you can take care of others. Give to yourself freely so you know what it's like to receive. That's what it feels like to other people when you give to them. Experience your gifts, and then pass them on to your children.

FIRST THINGS FIRST:

Affirmations, Visualization, Meditation, and Exercise

Lola wanted to get married and have children, but at the same time she was afraid of turning out like her mother: a perfectionist who had had difficulty finding happiness in her relationships with men. All of Lola's relatives told her that she resembled her mother much more than did any of her four sisters. She and her mother both had blue eyes and had the same coloring, and their personalities were similar.

At first, this made Lola feel special. Then, as she grew older, she feared becoming too much like her mother. When she first came to see me for counseling, I realized that she overate when she was depressed or unhappy.

"My mother seemed to be unhappy a great deal," Lola remembered, as we sat piecing together parts of her childhood. "She and my stepfather argued a lot and were always leaving each other. I felt that all of her children were a burden, especially me, so I kept my own problems and unhappiness to myself."

Lola was aware of her family dynamics, but the understanding she received through private psychotherapy sessions and from me was not enough to help her change her eating patterns. We made a little progress in a few months, but both Lola and I wanted more. Finally, it was an affirmation that enabled her to stop fearing she would turn out like her mother. The steps we took to formulate Lola's affirmation may help you as well.

"I'd like you to use an affirmation for a few weeks to see if it will help you understand the differences between you and your mother on a deeper level," I suggested. "There may be a few little aspects of your personalities and experiences here and there that are similar, but there are huge differences. She got married at a young age and had lots of children; you chose not to get married. That's an enormous difference. Right now, you can never be like a mother with children. Do you see this?"

She nodded slowly, but I could tell she was still afraid of becoming like her mother.

"How's this?" I asked, beginning to formulate an affirmation for her: "I am different from my mother."

Lola's face brightened.

"Your fear is that you will be *exactly* like her—that you will try to be perfect and fail. But if there are aspects of her personality you see in yourself that you don't care for, you can say, 'I would like to change this part of me,' and work on changing it. And you can also look at the parts of her that give you something positive and say, 'I'd like to keep that quality.' "

"I never admitted it before," Lola said, after thinking about my comments, "but I didn't look at her positive qualities. I was too busy trying to avoid the negative ones."

"What do you like about your mother?" I asked her.

A smile spread over Lola's face as she began: "All of us children turned out well. We were all smart; we never got into trouble. There was always enough food when we were growing up, even during the hard times. Mother was creative. She always made things work. If she got lemons, she made lemonade. I really admire that in her, and I never said it before." Her eyes held back tears, and her voice was thick with emotion.

"You do that, too, you know," I told her. "No matter how hard things are, you look for a solution until you find it. You're very much like your mother in that way." Lola sat quietly and took my comment in. She could accept being a survivor, like her mother.

"Did she do the best she could?" I continued.

"Yes," Lola answered, "my mother did the best she could. She did. She had a lot of adversities and a lot of limitations that she'd gotten from her own mother. Let me add that to my affirmation." She said the words slowly: " 'My mother did the *best* she could.' Oh, boy," she sighed. "That feels good."

"Do you do the best you can in your life?"

"Most of the time, I do. I would say I do the best I can a lot of the time."

"Is that all right? Is it okay not to be perfect all of the time, even though you would like to be?" Lola nodded. "So," I continued, "you do the best you can most of the time. Just like your mother." She smiled.

"I think we have your affirmation," I told her. "Try this one on: 'My mother did the best she could. I am responsible only for my own happiness, and I am the happy, healthy, balanced person I always wanted to be.' "

"I don't know about that last part," Lola disputed. "I don't feel happy or balanced now."

"I know. But an affirmation is an expression said in the present tense, even though it may not be true at the moment. Try it on for size. Say that part out loud a few times."

She did this, but the last sentence still didn't feel comfortable to her. "It brings up a lot of emotions inside me," she said.

"Good. I think you feel these emotions because something inside you recognizes the truth in this statement. There is a part of you that is happy, healthy, and balanced. When you feel emotions well up inside you, it is an indication that your affirmation is true.

"The more you say it, the better it will feel, because you'll hear and see more of the truth in it," I continued. "At the beginning, you didn't realize that your mother's limitations were no different from yours. And your limitation of not being perfect at times, while still doing the best you can, came from watching her do the best she could."

"There's a lot of forgiveness in what you're saying," Lola said to me. "Self-forgiveness and forgiveness of my mother. I haven't had a lot of that in the past."

We met a few weeks later, after Lola had repeated her affirmation for about ten minutes each day. She was looking and feeling much better and had not overeaten as frequently as she had in the past. She admitted that something inside her was slowly changing.

"I know you were skeptical about using affirmations the last time we met," I said. "How do you feel about them now?"

"I used to have a lot of doubts about them, because I thought they were taking me out of what was reality. But what I thought was real was only part of the truth," she admitted. "I thought affirmations were silly, that they were about things that weren't going on. I don't feel that way today."

Lola's fear of becoming like her mother and her resulting unhappiness was a major theme that wove its way through her life and affected many of her relationships. The affirmation she used helped her to look at her fear more realistically and see that she would never be like her mother. While she had denied it in the past, Lola was now able to admit for the first time that her mother had qualities she admired and that these are qualities Lola likes in herself, as well.

AN EASY WAY TO START

Whether you are held captive by biochemical or emotional bonds, it takes more than intellectual understanding to break them. Just knowing what's been going on is not enough to eliminate the negative eating patterns you've had most of your life or to help your daughter change patterns she has learned from the person she trusts most in the world—you. These patterns have been reinforced by beliefs and actions, and to replace them you need to combine understanding with substituting other actions. Daily affirmations and meditations can help you do this.

Begin your day with these techniques. They will set a tone that permeates your thoughts and actions. Each Taking Action section in Parts Two through Five begins with an affirmation to help you move into new patterns. The importance is in regular, daily practice, not in any particular technique. If you want to replace a technique given here with another one, by all means do so. Just use it daily.

Why daily instead of occasionally? Because food patterns are daily patterns. You have been eating every day, and you have been repeating many of your thoughts and feelings about food to yourself for years. They have become part of you.

Affirmations, visualization, meditation, and both physical and emotional exercises will all contribute to changing your inner and outer patterns—if you practice them. They won't help you if all you do is read about them. If you are skeptical, use your skepticism to find out for yourself what they can do by using these exercises for a few months. These techniques have a venerable history of success, and a growing number of medical doctors include them as part of treatment. If you use just one-tenth of your past dedication to unhappiness to rededicate yourself to healing by making time in your life to practice these techniques, they can help you change your life. Surely, your happiness, and your childrens', are worth half an hour a day.

Affirmations, Visualization, Meditation: What's the Difference?

An affirmation is a verbal technique that helps you reprogram some of your basic belief systems. When you tell yourself throughout the day, "I can't stand myself—I go right on eating foods that give me headaches and make me gain weight, even though I know better. I'll never feel good or look good in clothes," you reinforce your belief that you are a person who will constantly fail and will continue to eat the wrong foods. Affirmations can help you change your belief. A statement like "I'm slender and eat only those foods that nourish me" is an affirmation that can be used to counteract this negative belief.

We're constantly talking to ourselves, giving ourselves messages, and reinforcing our attitudes. An affirmation is a technique for changing this kind of programming from negative to positive.

Visualization, another technique for reprogramming, is like a visual affirmation. Instead of saying "I am slender and eat only those foods that nourish me," you imagine yourself as being slim, choosing healthful foods in appropriate quantities, and enjoying them. By repeating this visual image, you slowly counteract the way you have been seeing yourself: heavy and eating junk food, or eating too much. The visualization makes it easier for you to change your outer response.

Meditation has come to have different meanings to different people. When I speak about meditation, I'm not talking about just being relaxed, or about contemplating your navel, or about anything else but a mental discipline. Meditation is a technique that teaches you to be focused and to pay attention—not only to food, but to everything in your life.

Meditation teaches you to listen. A short, daily practice of meditation is one of the best methods I know for learning how to listen to the information that comes from within. Your body has innate wisdom. It will tell you what it needs if you only stop long enough to listen, so you can follow its directions. Meditation will help you identify your emotions when you are confused and don't know what you're feeling, or why. The answers are inside you. Meditation teaches you how to get to them.

Meditation does not necessarily have anything to do with religious beliefs or spirituality. No matter what religion you practice, meditation can be a comfortable and appropriate tool to use to help you retrain your mind and change your attitudes about yourself, food, and people around you. It is one of the most powerful techniques I have experienced. I urge you to incorporate ten or fifteen minutes of meditation into your daily life to see for yourself how beneficial it can be. A simple meditation technique is included later in this chapter, and several books that can teach you other meditation techniques can be found in the Resources section. Not everyone will be drawn to meditation or will be willing to try it. But for those who are, the rewards include much more than breaking free from eating patterns.

Meditating for ten minutes daily, doing affirmations five minutes or so a few times a day, writing down an occasional exercise in a notebook or diary, and taking a brisk walk or doing other physical exercise four or five times a week will result in a well-rounded program that retrains your mind, body attitudes, and perceptions. I strongly suggest that you use all types of techniques, rather than one kind alone, to support changes on both inner and outer levels.

Affirmations

An affirmation is a positive statement made in the present tense that talks about who or what you would like to be in the future. By repeating it you become more receptive to its truth, which can allow the statement to eventually become part of your reality. You do not need to believe an affirmation in order for it to work. You can be skeptical, as long as you repeat the affirmation and give it a chance to sink inside you with its truth.

Each section of this book contains a specific affirmation designed to help you change your emotional or physical responses to situations in your life. Feel free to change any of them to suit yourself more precisely, but use them. Repeat each affirmation for five or ten minutes at a time, several times a day, to help you move through your problem areas.

An affirmation works best when it speaks to an inner truth or state of development—for example, "I am a good person" or "I love myself"—even if you don't completely believe it at the time. One of the most beautiful and simple affirmations I know is one from Emile Coué, a nineteenth-century psychotherapist: "Every day, in every way, I am getting better and better."

Affirmations work to help you change your attitude, and your attitude determines your outer reality—that is, what you do. The idea is not to change your outer reality with these phrases, but to change your inner reality. When your inner reality changes, it supports an outward change.

If you overeat to avoid feeling the pain of abandonment, an affirmation like "I am safe. I am secure. I am loved and comforted" will help ease that pain and, hopefully, will lead to less pain to cover up. Then you can look at the idea that maybe you don't have to eat as much, because there's less pain. Perhaps when you are in less pain you will be able to see more clearly that eating isn't a very good way to handle that kind of pain anyway, because it only works for a short time, is not very effective, and ultimately causes you even more pain.

Doing Affirmations. Keep each affirmation short, positive, and always in the present tense. To avoid being too scattered, limit yourself to working with no more than two or three affirmations at a time. Write down each affirmation on a three-by-five-inch index card, and carry the cards with you wherever you go.

Read them over carefully and thoughtfully for five minutes, either when you wake each morning, before you go to sleep, or during the day. Whenever you can, say the affirmations out loud. You might do this in the car or in the bathroom. Take them out and read them before you eat lunch, when you have time. If you are standing in line at the supermarket, bank, or post office, repeat them silently to yourself. Don't skim over them quickly to finish them as soon as possible. Changing reality takes a dedicated attitude.

If you reinforce your inner reality throughout each day by repeating affirmations, you should notice the beginnings of change within a few weeks. This slight change can be enough to encourage you to continue. It might not seem like much, but it may be a lot compared with what you've already accomplished—and the slight movement of a pebble has been known to start avalanches.

Visualization

A visualization is a pictorial affirmation. It works beautifully for people who are visually oriented. Some people are not; they respond to other senses, like hearing or feeling. You may respond on more than one level and decide to make an audiocassette tape with a visualization combining descriptions of images with the sound of your voice. To heighten your perception, you may want to use other senses in your visualization, like smelling the salty ocean air or feeling a warm breeze.

Use visualizations like affirmations, doing them several times a day, and more whenever possible. Don't be concerned if you "sense" an image rather than see it clearly. You may be one of the many people who do not get clear images. That's fine. Neither do I. I remember talking with friends many years ago about a visualization we were all doing. I felt awful when I realized they saw clear, sharp technicolor pictures in their minds, while my mind held more of a memory of the image than the image itself. I felt left out (one of my issues since childhood), incapable, discouraged, and as though I were a total failure. I felt like giving up, but I was too stubborn. I was surprised to discover my visualization worked for me as effectively as others' did for them, and I came to learn that the impression in my mind was as effective a tool for me as their clear pictures were for them. If you don't see or sense pictures at all, perhaps you're just not a particularly visual person. There's nothing wrong with that; you simply relate better with other senses, and you can choose to use a nonvisual technique, like affirmations.

Meditation

Some people feel as if they've meditated after sitting quietly and listening to relaxing music, taking a walk in the country, or jogging along quiet streets. These activities can have a meditative or contemplative quality to them, but they are not what I'm talking about when I speak of meditation. What I'm speaking about is *active* meditation.

Active meditation is a mental process whereby an attempt is made to focus all of your mind's attention on a particular focal point. This is difficult for most people, and it may seem impossible to you. You may not be able to place 100 percent of your attention on anything for more than a few seconds, at best. And yet, even though you know it is difficult, you can persist. When a distraction appears, take a passive attitude toward it, release the distraction, and bring your attention back to the focal point. This is what I mean when I speak about meditation.

This kind of meditation helps you to become more aware of everything you do. As you train your mind to pay attention to a point of focus during meditation, you are training it to pay attention to details and actions in your daily life. For example, you may sit down to eat dinner in front of the television and, several commercials later, look down at an empty plate. You don't remember tasting the food, and you don't remember chewing it. Somehow, your food went directly from your plate to your stomach!

If this sounds like you—if you repeat some of your negative eating patterns unconsciously—meditation may be a useful tool for you to use. It is a form of mind training that involves gently coaxing your mind to be a little more concentrated, a little less scattered, and a little less agitated. It increases your awareness of "here and now." If you eat mindlessly, or if you are so caught up in other things that you don't pay attention to what and how you're eating, meditation can be very valuable in helping you to become more aware of your actions. As you become more aware of them, you can begin to change them.

The Right Way to Meditate. If you're doing anything that helps you make any progress, you are meditating correctly. There are no "wrong" ways to meditate; there are just ways that are more effective than others. Most of the time, when people say they haven't meditated correctly, it's because they have incorrect expectations about what meditation should be like. It's very easy to build failure into the practice of meditation, because it's an unfamiliar technique that doesn't lead to immediate results.

Understand that meditation is a process, not a goal, so if you don't quiet your mind right away (". . . like in the first three years," laughs psychotherapist and meditation teacher Dr. Fred Wilkey, knowingly), it's no big deal. You will get results from meditation even if you can't stay focused and quiet your mind.

Meditation calls for practice, and it improves with practice. It's best to do it daily, sitting up, at about the same time and in the same place. The routine of doing the daily discipline of meditation is part of your retraining. Use meditation as part of a whole program rather than as the only technique you use to change your life.

In meditation there is always a point of focus. It may be walking, it may be looking at a flower, it may be a point on or in your body (for example, your heart), it may be a physical process like breathing, or it may be a repeated thought. You are attempting to put all of the attention of your mind on this focal point. The task is almost impossible, but you do it anyway, because that's what meditation is.

As noted earlier, whenever you become aware that your mind has scurried off to something else, you passively say, "Oh, well," without condemning or judging yourself, and release the distraction. Then you bring your attention back to your focal point. Repeat this again and again and again for as long as you meditate. This may sound boring, but it's actually not. (Well, occasionally it *may* feel boring at first, but that, too, passes!) I find meditation to be the time when I center myself each morning and find a quiet, peaceful place inside myself. From that point, I begin my day. Gradually, I have become more and more aware of details both inside and outside of me.

Often, the benefits you gain from meditation will appear to be coming from sources other than the meditation itself. You may find that you're not as bothered as you used to be by a next-door neighbor, or that you don't fly off the handle as often at the little things. You may attribute the change to something "out there," when actually it's a change inside yourself. Meditation changes the way you experience things.

An Easy Meditation. There's no one way to meditate that works for everyone. There are dozens of meditation techniques, ranging from the very simple to the very complicated. Don't set yourself up for failure by deciding to use a technique that's difficult for you. Set yourself up for success. One simple technique, described by Herbert Benson in his book *The Relaxation Response*, is not unique; Benson just formulated it in an easy way. This technique combines a mantra (a word or phrase repeated over and over) and breath.

With this technique, you can pick a word or brief phrase that feels comfortable to you in relation to your particular spirituality, or you can use a very general affirmation or even a neutral word. A very simple phrase like "I am love," "God is love," or "balance and harmony" will do. Or you may pick a word like *peace, joy, love* or *one.*

The Southwest American Indians have a very beautiful phrase, "walk in balance." It refers to the concept of walking in balance with the entire universe, letting every action you take be in tune with the flow of the universe. You could choose to use this phrase in your meditation.

Mentally repeat the phrase or word you have chosen every time you exhale. Keep your phrase short so that you won't get out of breath. Don't try to regulate your breathing. Sometimes your breath will be short, sometimes long. Your breathing may vary from shallow to deep. Just say your word or phrase on every exhalation.

Whenever a distraction comes along, say, "Oh, well," and go on to the next exhalation and the next repetition of the word or phrase. That's all there is to it.

How Long Should You Meditate? Begin with five to ten minutes a day. If you end up doing ten minutes, that's excellent. If you can gradually extend your meditation to twenty minutes, that's wonderful. Almost everyone will benefit from meditating for ten to twenty minutes once a day. And doing it twice a day is a real bonus.

You may not want to meditate more than twenty minutes twice a day, Dr. Wilkey suggests, because doing so can stir up some deeper mental/psychological processes that most people are not ready for and don't want. If you eventually decide to meditate longer, you may want to find a teacher to study with who can help you understand the experiences that come from longer meditations.

DAILY EXERCISE FOR YOUR BODY AND EMOTIONS

Physical Exercise

Physical exercise gets your body moving. Moving is the opposite of being stuck, and you may feel stuck in old patterns. Not only will you benefit physically by doing some exercise regularly, but you will also benefit emotionally by creating a pattern of movement where little movement may have existed in the past.

You may not feel much like exercising after you overeat. That's certainly understandable. But remember that you want to change some very old negative patterns, and exercise is one method that can help. Don't use it as a punishment for overeating. Just start to include a walk in your schedule as often as you can. It might be ideal for you to exercise daily, but be gentle with yourself. A ten-minute walk twice a week may not seem like much to someone who jogs five miles every day, but for someone who had done nothing, it's a beginning. It's better than no exercise at all, and you can eventually increase the frequency and length of time you exercise.

Walking is one of the best exercises you can do. Start with a ten-minute walk around your neighborhood or a nearby park on weekends, and gradually expand this to twenty minutes, four times a week. Aerobics, bicycling, or jogging are also very good exercise choices.

Exercise can actually effect a metabolic change, helping you burn calories more quickly and leading to the production of chemicals in the brain called endorphins. Endorphins make us feel good and can even block pain. They also tend to take away feelings of hunger, so after you exercise you may feel less hungry than you do when you don't exercise.

If you're the exception rather than the rule, have a glass of water or a piece of fruit after your workout. You may just be a little dehydrated, or your blood sugar may be a bit low. If you're eating at regular intervals, adding exercise into your schedule will likely make you more thirsty than hungry. Drink more water throughout the day. Then, when you think you're hungry, pay attention to what your body really wants, instead of responding automatically with a particular food because of its taste.

Don't use exercise as an excuse to overeat. Even a brisk thirty-minute walk won't offset dessert or a bag of potato chips. The idea is to use up some of your excess fat and tone your muscles. When you feel healthier by including exercise in your daily schedule, you will be more likely to want to continue having this feeling by eating healthful foods in appropriate quantities.

Emotional Exercise

The Taking Action sections at the end of each chapter in this book are your emotional-exercise program. They are an essential part of your success in overcoming your overeating. Writing down thoughts or memories from the past, keeping a food journal, and listing options for your actions so you can refer to them easily can be particularly beneficial exercises for both you and your child. As you understand yourself better and learn where your patterns originated, you will be able to talk with your child about your realizations. Encourage her to share her feelings with you.

Some of the techniques in these sections will help you to understand the emotional origins of your negative eating patterns. Others can help you to identify the presence of physiological imbalances and enable you to take steps to correct them. If you like, you can arrange these techniques in categories in your notebook to chart your progress. One category might be "My Family's Eating Patterns." Another could be a monthly calendar, with a place to check off your daily meditation, affirmations, physical exercise, and other activities that lead to your healing. You may want to have a section that includes exercises you do with your child, and the results of these exercises.

HOW TO BEGIN EACH DAY

The most important "food" to put into your body every morning is a positive thought. During the first fifteen or twenty minutes you're awake, recite an affirmation or read a scriptural passage or a page from an uplifting book. Start the day with a prayer, a forgiveness, or an affirmation. Then sit in meditation. Starting the day with a positive thought can change the character of your entire day.

I often start the day with a simple statement such as this: "Thank you, Lord, for this day. Show me how I can be of service to you." I find that I pay closer attention to the details of my life and take better care of myself and other people when I take a minute to center myself with a positive statement. Then I meditate.

Remember, meditation helps you listen to your body and hear its messages. You may want to begin your day with meditation to allow yourself to be more focused and calm. Then, depending on your preference and your schedule, you may do some physical exercise before starting your day's activities, or you may prefer to take a brisk walk after work. Affirmations or visualizations can be scattered throughout your day or placed into your schedule.

Begin slowly and gradually to add techniques and to increase the length of your practicing them. Don't push yourself too much. Find your comfort zone, and stretch yourself by doing a little bit more. Just remember to always begin your day with a positive thought. This is your first step in taking action and changing your old negative patterns.

PART TWO

In the Beginning— and the End—Was Food

Judy was two years old when she wandered into the kitchen and saw her mother sitting at the kitchen table with her grandmother. Her mother was crying uncontrollably. Judy had never seen her mother cry so hard, and she suddenly became very frightened. She didn't know that her mother and father were newly divorced and that her mother was crying from the pain and loss. She only knew she wanted her mommy. She desperately needed to feel her mother's love.

Judy's grandmother looked at the child, who had run over to her mother for comfort. She handed Judy a cookie and gently pushed her toward the door. Judy thus learned at a young age that food is love, and that it is often the solution to being upset. When there is nothing to comfort you, to hold you, to tell you you are loved, food is there.

Food is a constant in our lives. We eat every day unless we are sick or fasting or are the victims of a food shortage. When we are infants, mother is food. At that stage in our lives, food and love are one and the same. Food may continue to be used as an expression of love, or it may change into a means of gaining approval, a symbol of control or of a power struggle within a family, or a nonverbal means of communicating any number of things. We use it as a reward or as punishment, as an expression of denial, or as a way to keep busy, to calm down, or to get energy. For many of us, food is seldom used only as nourishment. It has taken on added meanings, which we rarely discuss and may not even be aware of.

Food is an important part of the way we celebrate special personal, historical, and religious occasions. When we eat overly sweet or fatty foods at these times, we may simply be entering into the spirit of the celebration, suffering little or no consequences. But when such eating becomes obsessive behavior, or when we are out of control, we have to look at whether or not we are using food in an appropriate and healthy way.

We come together in this country from many cultures, each of which has its own food and eating habits. We begin by eating like our parents. While we change a bit as our lives differ from theirs, many of the foods we now eat and many of our relationships to food come from our childhoods and from the roles played by our mothers, aunts, or grandmothers.

What and how we eat have become the subject of much controversy. While we continue to argue about which foods are the most healthful and how we can manage to find enough time to prepare them, we continue eating two or three times a day, sometimes more. Many of our mothers overate. Whether or not we are conscious of imitating our mothers, a tremendous number of us eat for the same reasons they did.

We gain weight and find that it is not culturally acceptable, so we look for a diet to help us control our eating habits—but without looking at how and why these patterns began in our families. We discover a new diet or nutritional program and become enthusiastic over its possibilities—until a friend shows us an article invalidating it and calling it a fad or, worse, dangerous.

No wonder we're confused. No wonder we give up and eat whatever we want. No wonder we overeat. It's time to take a closer look at how we eat, what we eat, and why we eat the way we do. We need to examine the various meanings we have given to food beyond its original one. When we understand the hows and whys surrounding our negative eating patterns, we begin to break the particular chains of overeating that exist in our families. When we know what we're doing, we can replace the patterns that have never worked for us with patterns that put food in its proper perspective. We can use food to keep us healthy and give us energy, and we can use mealtimes as occasions for sharing and enjoying our families as well as our food.

Our journey begins with a look at the many meanings food takes on in our lives as we grow. In the beginning food is love, but depending on our family, its meaning changes.

Chapter 2

FOOD AS LOVE

As infants, we associate food with love. Later, food becomes a substitute for love. Eating may give you a warm, comforting satisfaction that's so close to how you feel when you feel loved that you may get the two confused. You may overeat when you actually want to feel close to someone and there is no one to fill this emptiness. You might even choose foods that remind you of baby foods or foods from your childhood—for example, ice cream, mashed potatoes, or pudding—in an effort to recapture the feeling of being held and comforted as a child. Or you may deliberately withhold food from yourself because you believe that you must be a terrible person if no one loves you.

Feeling unloved is a major theme that runs through various eating-disorder patterns. Whether we see it clearly or whether it's hidden behind our need for attention and approval or our feelings of abandonment, loneliness, or anger, not feeling enough love is often at our core. Because we grow up with this association of food with love, we extend it to others. When we feed others, it is because we love them.

When I remember Grandma Drimmer, I remember her squeezing me until I thought I would suffocate and pinching my cheeks until I wanted to cry out—and I remember her always cooking. Grandma Drimmer wasn't much of a talker, but she was some baker. "Eat some cookies," she would insist whenever I visited, pushing a plate in front of me. And I sat at her kitchen table eating cookies while she watched me, smiling and refilling my glass of milk.

Grandma Drimmer was not my real grandmother. She was the mother of my mother's best friend, and she lived a few houses away from us when I was a child. Many years after she died, my mother happened to mention her. "She loved you very much," mother reminisced.

"Yes, I know," I answered. "She was very affectionate to people, but I never saw her squeeze and pinch other people as hard as she did me! And she always made me sit down with her and eat cookies, even if I wasn't hungry." I don't remember having had a single conversation with Grandma Drimmer, but I remember the love in her cookies.

Grandpa Fuchs (my real grandfather) never told me he loved me either, but somehow I knew he did as well. Whenever he visited he pulled packages of Lifesavers out of his coat pocket for me and my brother. The candy meant to me that my brother and I were special and that Grandpa loved us. It was the closest he ever came to expressing his feelings. Fortunately, I heard his message. Unfortunately, I carried it over into my life and turned to cookies and candy when I needed to feel a bit of love. When I went out on a date in college and my date didn't say he'd call me again, I ate candy.

Grandpa Fuchs and Grandma Drimmer were just two of the many people in my life who taught me at a young age that food is love. As I've said, we get this message from our mother from the time we're born, and we hear it again from family friends and relatives as we're growing up. Often, the message comes from several sources. As a result of all this, we grow up believing that food and love are one and the same.

Until we learn to separate food from love, until we look at food as nourishment and at feeding the people we love—ourselves included—as only one way of showing this love, we are likely to turn to eating whenever we feel unloved or whenever we want to express our love to others. This is a trap. Eating when we want to feel or show love is no solution at all. We can't fill an emotional emptiness with something physical. Eat as we may, even stuffing ourselves until we feel sick, we cannot feel emotionally satisfied by food. If this is part of your negative eating pattern, you may be unconsciously passing it on to your children, teaching them to overeat when they are looking for a feeling of love and caring.

TAKING ACTION

1. **Affirmation:** I give and receive love to nourish my life. I eat only to nourish my body.

2. **Be aware of how you feel *before* you overeat.** How long do you feel satisfied when you eat to fill the empty space? Does it last only as long as you're chewing, tasting, and swallowing? Do you feel unsatisfied after you finish eating? Be aware of how you feel while you overeat and afterward. Remember how you felt before. This is how you will feel when you eat enough and not too much.

3. **Are food and love the same for you?** Write down some of your feelings about food and love in your notebook. Do you eat when you feel unloved? Do you turn to food when you feel an emptiness that is not physical hunger? Was food used as an expression of love in your home or by friends when you were growing up?

    See if you can identify the difference between your need to feel loved and your need to stop the feeling of hunger. When you begin turning to food to fill an emotional emptiness, try to fill yourself with love instead.

4. **The Loving Heart Exercise:** Sit with your eyes closed in a quiet place (the bathroom will do, if all else fails!) and place your hands in front of you, palms up. Cup them to make a bowl. Visualize someone in your life who loves or loved you, or think of someone whom you love.

    See this love as something tangible, a substance that has

weight and form, and visualize it filling your hands until you can't hold any more. Feel your hands growing heavy with this pure love.

Now bring your hands toward your heart, and taking a deep breath, allow the love in your hands to fill you. Breathe in slowly and deeply until all the love you have gathered in your hands is in your heart. Think to yourself, "I am loved. I have value. I am enough, and this love fills me."

Use this technique instead of eating when there is no physical hunger and you are looking to feel love. If it is difficult for you to tell the difference between the two, fill yourself with love first, before you turn to food. Notice whether you eat as much, or if you are satisfied with less food.

5. **Speak your love:** Do you tell your children that you love them? When you feed them as an expression of your love, do you tell them what you're doing? Do they eat when they're upset or when they think they're unloved?

When you fix something special for them out of love, give them the love first as something separate from the food. Tell them you love them with words. Tell them they have value. Explain that words can't always express the depth of your love for them and that sometimes you want to show them how much you love them by buying or preparing some special food, but you don't want them to become confused and think they're the same.

Teach them the Loving Heart Exercise. Explain how they can fill themselves with your love whenever they need it. Being able to receive love can transform and nourish us more completely than anything else. Teach your children to receive your love and to love themselves. Teach them the difference between stuffing themselves with food and feeling filled with love.

4

FOOD AS ATTENTION
AND APPROVAL

Sonia put sprigs of parsley around the roast chicken, sprinkled paprika on the mashed potatoes, and added a few cherry tomatoes to the mixed salad. When everything looked picture perfect she brought it out to the dinner table. It was an ordinary night with no company.

Preparing meals day after day was boring. In fact, being a mother wasn't what Sonia had thought it would be. Instead of continuing to be the bright, creative woman she had been when she was first married, Sonia had become cook and housekeeper to a family of four. She loved her family, but she hated her work. There was nothing at all special about the daily routine of shopping, cooking, and cleaning. There was nothing in it that made her feel good about herself, and very little that made her feel she was worthwhile.

Although she often felt ignored throughout the day, dinnertime was when Sonia got attention for being a mother. She had noticed that her family fussed over her when simple meals looked pretty, so each night she tried to outdo herself. Who can blame her or any mother for trying so hard to be loved through food? Sonia's was a thankless job. For her, as for many mothers, being appreciated for the foods she cooked, arranged, and served was the answer to being ignored and the validation she sought that she was worthwhile and loved.

When my own mother wanted to please us she would buy our favorite dessert: Boston cream pie. If I had been ignoring her or if I had been particularly difficult that day, I suddenly became as sweet as that delicious pie. Oh, I would thank her over and over and tell her how much I loved her, just as I remembered to thank her and tell her what a wonderful mother she was when she baked the best choco-late-chip cookies I've ever tasted or made us chocolate pudding (especially the kind with nuts!). I remember thanking her often for the foods she prepared, and I also remember clearly the pause of expectation that preceded my thanks.

We feel loved for who we are or for what we do. Many of us did not grow up feeling that who we were was enough. We had to do some-thing tangible to "earn" a parent's love: get an A on an exam, write a poem, clean our room, or fix an elaborate meal. When we know we're loved, when we feel good about ourselves and do not need to find value through other people's eyes, a hug or a kiss can be enough.

But sometimes the people in our families seem to take us for granted. They may not see everything we do for them every day, and if they do, they may not tell us or show their appreciation. It's easy for a mother to feel discounted, especially if she doesn't see her own worth. Chances are that Sonia's mother was valued for being the family cook. My mother's grandmother, the person in her family who raised her, was a terrific baker who was praised for her cooking. No wonder my mother wanted to be appreciated for her special cooking skills.

But the message my mother gave me, and that Sonia is giving her daughter, is that you don't have value unless you do something out of the ordinary. You won't be appreciated for just being a caring person. The work you do every day is not enough. If you want some-one to pay attention to you, you have to go out of your way and make a special effort. You are not enough.

This is not the only reason women prepare food to get attention and approval. You may see your mother as a negative role model and want to be as unlike her as possible. If she happened to be a terrible cook, if she relied heavily on fast foods to keep the family fed, or if she simply didn't enjoy preparing meals, you may overcompensate by becoming an excellent cook. Where your mother sought approval in other areas—in her job, as an artist, as a volunteer for service organizations, as an organizer, as a good friend—you may look for attention from the elaborate meals you fix. You may use food to get attention and approval, not because you feel you are not enough, but to separate yourself from your mother.

If being a mother is your primary job but you feel less than worthwhile in this role, you may be looking for appreciation from your family. If you are seeking approval by preparing particular foods rather than simply believing that your role in the home has immense value, this is what you are teaching your children. When you do not feel you are enough as a mother, you pass on this feeling as well. Your children will grow up knowing somewhere inside them that being a caring person is not enough for them, either.

When you prepare something special, it can be a gift of compensation—a way of feeling less guilty for not spending more time with your family. If you have another job besides that of being a mother, fixing foods your family likes may be one way to continue feeling good about yourself in your role of homemaker. If you do not enjoy the rewards of being a homemaker, you may be teaching your daughter that being a wife and mother is less satisfying than having a job outside the home. It is important for you and your children to realize that both of you are enough as you are.

We don't always feel we have value for just being who we are, so we place value on the work we do. Being a loving person is enough. Sometimes we place too much value on outside jobs, but all the work we do has tremendous value. Raising a child to be happy, healthy, and loving may be the greatest contribution any person can give to the continuation of life on this planet. Everything you do has value, not just cooking meals or preparing special foods for family and friends.

When the work you do is fulfilling to you, it's not necessary to seek approval or recognition from other people. You know within yourself that you've done a good job, and that gives you satisfaction.

Even packing your childrens' school lunch can be a source of satisfaction when you become aware that you are providing them with nutritious foods that taste good and you are being a role model. When you prepare food mindlessly and see it as a dreary chore, you are overlooking both its importance and yours.

If you enjoy cooking and preparing elaborate meals in an attempt to be different from your mother, you may want to put the attention and approval you gain from this in its proper perspective. While it's gratifying to have friends and family praise you for your meals, learn to enjoy the feeling of satisfaction you get in the preparation. Don't put all the emphasis on the comments of others. Your comments have value. Your own praise and recognition of the meal is sufficient.

Your real value in life comes from being a loving, caring person. If you go out of your way to find or fix particular food that friends or family members enjoy, just knowing how much they enjoy it can be enough satisfaction. If they give you no thanks or recognition when you serve it, it may be because they are preoccupied or upset. Even if they say nothing, their taste buds recognize the food; you are giving them enjoyment whether or not they thank you. The attention and approval of other people is not as important as your own recognition of your worth.

TAKING ACTION

1. **Affirmation:** Who I am is enough.

2. **Getting attention from food:** Did your mother look for compliments after she made a special meal or favorite food? Pay attention to your motives for buying or preparing foods your family especially likes. Keep a list of people-pleasing foods you buy or make for one week. Make a note of how you feel when you serve one of these foods and whether or not anyone tells you how much he or she appreciates you. Did you offer this food as a gift from your heart, or did you wait for a response to give you a feeling of completion?

3. **Feeling appreciated:** Do you feel empty or unappreciated if your family does not thank you for making a particular food or a special meal? Do you feel taken for granted as a mother? Do you tell your family how much time you spent fixing a special dish, in the hope that they will thank you and make a fuss? The next time you make food for your family and look for approval from them, tell them that you often feel valued for serving their favorite foods but not for doing the many other things you do throughout the day. Let them know how much we all need to feel appreciated.

4. **Watch your motives:** Do you fix something special to eat for someone else when you need attention? How do you feel if the person shows you appreciation? How do you feel if the person says nothing? Are these foods that you yourself enjoy, or are you only thinking of the other person's likes and dislikes? Take a few minutes to reflect on these questions, and make notes in your notebook that you feel may be helpful to look back on later as a reminder of your motives for cooking.

5. **Family Appreciation Day:** For one week, ask family members to express their appreciation once a day to everyone in the house for some little thing done or said. At the end of the week or at the end of each day, talk over how each person felt when someone thanked him or her for doing something minor. Repeat this exercise by setting aside one day a month as Family Appreciation Day. Be sure you include appreciation for being a loving person as well as for doing something tangible.

6. **Passing on your gifts:** Do your children ever help you prepare food? When they do, what is the most important aspect of your cooking together: your teaching them about healthy, good-tasting foods; doing something together; or their getting approval from the rest of the family after the dish has been served?

    Prepare a meal with your child. Choose a time when you will not be rushed and can show him or her how they can help without your becoming impatient. Be aware that you are teaching them something they may someday teach your grandchildren.

Understand that the time you spend and the enjoyment you receive from working together is more important than any reaction you get from people when you serve or eat the meal. Tell them how much you enjoy doing things with them and teaching them what you know. Let him or her know you love them more than the food they make or the help they give you.

5

FEEDING OTHERS
AS CAMOUFLAGE

Every evening after dinner the ritual took place when our family gathered together in the living room to watch television. "Who wants something?" my mother would ask, rising from her chair. There was silence. "Anybody hungry?" she continued, moving toward the kitchen.

"No, thanks," my brother and I answered in unison, knowing a response was mandatory before we could go back to our program without further interruptions.

From the living room we heard the refrigerator door open. Our mother's voice cut like a sharp knife through the show we were watching: "How about some chocolate pudding?"

"No, thanks, Mom."

"Would you like some fruit? I have nice plums!"

"No, thanks."

The litany went on through the melon, carrots, Jell-O, potato chips, and leftover cake to the cookies and milk or, in winter, to hot chocolate with marshmallows. I usually succumbed. Sometimes I gave in because the food sounded so good and I had room to fit it in my stomach, not because I was hungry. Sometimes it was only to be allowed to watch TV without any further interruptions.

Mother returned from the kitchen with food for all of us. She had a look of satisfaction on her face as she passed out our snacks, then sank into her chair to eat hers with great enjoyment. On those occasions when I felt belligerent and wanted to irritate her, I refused her offerings. Then she would sit down and look over at me with a guilty expression, chewing a morsel of her snack. "This is very good," she would say. "Are you sure you don't want any?"

"No, thanks."

She continued eating, but it seemed as though some of the enjoyment was missing for her when we didn't share this extra meal with her.

Some mothers feed their children because they feel guilty about eating alone. One way of drawing attention away from their own overeating is to focus on their children. When you press food on your family, they may not notice how much you're eating, but they will pick up on your motivating guilt. If you eat and feel guilty, even if you are trying to cover up your overeating by getting others to join you, your guilt will likely become your childrens' guilt. Your attempt at creating a smokescreen so others will not notice how much you are eating is behavior you may be teaching them.

Other mothers watch their weight to such a degree that they derive a vicarious pleasure from forcing food on their daughters and other people while denying it to themselves. This form of denial can cause problems for the mother and give confusing messages to the child, who does not know whether to believe her mother's words or her actions.

I don't think my mother saw her behavior as overeating. I think it was her attempt to feel loved. Looking back, I see that none of us could have been very hungry after her substantial dinners, which always concluded with dessert. In fact, hunger rarely entered the picture. We ate when we had room for more, not because we were hungry. It was a cultural pattern my mother had learned in her family, one that she passed on to my brother and me.

The look on her face, which I interpreted as guilt, is one I remember. My inclination since then has been to eat with people when they're eating, whether or not I'm hungry, to keep them from feeling guilty. And there have been times when I pressed food on friends so I wouldn't feel guilty eating alone.

TAKING ACTION

1.   **Affirmation:** I always eat with my best friend—me.

2.   **Eating with your mother:** Was shared eating your mother's way of camouflaging her overeating when you were a child? How did you feel when you joined her? How did you feel on those occasions when you didn't eat with her? Write a paragraph or two in your notebook about the feelings you had when your mother overate and you were a child. Write another paragraph or more about your present feelings when you overeat.

3.   **Eating alone and with others:** Would you rather eat with someone else than eat alone? Do you feel guilty or uncomfortable when you eat alone and other people are around you? Do you tend to eat more, less, or the same amounts of food when other people don't join you? Keep a diary in your notebook for a few days showing how much you eat when you're by yourself and how much you eat when you're with others. If there is a difference, try to find the reason for it, and make note of this reason at the end of your diary.

6

FOOD REPLACES FEELINGS

Lee was eight and her brother was six. Still, they were old enough to give a surprise anniversary party for their parents, complete with a fancy tablecloth and real napkins, not just the paper kind. They invited some relatives and a few of their parents' friends to make it a proper dinner party. The dining-room table was set perfectly. At each place setting was a dinner plate from the family's best china, and on each plate was a little bunny salad: the bunny's body was made from canned pears, and it had a cottage-cheese tail, raisin eyes, a cherry nose, and almond ears. It had taken Lee and her brother all day to make the meal, and they had spent a lot of time calling the guests and keeping the whole meal a secret. Lee was bursting with love for her parents, and this meal was the only way she knew how to show it.

All her life Lee's mother, Helen, made elaborate dishes for her family and friends. She never said "I love you" with words. Lee eventually learned that this was what her mother meant when she prepared a special food or meal, and it became the only way Lee knew for expressing her love for others.

Helen didn't feel close to her daughter any more than she had to her own mother. She and Lee were so different; she was a mother, an adult, and her child was . . . well, so young. Helen's mother hadn't spent a great deal of time with her when she was little, and Helen had had no one else to pattern herself after. One of the only ways she knew of sharing was to bring the family together at mealtimes. Without words, she said, "I want to be close to you and share something with you. You and I are so different. This is one of the only times I feel close. Anything more than this feels uncomfortable to me."

When Helen fixed a special meal for the family, Lee came to understand from her mother's attitude that this was an expression of love. Her mother wasn't looking for approval from anyone; instead, cooking was her way of expressing love. But because Lee wanted to hear the words, she always felt that something was missing. She felt an emptiness, and she overate in an attempt to fill it. But as stuffed as she became, she was never filled with the "food" she was looking for: the talks with her mother that she knew her girlfriends had with theirs, the words of praise for just being herself, the daily hugs and kisses and "I love yous."

Lee now understands what she missed as a child, and it's easier for her to find love outside food. With the help of a psychotherapist, she's learning to use words more to express her feelings, and with nutritional counseling she's learning to use food to nourish. There is a shyness, a tentativeness about her that is lovely; it is the innocence of a child who is becoming aware of the importance of saying how she feels. There is, too, the strength of an adult who sees the gift that both people receive when one tells the other that he or she is special.

Using food as a replacement for talking can be an easy way of sharing when you and your child find it difficult to communicate with words. Like Lee and her mother, you may eat or prepare foods instead of expressing your love verbally, or you may fix a meal for someone or overeat by yourself instead of talking about a disappointment or a situation that has left you anxious.

It was a hot summer night, and I was feeling upset and lonely. Since I didn't feel like reading, food would be my companion. I drove to a convenience store for a pint of ice cream and instead found myself buying a half-gallon. I had to be very upset to buy that much, and this night, I was.

Back in my apartment, I began eating the ice cream from the carton. At first it tasted delicious, then a little less good, but still good enough to continue. Besides, I was feeling comforted by its creamy sweetness. Although it was one of the hottest nights of the year, I began to get cold from the ice cream. Dairy products can lower your body temperature, which is one reason some people tend to eat ice cream or frozen yogurt more in summer than in winter. I was shivering, but I continued to eat.

I can still see myself standing in front of a lighted gas wall heater eating ice cream from that carton, although it was over ninety degrees in the room. I just couldn't stop. Half finished and afraid I would become sick if I continued, I reluctantly put my friend in the freezer and went to sleep.

The next morning I felt better emotionally and thought about whether I wanted cereal or toast for breakfast. But I remembered the half-eaten carton of ice cream waiting for me in the freezer. Although I tried to resist it and realized it would be there to eat at a more appropriate time, I finished that ice cream for breakfast. What I could have done the night before was to reach out and call a friend. The ice cream did not take away my loneliness, it just masked my feelings.

Overeating when we're alone and upset is common. It's also not unusual for two people to eat together when one of them is upset about a relationship or a job, even when neither is hungry. The food does not have to taste good or be special. It is the act of eating with someone that gives the illusion of sharing feelings. But the sharing that comes from food doesn't come close to exchanging feelings and ideas with words.

Deeper interaction is absent when you speak through food, and the message you give your children through your actions can be confusing. You are encouraging them to do the same in their life. You're telling them it's all right to communicate by fixing a special meal instead of by saying, "I love you. I appreciate you." They try to share their emotions without words; they know no other way. Because this kind of communication leaves a great deal unsaid and unshared, something feels missing. And the most familiar substance to fill that space with is food. This is a negative eating pattern that can lead to your childrens' overeating even when you don't.

As difficult as it may be for you to share your feelings or even, at times, to identify them, it is important to learn to share them if you want to help yourself. It could help you to recognize that your own pattern of expressing yourself through food rather than words may have originated with your mother.

It is only quite recently that we have begun to talk about our feelings. Twenty years ago and more, it was common to suffer in silence, to not confront, to not upset anyone or burden them with our problems. Today, we are moving away from denial toward sharing more of ourselves with one another. This sharing becomes deeper, more valuable, when we speak with words.

THE SHAMEFUL BURDEN: CHILDHOOD SEXUAL ABUSE

The more we understand eating disorders, especially overeating and bingeing, the more we see a connection between stuffing ourselves with food and keeping down the painful memories of childhood sexual abuse. Also, many people overeat to separate themselves from both their feelings and their bodies as a result of this abuse. This separation from your feelings may have occurred when you were very young, without your being aware of its origin.

There seems to be a direct correlation here between the mind and body, and the large number of people with eating disorders who have a history of abuse. If you are aware of having been abused sexually, it is important to work with a psychotherapist who is familiar with this violation and who understands that one way of not dealing with the horrors of the past is to eat uncontrollably. Please look for a therapist or therapy group in your area and get professional help for this aspect of your overeating.

You may be overeating because of physiological reasons as well, but sexual abuse, whether recognized or buried in your subconscious, will not go away. It will leave you with some kind of compensating pattern—like eating to dull the senses, pushing down painful feelings, or keeping you separated from your body—until you are able to release the burdens of the past.

TAKING ACTION

1. **Affirmation:** I know what I feel, and I feel comfortable expressing my feelings with caring friends and family.

2. **Talking with your mother:** Did you feel close to your mother when you were a child and talk with her about your feelings as well as your daily activities? Did you feel separated from her and not talk much to your mother at all? Did she ever talk to you about herself?

    This exercise involves writing a letter to your mother that is not meant to be sent to her. It is a way for you to get your feelings out on paper, where you can look at them. It is not important whether your mother is alive now or not. This letter is for you.

    The "I-Never-Told-You" Letter: Write a letter describing an incident from your childhood that you were unable or unwilling to share with your mother. Pay attention to how you feel before you write the letter. In it, tell your mother how you felt when the incident took place and why you didn't feel you could talk with her about it at the time. Describe your feelings in detail. Be as specific as possible. Tell your mother now what you wanted from her then—to have her listen to you, offer you advice, give you a shoulder to cry on, hold you.

    Read the finished letter to yourself. How do you feel after having expressed yourself with words? Do you feel more satisfied or relieved after writing down your feelings, even though your mother didn't hear them? As an adult, could you talk with her more openly?

3. **Talking with a friend:** Do you talk about your feelings with your friends? Are your friendships based on sharing thoughts, or are

they more superficial? Do you feel uncomfortable talking about yourself? Do you feel that it's "too personal" to verbalize?

"True Confessions": Designate a time for you and a friend when you can talk about your feelings. Ask her to just listen, and share an incident with her from a time when you felt hurt, angry, or happy. It's not important whether the incident involved her. The idea is to feel more comfortable about sharing your feelings with someone.

When you are finished, tell her what you are afraid she will say. This, not the story you told her, is your true confession: for example, "I'm afraid you'll think I was silly" or "I'm afraid you won't like me for what I did."

Now let her tell you what she really felt. Is it what you thought, or were you projecting your fears onto her? Perhaps she'll tell you, "I feel bad that you couldn't tell me that before." Begin to share more of your current feelings with her.

4. **Keeping family communications open:** Was it easier for you to share food with your mother than thoughts and feelings? Is it easier for you to feel close to your friends or your children when you eat together than when you talk? Do you talk with your children about your feelings as well as about more concrete things, like daily activities? Do they come to you for advice, or do they go to their friends or others?

   If your children are old enough, begin by sharing something about yourself with them and asking for their opinion. Tell them how you feel about the problem or incident, rather than just describing it. Let them know you value their input and that you feel you've been missing something by not sharing more with them.

5. **Get professional help:** If you know or suspect you have been sexually abused as a child, seek professional help from a trained psychotherapist or hypnotherapist who understands and has worked successfully with this problem. Do not try to do it alone, and don't continue burying your memories. It was not your fault. An adult took advantage of a child and was abusive to you. You have the right to be whole and heal from these wounds.

7

FOOD AS REWARD OR PUNISHMENT

FOOD AS REWARD

I had skinned my knee badly enough for my mother to take me to our family doctor. It hurt like the dickens when he cleaned bits of gravel from the wound with tweezers and scrubbed it with cotton dipped in a stinging medication. By the time my knee was bandaged, I was cranky and on the verge of tears. I limped toward the door while my mother was still saying good-bye to the doctor. "Have a lollipop, Nan," Dr. Teitelbaum called to me. I rummaged through the large glass bowl filled with candy until I found my favorite flavor—grape. I knew if I had cried a lot or misbehaved I would have been rushed out of the office without my candy. I had learned at a young age that food was a reward for good behavior, especially during difficult times.

As I grew older I continued to be rewarded for going to the doctor or the dentist or for surviving a day of shopping with my mother. Sunday school was often boring, but the large, juicy, garlicky dill pickles my brother and I chose from a barrel at the grocer's as we walked home made it more bearable. When I was on my own I found my life filled with traumas, each accompanied by a reward I could eat or drink. After an exam in college I stopped off for a milk shake instead of joining classmates in the cafeteria for my usual cup of tea. This pattern of using food as a reward contributed to my overeating. There was always something to reward myself for. The excessive use of food as reward for both major and minor reasons became a problem.

Little Pauline followed her mother into her daddy's office. She didn't like being there ever since he had died, but her mother had to be there and Pauline had to come with her. She sat at an empty desk and began drawing pictures to make the time go by more quickly. Every time she walked into daddy's office she felt sad. She wished there was someplace else she could go, someone she could visit, instead of coming here.

After her mother was finished they walked around the corner from the office for their treat. Pauline's mood was instantly transformed as she skipped over to the Orange Julius stand and ordered her hot dog, drink, and potato chips. This is fun, she thought. She bit into the crisp hot dog in its soft bun and took a sip of the creamy orange drink. Her sadness disappeared. Pauline and her mother always ate fun food after an unpleasant experience, and even today Pauline thinks in terms of two kinds of food: regular food and fun food, with fun foods being rewards.

The taste of certain foods can remind us of life's sweetness or distract us from its bitter moments. We turn to these kinds of foods when we feel so joyful that we don't know what to do with our feelings, so we sedate ourselves with food, or when we're so overcome by unpleasant feelings that we distract ourselves with food. In fact, many women use food as their "drug of choice." This negative eating pattern, developed in childhood, becomes one we repeat later in our lives under similar circumstances.

As children, we often associate special foods with rewards for having survived difficult physical or emotional events. Sometimes this is appropriate, like treating yourself to a meal in a nice restaurant after studying all day for an exam or spending your day off painting the kitchen. But at other times it can become a habit that gets out of hand. When we become adults we continue this reward system. We stop off for a drink with a friend after a difficult day at work. We get bad news about the car from the mechanic, so we stop off for some ice cream. We spend the weekend cleaning the house or apartment instead of relaxing and enjoying ourselves, and then we indulge in a rich meal we would not ordinarily eat. This is what our mothers taught us to do, isn't it?

If this is what you are doing, it is also most likely what you are teaching your children. Take a look at your own childhood and see where this pattern of using food as a reward began.

TAKING ACTION

1. **Affirmation:** Feeling love is my greatest reward.

2. **Getting treats:** Do you remember being given treats after an unpleasant experience? Did your mother bribe you with food so that you would behave yourself when you were in public places with her? Were you rewarded with food for an achievement like having a good report card or cleaning your room without being reminded? Do you reward your children with food in some of the same ways your mother rewarded you?

    Write a paragraph or more in your notebook about the role food as reward played in your life when you were a child. Was it used in an appropriate or inappropriate way? Have you continued this pattern out of habit and thus passed it on to your children?

3. **The Reward List:** Make a list of rewards other than foods that you would have liked when you were young. Did you want to spend time playing games with your parents? Would you have enjoyed staying up later at night for a special event, or having someone read your favorite book to you? Or would you have been happy if your mother had just told you how wonderful you were and given you a big hug?

    Next, make a list of any nonfood rewards you would like now. You might give yourself extra time to read, to pursue a hobby, to take a walk or drive in the country, to go to a movie, or to have a manicure or pedicure. Consider a bubble bath with your favorite music playing. Look for treats that have nothing to do with food.

4. **Your Child's Reward List:** What kind of treats do you give your children? Are the rewards you give always, or usually, food? What would they like other than this? Have you read them a story lately, taken them to a movie, or given them a hug and told them how proud you are of them?

    Make a list of other kinds of rewards you could give your children besides food. Ask them for some suggestions. Along with the reward, tell them that while you appreciate all they do, you love them for just being themselves. We don't need to be rewarded with food for every difficult experience we have or to recognize our achievements as much as we need to feel valued and loved. Put these rewards into effect. Place less emphasis on food.

FOOD AS PUNISHMENT

Donna sat down at the kitchen table to eat her dinner. Uh-oh, she thought, Mom must be angry again. Donna wasn't sure what she had done, but by the looks of her dinner she must have done something pretty awful. On her plate was a small hamburger patty and a few string beans. She counted them. There were six. Six string beans and a little piece of meat for a growing eleven-year-old girl? Donna didn't know why she was being fed so little, but she was determined to get even with her mother somehow. She would refuse to clean her room for a week. That always made her mother angry.

She had noticed that her mother gave her smaller portions than usual when she was upset with her. Why didn't she just *tell* Donna what was wrong? And what made her angry so often, anyway? Donna ate slowly, hoping the food would last longer. When she left the dinner table she was still hungry.

Ethel, her mother, was angry with Donna for having misbehaved.

Donna never did anything she asked her to do to help around the house, no matter how often she reminded her. Donna's room was messy, the bed hardly ever made, and she refused to help with any chores. Ethel was tired of harping on the same things. She had stopped trying to reason with Donna years ago. Life was enough of a struggle without the burden of having a daughter who refused to do her share.

The only retaliation Ethel could think of was the punishment she had received when she was a child—hunger. If Donna was hungry often enough, maybe she'd get the message and do some work around the house to earn her keep. Like her mother, Ethel kept her cupboards and refrigerator bare and fed Donna only enough to keep her from being malnourished. Maybe it was mean, she thought, but Donna was impossible.

As Donna grew older, she adopted this negative pattern for herself. Whenever she felt bad about herself without knowing why, she punished herself by not eating. When she had done poorly on an exam or flunked her driving test, she starved herself. And when she was ready to forgive herself, she did what she had waited for her mother to do for her—she rewarded herself with food and overate everything she liked best.

Some parents withhold favorite foods as a form of discipline: "If you don't clean your room you can't have dessert tonight." This can be an appropriate punishment that carries an effective message; missing dessert while others in the family are enjoying it may awaken a child who has been sleeping through your admonitions. If you promise a special food and rescind your promise in response to misconduct, explaining your reason for the change, the child may even feel relieved at being punished. You may remember, as I do, being sent to your room without dinner. In my family this punishment was given for unacceptable behavior, such as lying.

When carried to an extreme, however, withholding food can be a cruel way of expressing anger and resentment. Punishment should help a child understand she has misbehaved and encourage her to think about her actions and act differently in the future. It should not be used in a hurtful way without explanation.

A child who is deprived of food and feels hungry when she knows her parents can afford to feed her becomes confused and angry. We all have the right to be sheltered, clothed, and fed—not just some or most of the time, but daily. When food is reduced to a bare minimum, this form of punishment constitutes emotional abuse and physical neglect, according to the National Committee for the Prevention of Child Abuse.

In addition to being immoral and illegal, punishing a child in this way leads her to believe that she must be a terrible person to deserve this kind of punishment. It may take many years for her to understand why she was punished so severely by being deprived of food. Or she may never understand it, continuing the pattern by using food to punish herself and others.

In another example of food used as punishment, a woman may overeat in order to deliberately make herself feel bad, either physically or emotionally. When you think you need to be punished or you feel self-destructive, you may turn to eating foods you know will cause bloating, gas, or diarrhea, or you may just eat too much because you believe you deserve to feel sick. This kind of punishment does more than just make you feel uncomfortable for a few hours or a day. It could result in digestive problems that may take years to repair and could lead to serious stomach and intestinal problems or in food sensitivities from eating the same foods over and over.

Chapter 21 looks at food allergies and sensitivities in more depth and describes some of the damage these can create. If you overeat to punish yourself, you may want to look at this chapter to see some possible effects of your action. You may want to find appropriate ways of admonishing yourself that are not physically harmful—or you may want to eliminate the problem completely by giving yourself the gift of forgiveness. There is nothing you can do or have ever done that cannot be forgiven.

If you stuff yourself and then feel guilty, branding yourself as "bad" to reinforce your belief that you're no good and that you've known it all along, there's no question that you're using food as punishment. Perhaps as a child you were told that you were bad or that you never did anything right. This may have been the way some adults dealt with you in an effort to get you to change your actions. This is the time to move beyond their punishments and to forgive them for not understanding you or being able to handle the situation with more love.

TAKING ACTION

1. **Affirmation:** I am lovable, and I forgive everyone who is unable to see this part of me.

2. **Looking back at punishment:** Did you go hungry often as a child because you were being punished? Did it feel like appropriate punishment, or did it seem to be more than was necessary to get the point across? Did your mother explain the reason for this punishment? Was she a person who told you in words how she felt, or did she show you through her actions instead?

   Do you punish yourself now by depriving yourself of food in any way? Perhaps there is no need for punishment but instead a great need for forgiveness. Can you understand why you acted as you did, realizing that you did the best you could or that you can be more aware and act differently the next time? Can you forgive, rather than punish, yourself? Can you forgive your mother for punishing you with food, for not knowing how else to handle a situation?

   Begin by just thinking about the ways in which you or your mother has used food as punishment. If you like, you can write some of this in your notebook, but you may just want to let these unpleasant memories go after you have remembered them.

3. Write a **"Dear Mom" Letter** expressing your anger to your mother. Tell her how you felt when she punished you with food. It is not necessary to send her this letter, but it *is* necessary to express your anger in a safe way. After you have expressed your anger, reread the letter.

   Next, write a second "Dear Mom" letter, forgiving her. Explain that you understand she did the best she could at the time, but the punishment hurt you more deeply than she perhaps realized. Tell her how you feel about your right to be fed. Talk about other kinds of punishment that would have been more appropriate. End the letter by saying something like, "Even if I don't completely understand why you did this, I forgive you."

When you forgive someone, yourself included, you free yourself from hidden anger. Your anger will not grow into anything positive, so learn to let it go. Otherwise, it becomes destructive, and you must constantly build and rebuild. Forgiveness has a place in your life; unexpressed anger and festering resentment do not.

A variation would be to write a letter to yourself, forgiving yourself for having used food inappropriately as punishment, either with yourself or with your child.

4. **Punishing your children:** Do you punish your children by withholding food or by insisting that they eat the foods they dislike most? Begin by talking with them. Explain that you are going to use different methods of punishment in the future, and that the purpose of any punishment is to help them understand the need for them to act differently. It is not to make them feel bad or angry.

    If they have misbehaved, you may find that after you have talked with them, no punishment is necessary. Reasoning and understanding may be sufficient. If you feel that punishment is necessary, talk with them about doing something that can leave them with a feeling of accomplishment, like cleaning their room or doing the family laundry. Help them understand that the severity of any punishment should reflect the seriousness of the offense. Explain that as their mother you want to teach them, not hurt them. Ask their forgiveness for your having used food as punishment in the past. Their forgiveness will free you both.

8

FOOD AS POWER STRUGGLE

When I was a child I had to eat everything on my plate, no matter what. Occasionally a food I could not stand to eat appeared, like the infamous plate of creamed spinach. Then there was trouble. I began by complaining about the food, saying what it was I didn't like about it. "Think of all the poor, starving children in China," my mother retorted, eyeing my plate, which still contained substantial remains from my meal.

"You can send this to them," I answered, convinced they would *have* to be starving to eat stringy, sandy, black creamed spinach. There were times when I could bargain with her and eat only some of the food. But this time there was no bargaining. One bite of the spinach caused me to gag. I don't know if it was the long, stringy spinach stems or the loud grinding sound of sand against my teeth, but this was one food I would not eat. Ever.

I sat at the table, the rest of my meal eaten. Before me, in a clear glass dish shaped like a bunch of grapes that I can see in my mind today as distinctly as I did on that terrible evening, sat the creamed spinach I refused to touch. "You can't have any dessert until you eat your spinach," my father reminded me, prodding me to eat it and get this whole incident over with.

"I don't care." Nothing was worth gagging over.

"And," my mother continued, "you can't have anything until you do finish the spinach."

I had no concept of what that meant. All I knew was that I wouldn't budge, and neither, it seemed, would my mother. "Fine," I said, excusing myself from the table. The next morning I came into the kitchen expecting my usual bowl of cereal. At my place was the dish of creamed spinach, cold and darker from spending the night in the refrigerator. I went off to school hungry.

When I returned home for lunch it was still at my place. In a conciliatory gesture, my mother had warmed the dish to make it a little more palatable. I knew it was the most she would bend. I somehow gagged it down without getting sick. All I knew was that I had lost the battle of the creamed spinach. My mother had won the power struggle, and for much of my life I felt powerless. I still find it difficult at times to question authority. And, of course, it was years before I could face spinach again—and never when it was creamed.

In many households, a parent's will dominates. As a parent, recognize that there is sometimes a fine line between exerting your will and setting limits. Look at what you are doing and at the motives behind your actions. Sometimes forcing a child to eat a dreaded food is the way mothers show their power over their children. Never make food a battleground. There are appropriate ways of encouraging children to try new foods or to eat enough to get the nourishment they need. Forcing a child to gag down cold, blackened creamed spinach is not one of them. The consequences of these battles of will may not be seen for many years. I learned from many incidents—the spinach was only one of the more dramatic ones—that I had no power in my home. This feeling carried over into other areas of my life.

Even today when I eat in a restaurant I am tempted to eat all the food I'm served. If it isn't prepared correctly, or if it contains an ingredient I no longer eat, my first reaction is to say nothing. At times I still feel like a helpless child to whom no one will listen.

There are still occasions when I feel that my choices have been taken away by someone stronger than I am. Now I am getting better. I can send back a dish that is not to my liking. I do so respectfully, but I don't eat poorly-prepared food or eat something that doesn't agree with me. And I feel powerful by taking this small step.

For many years I would not challenge anyone who spoke to me in an authoritative manner. If I disagreed with that person I kept quiet, certain I would lose any argument. Rather than talking over a problem, I became silent and walked away. My relationship to food taught me how to act in other relationships, and power struggles have been an issue throughout my life.

Feeling defeated can come from more than having a dominating mother. It can come from feeling powerless over circumstances in our lives. If you think of yourself as worthless, as a failure, then at least you can feel "successful" when you binge. This power struggle is not with a person but with life itself. When you stop struggling because you feel powerless to overcome difficult situations, food may be the only area where you feel in charge.

Overeating can begin in early childhood as a response to unreasonable demands, demands that you feel you can't meet ("I want to see all A's on your next report card!"). And it can be a response to feeling like a failure at home ("Can't you ever do anything right?").

As a child I was told almost daily for many years that I was "the laziest thing God ever put on this earth." No matter what I did, I felt criticized for whatever I hadn't done. One day I decided to surprise my mother by dusting the living room without being asked to—but then she asked me why I hadn't vacuumed as well. From her point of view it made perfectly good sense: you wipe the dust off the tabletops and lamps, and then you vacuum it up so it's gone, not just spread all over the floor. But I felt like a failure once more. The only area of my life in which I felt I could succeed at pleasing her was eating. To show how truly successful I could be at something, I overate.

Overeating as a form of control has two sides. When you feel you can't win at anything in your life and you want to give up, sometimes all you can do is give up your final control over food and eat poorly or stuff yourself. Overeating may also take the form of a rebellious statement when you want to, or feel you need to, assert yourself. Some children use this control issue to starve themselves, becoming anorexic. Others binge and then go on strict diets, or overeat and deliberately get fat. The idea that you'll "show them" is one that backfires. You may win the control issue, but your body and your self-image will suffer.

TAKING ACTION

1. **Affirmation:** I am powerful and have great value, and I respect the power of others. I am a loving, capable, strong person.

2. **Standing up for yourself:** Were you forced by your parents to eat foods or quantities of food that you found difficult to eat? Did you have any say in how much or how little you ate? Did your mother or father impose his or her will on you with food?

   Did you feel powerless as a child? Does that feeling extend into your life now, and do you still feel powerless in situations in which others seem to find it easier to maintain a sense of power? Do you defer to authority because you don't believe you can stand up to it?

   The Restaurant Test: The next time you are at a restaurant and are served food not to your liking, send it back. If you asked for a dish with the sauce on the side and it comes with the sauce over the food, have the waiter get you the food you ordered. Be kind, but assertive.

   When you are given too much food at a restaurant, ask for a doggie bag or leave the food on your plate. Don't eat more than you want or need. No one in China or Ethiopia will benefit.

3. **Be gentle with your children:** Are you an overwhelming authority figure to your children, or do you speak directly to each other and make conciliations? Do you force your children to eat certain foods or amounts of food even when they insist they can't? Is some of the food distasteful to them or too much for them to eat, or are you engaged in a battle of wills?

Examine the ways in which you use your power with your children, and encourage them to discuss matters with you. They have as much of an ability to understand you and reason with you as you had when you were a child. Talk with them about the reasons for your actions. Help them to understand that when you want them to try eating various foods, it's because they have nutrients their bodies need to be healthy or because you would like to help them develop a taste for a variety of foods to make life easier and more enjoyable for them as they grow older.

4. **Talk more with your children about food:** Find out which foods your children dislike the most. Ask them to remind you gently or humorously when you fall back into the "dreaded-dish syndrome"—and lighten up, mother. Don't force your children to eat *all* of a particular food if they are willing to eat at least some.

    If your child has a serious eating problem, like only eating junk foods with no vegetables or whole grains, find a nutritionist who is skilled in working with children. Use this person to help you find ways to prepare foods your child will eat. For example, you can puree a few cooked carrots and add them to marinara sauce without altering the taste. Pureed vegetables like summer squash and broccoli can be added to soups.

5. **Change your style of eating:** Serve food family-style, letting each person serve him- or herself. Force yourself not to monitor what your children eat or do not eat. Let them choose smaller portions, if this is what they want.

    If any of your children truly eat too little at meals, find out whether they are eating too much between meals. Look at the kinds of snacks they're eating. Those high in fats, such as peanut butter or chips, may remain in their stomach for several hours and give them a feeling of fullness. Replace them with low-fat crackers spread with a little fruit jam, or with a few pretzels, a piece of fruit, or unbuttered popcorn.

9

FOOD:

The Mother Who's Not There, or Never Was

THE MOTHER WHO'S NOT THERE

Jennifer is a sculptress trying desperately to succeed in the complex art world of a large city. The competition is fierce, and she is unsure of herself and her work. The piece she is working on now is frustrating. It was difficult enough to sculpt in clay, but when she moved on to stone the problems multiplied. One wrong strike of a hammer and chisel—like today, when the chisel slipped—and her whole concept is changed forever. How is she ever going to solve this problem or get the piece ready in time to enter next week's art show?

Jennifer has no one with whom she can talk over this problem, no one to assure her that everything will work out. She feels very alone. Accompanying her frustration is a feeling of emptiness. She drives to the nearest coffee shop and orders two side orders of mashed potatoes and gravy. She begins to feel a little better, and when she's finished she orders another serving and eats until she's stuffed.

Jennifer is completely unaware of why she's doing this, but stuffing herself with mashed potatoes always makes her feel better. If she can't easily find mashed potatoes she will eat ice cream, a food that also calms her down. But feeling filled with mashed potatoes is her favorite. It's a food her mother fed her often when she was young, and it's the food she most associates with "mommy" and with being loved.

Jennifer is looking for support and comfort. Without knowing it, she is looking for her mother's love. When she was a little girl, her mother held her and nurtured her. Today Jennifer wants to be held and reassured. She unconsciously turns to foods that most resemble baby food and remind her of that time in her life when she was cared for and comforted: mashed potatoes, ice cream, pudding, applesauce. She eats too much in an attempt to fill the emotional emptiness that food can never fill.

When life feels overwhelming and you want someone to make everything better—when you "want your mommy"—you may turn to foods that remind you of your mother. And if you, like many other people, associate that stuffed feeling with feeling content, you may overeat these foods. If you feel lost and alone in the world for long periods of time, overeating may become a pattern.

One of the most common comfort foods from childhood is ice cream, but you may turn to other soft foods or to a food your mother gave you as a treat—for example, french-fried potatoes, chocolate cake, or cookies. Any food that you associate with your mother may be the food you choose when you feel lost and alone and miss her presence.

If you turn to foods from your childhood when you feel lost and want your mother, perhaps you're encouraging your child to do the same.

TAKING ACTION

1. **Affirmation:** I love myself. I am loved. I find healthy ways to nurture myself.

2. **"Friendship Coupons":** Talking with someone and being held is a better solution than eating when you feel overwhelmed and want someone to take care of you. Look to see whom in your life you could turn at these times instead of eating. Make some "Friendship Coupons" for you and a friend, redeemable for a talk, a shoulder to cry on, a hug. Exchange these coupons and redeem them when you need to have someone be there for you. Or give them to the "mommy" inside yourself, and turn to her for support.

3. **Comfort foods:** Think back to your childhood and to the foods your mother or other relatives fed you when you were upset. Now look at the foods you turn to now when you're looking for comfort. Is there a similarity between them?

   If you think you turn to foods from your childhood that evoke a feeling of comfort at times when you need comforting, pay attention to how you feel before, during, and after eating them. Write down how you felt when you realized you wanted a particular food. What was the event that triggered this feeling?

   Write down how the food tasted. Did that taste bring back any memories or feelings from your past? Write down, too, how you felt after you ate it. Did you feel satisfied, content? Was this the feeling you wanted from a person rather than from food? Was food a substitute in this instance for your mother or for some other caretaker?

   Make note of how long the feeling of satisfaction lasted and whether or not you ate to the point of discomfort. Did you feel guilty? Did you feel stuffed, and did the food give you any pains or gas? If so, did the uncomfortable feelings take the place of your need for comfort and distract you?

   Look at what you've written. Did food successfully replace mother and give you all the positive feelings you wanted? Did it make everything better? If your mother distracted you with food, then perhaps this food did seem to make things better. But that didn't solve anything when you were a child, and it doesn't solve anything now. It's just another form of denial. If in addition to giving you this special food, your mother held you and talked with you about your anxiety or problem, the warmth and interaction may have been what worked.

4. **Food is not your mother:** We all have a little child inside us who screams for attention at times and can push us into troublesome areas. This is the part of us that is carried over from our childhood, the part of us that hasn't grown up. It pushes aside all reason and disregards our good intentions in favor of instant gratification. It yells for ice cream or candy until we give in. We also have a mother, a caretaker who keeps this little child from doing dangerous things, like riding her bike in rush-hour traffic. The little child inside you is the part of you that pushes you toward familiar foods. But this is no time to let an anxious child run your life—this is a job for mother.

   If your child was like this little one, would you give in to her? Would you let her boss you around, and would you buy her sweets or other foods that might not be good for her or let her overeat until she felt sick? If not, why are you doing this to yourself? Be the same firm, loving mother to the child inside you that you are to your physical child. Talk to that part of you, explaining why food can't replace feelings of caring and support. Tell the child in you that you realize she's frightened and feels alone, and let her know she is never alone. You're the mother who will always be there for her. *Food is not her mommy—you are.*

5. **There are no forbidden foods if you can control your portions:** When you deny yourself the food you want when you are looking for comfort, do you feel satisfied eating anything else? If not, you may overeat. No foods are forbidden foods. You can have anything you want, as long as you watch the portions. If you can control the amount you eat, have a small serving of the food you particularly want. Be very aware that it is only a substitution for a physical or emotional comfort, not the real thing. If it works for you, it could be a good answer until the realization that food is not mommy sinks in. It may work better for you to eat a small dish of ice cream and feel satisfied than to eat some carrot sticks, feel unsatisfied, and continue by eating some chips, some cheese, and some fruit.

THE MOTHER WHO WAS NEVER THERE

Infants being held by their mothers and fed when they're fussing is only one possible scenario. Not all babies are held, for a number of reasons. Joan's mother, Charlotte, was afraid of her tiny daughter. Charlotte was a successful businesswoman at a time when few women held positions of importance in the work force. To reach this pinnacle she had learned to suppress her emotions and to act "businesslike" at all times. While many women can be successful in business and still be nurturing, Charlotte could not.

Charlotte learned how to play the game and be "one of the boys." She became a top sales representative for a clothing manufacturer, but she didn't know how to be an affectionate mother. Because she was terrified of hurting her daughter or making a mistake, she rarely touched her. She couldn't even bring herself to pick Joan up or change her diapers. The housekeeper or Joan's father cared for the baby so that she was always fed and dry, but as a result of the lack of bonding between mother and child, Joan and Charlotte were never close. As an adult, Joan, like Charlotte, had difficulty expressing herself emotionally or through touch.

Joan's father was a warmer, more expressive person than her mother, but he could not take Charlotte's place. Despite his care, something was missing for Joan.

As a young child, she developed an emotionally-induced asthma; it was the only way she knew to get her mother's attention and experience her caring. But the asthma only made Charlotte more afraid of her daughter. She was terrified of intensifying the asthmatic attacks and creating further harm. Rather than becoming more physical, she drew back even further. Instead, she expressed her love for Joan by taking her to the best specialists and by buying her expensive toys—or by giving her food.

Before Joan was born, Charlotte had had three loves: her husband, her job, and food. Her favorite means of entertainment had been to drive any distance to a restaurant known for a special dish and then to indulge in great quantities of food and drink. Her husband shared in this enjoyment. They overate rich foods and talked often about restaurants they had visited. When they socialized with

friends they recounted past meals with great relish, remembering particularly delicious dishes and tasting them again in their memories.

In her role as mother, Charlotte spent time explaining things to
Joan, just as she would spend extra time at work solving a problem.
However, it never occurred to her to play with her daughter. To
Charlotte, play was eating.

A frightened mother, Charlotte always did the best she could,
just as many women do. It wasn't that she didn't love her daughter.
She did. She just didn't know how to show her love. Her references
had always been work and food, and she passed this way of thinking
on to her daughter. In fact, Charlotte gave Joan everything she knew
how to give.

Joan and her parents were family friends of mine, and Joan came
to stay with me for a few months when she was in college, at a time
when she felt lost and unhappy. Like her mother, she was unable to
talk about her problems or express her feelings with words. She ate
when she felt anxious, and for those two months she was a very anxious young woman.

I was overeating at that time myself, but Joan's eating habits
brought new meaning to the word. She was never without food in her
hand or mouth. My usually overfilled cupboards were emptied constantly by this unhappy young woman. Food was the mother she needed
and had never known, and Joan kept her "mother" close at hand.

Joan is now married and has a daughter of her own, who, much
like Joan, has been spoiled with expensive gifts from her parents.
The child is demanding, loud, and unpleasant to be around. Joan's
husband, like her father, is an expressive, loving man, but that does
not seem to be enough for the child. She is always looking for attention. Instead of getting sick, like her mother did, she has become
overbearing and demanding of attention. Joan's response is to rationalize with her young daughter at great length. She spends a good
deal of time explaining things to the child, but I have never seen or
heard of her holding her child. When the daughter wants a particular food, she gets it—and as a result she, too, is learning to associate
food with mothering.

When Joan visits her parents, the child runs to her grandfather
and sits on his lap. He holds her, hugs her, and wins her affection

even more by giving her ice cream, candy, and cookies. The child and her grandmother, Charlotte, ignore each other—the grandmother out of fear, and the child because the warmth she is seeking is not there. Since her grandmother and mother are so alike, how close can she feel to her mother?

A chain with strong links has been forged in Joan's family. It started generations ago. When will it end? Perhaps not until Joan or her daughter understands how food has replaced the mother who was never there. Food is not a substitution for mothering. It is a different kind of nourishment—physical nourishment. And *we can never fill an emotional void with a physical substance like food.*

Some people grow up without a mother in the home due to divorce or death. Some, like Joan, have mothers who are physically but not emotionally present because they don't know how to nurture. Still others live with a stepmother or other relative who is not close or warm, or they spend their early years in foster homes with strangers. Many of these people overeat. They feel empty but don't know what they're looking for, because they never experienced that "something" when they were children.

A child who grows up without knowing her mother's love may overfeed her children, just as she overfeeds herself. If she associates food with love, feeding her children may be the only expression of love she knows.

A friend of mine, Michael Sun, wrote a song that says, "Love is the strangest thing that I know. You keep it around by letting it go." When you want love in your life and don't have anyone there to give it to you, give your love away. When you give it to your child, she will know the love you missed when you were young. You will change her experience and give her everything that you were looking for as a child but never received. What a gift to give! How different your life would have been if someone had done that for you.

TAKING ACTION

1. **Affirmation:** My loving mother is inside me. She is always there to love me.

2. **Is it food or is it mommy?** Has food become a substitution for your mother? Was it used instead of love in your family? Did you turn to food when you were a child and your mother wasn't there? The emptiness you try to fill with food can't be filled with anything physical. When you feel empty and want to eat, fill yourself with love instead. Use the **Loving Heart exercise** given in the Taking Steps section in Chapter 3, "Food as Love."

3. **Love means taking time for yourself:** Are you able to give love to yourself? Begin by looking at how you feed yourself. Do you make time to shop for nutritious foods? Do you cook for yourself? You don't have to spend a lot of time preparing foods. Since food, love, and nourishment are all wrapped up together, make an agreement with yourself to feed yourself a nourishing, tasty dinner every day for at least a week. You can find instant soups to serve with a salad and good bread; make stir-fry vegetables with chicken and serve over instant (or pre-cooked and frozen) brown rice; or make a hearty stew or soup in a crockpot that will give you many meals. Pasta with a marinara sauce topped with steamed frozen green beans or broccoli can be a simple dinner you can whip together in a few minutes.

   If you have difficulty doing this alone, have a few sessions with a nutritionist who can give you other ideas of healthy, good-tasting foods you can buy and quick meals you can prepare which your taste buds will enjoy.

PART THREE

Emotional Answers
to Emotional Problems

Each chapter in this section elaborates on a different emotional reason for overeating or misusing food and takes some of the problems we've seen to a deeper level. Many of these problems originate from your not feeling good about yourself. For example, you may "eat for the future" by stuffing yourself before going to work, because making time to eat during a busy day would mean saying that you're more important than your work. Or you may eat when you're lonely, because you don't like your own company enough to spend time with yourself.

Other negative emotional eating patterns come from our being unaware or uninformed. A woman who eats constantly out of habit is in denial and is not aware of her true feelings of hunger. A child who was not taught to eat well and was not allowed to make decisions about food grows into a woman who does not know her options and continues to eat poorly. Denial plays a part in many of these patterns. The reasons for your own negative emotional eating patterns may be included in one or more of these chapters.

The scenarios in this section are meant to serve as windows for you to look through, so that you can begin to see the details of your own life more clearly. Your story may vary from those presented here, but the struggles are similar. As you see yourself in the lives of these people, be willing to remember some of the painful incidents in your life that you have pushed aside. The Taking Action steps at the end of each chapter are designed to help you work through those incidents; a support group, a therapist, or a nutritionist can help you with any painful memories you cannot manage comfortably on your own. When you are willing to look at a problem in its entirety, you become capable of solving it.

Take a good look at the goals you have with food. Each goal is a choice. You can choose to continue eating the way you have been, or you can choose to change. Numerous choices add up to achieving each goal. Become more aware of the choices you make that are working for you rather than against you as you begin to change your eating patterns for the better. Remember that each area you look at has two components: your mind (emotions) and your body (physiological needs). Address one of them and you may continue to be going around in circles with a partially-solved problem. Address both of them and you'll be able to look back some day at the problems you used to have!

10

LEARNING THE MEANING OF HUNGER:

The Solution to Eating Constantly

M any people don't know the feeling of hunger. It is a foreign sensation to them. When I ask them if they're often hungry, these patients look at me with a questioning look and admit they don't remember being hungry. Some laugh uncomfortably and reply, "I haven't been hungry in years!"

There are numerous reasons why people grow up without knowing hunger. Perhaps their mothers or grandmothers practically lived in the kitchen where someone was constantly eating. A child in such a family would grow up knowing the familiar feeling of being fed very frequently, of having something delicious to eat whenever she wanted.

Another person may come from a farming family where cellars and barns were filled with grains, cheese, apples, squash, and other foods to tide them through the winter. Gigantic meals were prepared for and consumed by the men who labored in the fields. A child growing up in this kind of family would be used to eating large quantities, to mimic the grownups around her.

There are people whose ancestors lived through famines, food shortages, or the Holocaust. They often overcompensated with their families and made certain their children and grandchildren would never know the meaning of hunger. A child growing up in such a family may have learned that hunger is an enemy to be avoided.

In some families, an abundance of food and a lack of hunger expressed caring and love. A child who understands that cookies, cake, and the second and third portions urged on her at meals are an extension of love grows up eating even when she's not hungry. No matter how full our stomachs, we always have room for more love.

My brother and I grew up without knowing the meaning of hunger, except on those rare occasions when a meal was unavoidably late. Then we were usually given a snack to tide us over. Mother's cupboards were overstocked, just like mine have been. The two of us have always bought more food than we needed. I learned this from my mother, and she learned it from my great-grandmother, Nanny.

My mother grew up in a home where food was plentiful and her grandmother did most of the shopping and cooking. Meals were large, and the foods were rich—with lots of meat, butter, and cream—based on heavy German-Austrian cooking. There was more than enough food for snacks or meals if unexpected guests dropped in, and they frequently did. After my mother married, she cooked and stocked her pantry just like her grandmother had, although her family was now much smaller.

As I've noted earlier, my mother cooked fattening foods both because she liked their taste and to help my father, who was quite thin, gain weight. I became plump from eating great quantities of creamed foods, dishes with sauces, and desserts topped with whipped cream. And cheese. Mother always had plenty of cheese. It was an alternative to sweets when we'd had enough cookies. No sugar, but just as fattening.

I think she offered me food whenever her own stomach had room for more. If she had not been such a good cook, I might have escaped without overeating. Alas, she was and is an excellent cook, and no one in our family escaped.

When I moved out on my own, I carried some of my mother's

habits with me and continued to overeat. I overate for a variety of reasons: loneliness, boredom, unhappiness, frustration, anxiety—and because I had become used to overeating. I didn't know enough to eat only when I was hungry and to stop when I no longer felt that hunger. I ate all the time, and I waited for the familiar feeling of fullness. Like my mother, I had become used to it.

I have no doubt that if I had had children, they would have had the same tendency to eat whenever there was any room for more. If you don't experience hunger, if you eat to fill space whenever it's there, you may be passing this trait on to your children.

THE HUNGER MECHANISM

As you take a closer look at what hunger feels like, it may help you to know what's going on in your body when you eat, and how your stomach tells you it's full.

While you are chewing, your taste buds send a message to your stomach that food is about to be sent to it. "Get ready for some potassium and phosphorus," your taste buds announce, "she's eating a chicken sandwich. You're getting some vitamin A, some niacin, magnesium, and a little zinc. Oh, yes, here comes a little fat and an assortment of B vitamins, too. You know, the usual stuff that comes with chicken and bread."

Your stomach begins to produce hydrochloric acid, a substance that breaks down some of the raw materials in your food into smaller particles in order to release the vitamins and minerals it contains.

"Hold on a second," your taste buds continue, "there's more vitamin A than I thought. This chicken sandwich seems to have lettuce and tomato on it. Don't forget that means extra iron and calcium because of the tomato. Here it comes—get ready with some more of that hydrochloric acid!"

When your stomach doesn't have enough hydrochloric acid, or if this acid is neutralized by taking antacids, some nutrients don't get utilized. Iron and calcium, for example, need acid in order to be released from foods and assimilated into your cells. When you listen to your body enough to eat just when you're hungry and stop when the feeling of hunger leaves, you can digest your food better. Your stomach is not stuffed, and it is better able to produce enough digestive juices to break down the foods you have eaten. When you digest your food completely, the vitamins, minerals, and other nutrients it contains can get into your cells and nourish you.

But that's not the whole story. If your body expects certain vitamins and minerals that are never liberated due to insufficient hydrochloric acid, it may ask for more food. It expected, and didn't get, a lot of nutrients, and you may still be hungry shortly after you eat.

After your stomach is full, it sends a message to your brain that no more food is needed. If you don't hear this signal, or if you eat too quickly, you may overeat. It takes about fifteen minutes for your stomach to tell your brain that no more food is required. This is an excellent reason to chew well and eat slowly.

Another reason you may want to use hunger to measure the amount of food you eat is gas. Gas, or flatulence, is not just uncomfortable and embarrassing, it's a sign that your body is not breaking your food down into small enough particles to be used, so it's sitting around in your intestines fermenting. You are not what you eat. You are what you eat, digest, and absorb.

Your body will tell you which foods it wants and in what quantities, if you listen to it. Eating too quickly and eating too many fats keeps you from feeling real hunger. A healthy body doesn't need to be fed constantly. In fact, it works more efficiently when there is time between meals to thoroughly digest food.

STOP RUNNING AWAY FROM HUNGER

If feels good to eat when you're hungry; at this point, eating is both necessary and satisfying. Enjoy your food. Savor its tastes and textures. Enjoy the feeling of contentment you get when you put food into an empty stomach and the additional satisfaction of knowing that you're nourishing yourself.

Don't be afraid of feeling hunger by denying its presence. Hunger is not your enemy. It is your body's way of communicating with you. Open up a dialogue with your body by listening to its messages and following its instructions. Unless you have a real shortage of food, hunger can be a friend. Hunger tells us when to eat and when to stop. Those of us who eat too much place ourselves at a disadvantage by quieting or ignoring its voice. Then we are all alone, attempting to gauge the amount we eat by seeing how much it looks like on our plate and guessing whether or not it will fill us. The idea is to eat when your body needs food and to stop when you are no longer hungry. Let your body run on the fuel from the foods you eat and on your body fat, if you have an excess amount of this.

I stopped overeating when I stopped running away from hunger and began paying attention to its messages. Although these feelings were strange when I first began having them, I know now what they mean, and they have become familiar allies in my caring for myself. Now there are times when I feel a little hungry, when I suddenly become aware of an empty feeling or a slight growling in my stomach, the area just below my left ribcage. I've learned to watch for signs that my body needs food, such as this feeling of emptiness in my stomach or difficulty concentrating. The latter can mean a slight drop in blood sugar; a piece of fruit, a few crackers, or some diluted fruit juice will raise blood-sugar levels and restore the ability to concentrate in a few minutes.

Do not allow yourself to get hungry if your doctor has advised against it for an existing medical problem, but if you have nothing that gets in your way, hear it and feel it. And listen.

TAKING ACTION

1. **Affirmation:** Hunger is my teacher and my friend.

2. **What does your hunger feel like?** Allow yourself to feel hungry. Pay attention to how hunger feels physically as well as to any emotions it evokes in you. Then, wait ten or fifteen minutes

before you eat. During this time, tell yourself that you are fine and will be eating shortly. Remind yourself that you are learning more about yourself so you can take better care of your body.

3. **How much do you really need?** To see how little food you need, you may want to conduct what I call the **Quarter-Sandwich Experiment.** In the morning, make a low-fat sandwich—for example, turkey with lettuce and tomatoes or a veggie sandwich. Cut the sandwich in quarters. When you feel physical sensations of hunger, have one-quarter of the sandwich for breakfast. Wait to identify feelings of hunger before you eat.

    Do not eat anything else. Wait until you feel hungry again, and again pay attention to how it feels. Is your stomach grumbling and asking for food? When you have identified a feeling as being hunger, not just as your desire to eat, have another quarter of the sandwich. Don't eat anything else.

    See how long it takes you to eat that one sandwich. You may find that it lasts until mid-afternoon, or longer. Have one-quarter of the sandwich each time you have identified the feeling of hunger. Notice how little food your stomach needs for you not to be hungry. Think back to how much it can hold before you feel full. Don't look for your old feeling of fullness anymore; just expect a satisfied feeling of not being hungry. Although this may be unfamiliar at first, it will be more and more satisfying as you repeatedly eat to eliminate hunger rather than to achieve a feeling of fullness.

    Eat when you are hungry until you're not hungry anymore. If you want a little more of the taste, eat a few more mouthfuls. *Don't* eat until you feel overstuffed and uncomfortable. The absence of pain, guilt, and bloating will likely be new and unfamiliar. This exercise introduces you to a new, healthier eating pattern. It's not at all about denial. When you eat less you are not denying yourself food; instead, you're denying these feelings of discomfort.

4. **Filling foods:** The foods that make you feel satisfied are often high in fats. Because a high-fat diet is not healthy, you will want

to begin changing over to eating other foods. Dense foods like beans and whole grains are also filling. But because they are lower in fat, you can eat more of them without as much concern about weight gain.

Consult with a nutritionist or read some books on nutrition (any by Jane Brody, for instance) to get information on how you can feel full without risking your health.

5. **Talk about hunger with your child.** What does it feel like when she's hungry? When she feels full?

How can your child learn to feel more comfortable with a little hunger, rather than living with the constant discomfort that comes from feeling stuffed, guilty, and possibly overweight? Talk with her about the benefits you get when you listen to your body and hear the message hunger brings about when, and how much, to eat. Be a role model for your children.

11

LEARNING TO PLAN AHEAD:

The Solution to Procrastinating

Planning requires self-discipline and self-respect. When people around you make decisions for you, and you don't learn to make them for yourself, you grow up without this skill. The result is often procrastination. Learning to plan ahead means having enough discipline to make decisions and follow through with them. When parents are too busy to give attention to a child and to teach her that her opinions are worthwhile, the child may lack self-respect and feel that her decisions don't count.

"I don't plan my meals, I eat whatever's around," Susan told me when I asked her what she ate for dinner. "Sometimes popcorn, sometimes ice cream, sometimes a TV dinner. And a lot of fast-food take-out."

Susan is a single parent. She does the shopping and is completely responsible for stocking her cupboards and refrigerator for herself and her eight-year-old daughter. No one else buys the ice cream. When there's no food in the house, it's because Susan didn't buy any. If she planned ahead and bought differently, she would have healthful foods on hand. But, like many women, Susan does not plan her meals ahead. In fact, she doesn't plan ahead with anything. She procrastinates in all areas of her life and then feels disappointed when things don't happen.

If Susan felt better about herself and her ability to make wise decisions, she would take better care of herself and her daughter by planning her weekly groceries and eating healthful meals. But Susan grew up in a large family, with seven brothers and sisters. All the children had vied for their parents' attention, and Susan had never felt that her parents saw her as an individual or respected any of her decisions. She felt unhappy and left out much of the time, and she escaped into a world of fantasy in which she was a world-famous singer and actress who finally got her parents' undivided love and attention. Her parents didn't take Susan's daydreams seriously; they were too busy surviving and supporting their other children's more realistic aspirations.

Susan was serious about her dreams. Singing and acting were what she wanted to do more than anything. The more she talked about this, the more her family made fun of her. When other decisions she made were also ridiculed, Susan came to believe that she could not make good ones. Her solution was to stop making any decisions at all—unless she was forced to. And, predictably, her parents would then make fun of her. Because her parents didn't take the time to encourage Susan's creativity and instead eroded her confidence in her ability to make decisions, she eventually became passive and just did what she had to do to get by.

There was not much opportunity for the eight children in the family to decide what foods they wanted to eat, what clothes they wanted to buy, or which household chores they preferred to do. They did the chores they were told to do, wore the clothes that were given to them, and ate the food that was placed in front of them. No options. If they didn't do their chores, they were punished, but they were never praised for doing a job well. Susan's mother was either too busy to tell her children how well each had done with daily chores, or she simply didn't think of it.

As a child, Susan rebelled whenever she could get away with it.

When she was bored with the foods her mother prepared—peanut-butter-and-jelly sandwiches, spaghetti, hamburger, tuna casseroles—she skipped meals and ate sweets, like spoonfuls of jelly or sugar, or when she could afford it, candy. She knew this was not a good decision, but she had never learned to make good ones. In fact, Susan succeeded in the only area she could, by becoming the mistress of poor decisions.

When I met Susan, she was overweight and depressed. She continued to excel in one area: making poor decisions. Because she didn't know how to shop ahead or prepare foods ahead of time, she lived on cheeseburgers and french fries, and she indulged in chocolates, ice cream, and pie. And she was teaching her daughter to eat the same way.

Susan had developed a strong pattern of procrastination by this time. When a decision had to be made, she considered each possibility for a long time and often became immobile, unable to decide. When she did decide, she worried about her decision. Was it right? Was it the best? She felt uncomfortable either deciding or not deciding. It was easier for her not to plan meals ahead and not to be more responsible for herself and her daughter, even though she felt better physically and had more energy when she did.

Susan had had an unhappy childhood partly because she hadn't understood why her family operated the way it did. No explanations were given to any of the children; they just did as they were told. She never understood why her mother didn't praise her when she did well or made good decisions, and she didn't understand that the economy and simplicity with which her mother ran such a large family were necessary for the family's survival.

Susan had been a lonely child who had never felt enough love and hadn't received enough encouragement or attention. She had felt like a misfit, out of place and unsure of herself. Because her mother was so busy taking care of everyone else, she presented a role model to Susan of a woman who gave to others and did nothing for herself. Susan became passive in that area also, and she never learned to give to herself.

It was different for Susan's daughter. Susan gave her all the attention that she herself had wanted and missed as a child, but she coupled this attention with the reactions of the hurt, lonely, rebellious, and insecure child who was still inside her. She was still reacting to her mother's food and her mother's rules, and she was teaching her daughter these reactions as well: to eat anything she felt like eating, even if it was not healthful; to leave the house messy if she didn't feel like cleaning it; and to not plan ahead because her decisions were not to be trusted.

Unhappy and immobile, Susan came to me for help in changing some of her negative eating patterns. And she did change them all, with a little direction and a lot of support. Susan had two key issues: she blamed her mother for whatever she hadn't been given (praise, attention, information about what was going on in the family and why), and she didn't have enough self-confidence to make decisions.

Something in our relationship gave her the validation she was looking for and woke her up from her passivity. This is the affirmation we developed that helped give Susan the ability to trust her decisions: "My mother did the best she could. She taught me what she knew. Now I know more."

Within a month of doing this affirmation every day, something changed inside Susan. She became more aware of her power to make decisions and more comfortable in making them. Her dedication and progress astonished me. Suddenly, she knew what she was doing when she gave in to a food craving. She began watching her reactions and noticing how bad she felt after eating chocolates or french fries. Most important, she saw that her life had been made up of two extremes: working at a job she very much disliked, and gratifying herself with food. She realized that she deserved a better life than the one she had given herself.

The woman who couldn't make a decision when she first came to my office now decided to be healthy and happy, and she realized that to reach that goal she needed to spend time actively working toward her health and happiness by exercising, preparing healthful foods, and focusing on achieving goals rather than simply daydreaming about them. She gave up the fantasy that her mother would some day give her the attention she had wanted as a child, and she began giving it to herself.

During that first month, Susan took steps to move to another city. She had been wanting to move for years, but she had felt unable to take the first step. She found a more interesting job with the help of a friend, then an apartment she could share with another single mother who had a daughter the same age as her own. Some of the decisions she made were not perfect ones, but she saw them as good interim ones and accepted them along with their limitations.

Not all of Susan's decisions concerning food are good ones, either, but when they're not, she learns about herself from them. In fact, this whole journey has been about learning. Susan has learned that when she has to make too many decisions at once, she is likely to revert back to her comfortable old patterns and eat poorly. So, even though she'd like to do it all at once, she concentrates on making a little progress at a time.

She builds self-confidence with each workable decision she makes. Each such decision takes her to her next one. It is slow progress at times, but it is progress. Susan sees her failures as temporary setbacks and as lessons, nothing more. And she is teaching her daughter how to trust the decisions she makes and to take care of herself, so that she will not become an unhappy, overweight, immobile woman like her mother once was.

TAKING ACTION

1. **Affirmation:** My mother did the best she could. She taught me what she knew. Now I know more.

    Use Susan's affirmation, or another one if you prefer, to help you reprogram the inner messages that keep you in your old negative childhood eating patterns. Look at whatever is stopping you from making decisions and see yourself moving out of your passivity. Your affirmation may be one like "I am worthwhile" or "I have enough love and support in my life" or "I deserve happiness in my life." When you stand by yourself, you *are* worthwhile, and you *do* have the love and support you need. You are enough.

2. **Accentuate the positive:** Give yourself credit for the good decisions you make. Write them down in your notebook at the end of each day and look them over. Concentrate on the positive, and see all of your decisions as lessons that can help you at another time. The more you decide to eat foods that make you feel good and to enter into situations that make you feel comfortable, the easier it becomes for you to take better care of yourself.

3. **Take baby steps:** Don't try to do too much at once. Don't allow yourself to feel overwhelmed by the number of decisions you have to make at any time. When you feel overwhelmed, stop! Then, when you can, make the simplest, safest decision you know how, like deciding to open a can of lentil or vegetable soup for dinner.

   Be willing to make decisions for now that might not ultimately be the best ones possible. Make a decision that is better than none at all and better than a poor one. Accept this, and allow yourself to feel comfortable with each small decision. Be gentle with yourself.

4. **Ask for help when you need it:** When you are passive, you do not learn how to do things. You may first need to learn simple tasks, such as how to prepare nutritious meals or how to make out a shopping list for the week ahead. Although you may believe you should already know how to do these things, perhaps nobody taught you.

   Pick any task you have difficulty with and ask a friend, a member of a support group, a psychotherapist, or a nutritionist for help in learning how to do it. As you learn these things, you will be able to pass them on to your children.

5. **Share your process with others:** Let people around you know what's going on with you, even if you did not do this as a child. Share your feelings and progress with your children, so that their experiences will be different from yours. Encourage them to confide in you when they have difficulty making decisions. Help each other, and talk over the possibilities. None of you is alone.

6. **Pay attention to your child.** Tell her when she does something right, and give her the opportunity to make decisions more often. Ask her what she feels like eating and discuss the pros and cons of those foods. Make up a menu with three or four acceptable items, and let her decide what she would like to eat. Then have her help you prepare the meal. Use this time to teach her what you know or are learning about better nutrition and better eating habits.

12

LEARNING A "BETTER THAN" APPROACH:

The Solution to Being a Perfectionist

Some people draw their life boldly in blacks and whites, with no grays. They have an all-or-nothing approach when it comes to many aspects of their lives, especially eating habits. Either they eat perfectly, or they fail. Often, they fail. The approach they take sets them up for failure, because none of us can succeed forever in eating perfectly.

These people begin the day with good intentions, then find themselves eating foods they've designated as "forbidden" or "bad" and feel they've blown it. Since they've failed for the day, they continue eating anything, and often everything, that they had successfully been avoiding up to that point. They feel guilty, they feel like failures, and they feel worthless, because the entire day has been spoiled by a cookie, an order of french fries, or a dish of ice cream.

If this sounds like you, you're certainly not alone. And if this is your attitude, there's an excellent chance it will be your child's as well. The all-or-nothing approach that contributes to your sense of failure and your unhappiness is a negative eating pattern you are unwittingly teaching your child. It's time to look for another answer for both of you. Pauline found it by gradually doing "better than" she had in the past.

Pauline, thirty-six, is a photographer and has a young daughter. She became my patient some years ago when her compulsive eating brought her weight and cholesterol count to an all-time high. She was uncomfortable, unhappy, thought of herself as a failure in many areas of her life, and had little self-confidence because, as she said, "I can't even eat right!" Since a number of her relatives had heart disease, Pauline was as worried about her cholesterol as she was about her excess weight. She was determined to do something about both, but she felt very, very stuck. She loved fatty foods and ate ice cream every day, and she loved to drink with friends. She felt there was no way out, that it wouldn't be possible to stop drinking and eating what she wanted and still have any fun.

It was ironic to me that this talented photographer saw her life as being only black or white. While her photographs contained grays, she judged everything in her own life in terms of good or bad, success or failure—values she had learned from her mother. She was a failure with food because no matter how well she ate at times, eventually she overate and drank too much alcohol. Then, in her mind, she canceled all prior successes.

Pauline's mother had been critical. She had constantly picked on her daughter for numerous minor faults, such as "being lazy." Although Pauline never doubted her mother's love, the daily criticisms that sprinkled her life were too much for her, and she gave up trying to succeed. Unless she could assure herself of success in an area, she wouldn't even try. She'd rather do nothing than be criticized by her mother.

For example, she knew she could make her bed neatly, so she made her bed—but she didn't think she could act well enough to get a part in the school play, so she didn't go to the auditions. Immobilized by her fear of failure and by criticism, Pauline did, indeed, appear to be lazy. Actually, she was not. It was just that if she couldn't do something perfectly, she didn't do anything at all. She grew into a capable young woman who didn't see any of her abilities, except her ability to fail.

Pauline's mother had also been criticized as a child, and as an adult she admonished herself for her own shortcomings as much as she did her daughter for hers. She was "bad" because she could never lose weight. She was a failure because she ate too many sweets and had become a diabetic. Pauline grew up with a role model for failure. And she perceived her father, who died when she was young, as having failed her by dying.

Children who grow up in homes with critical parents often go on to reprimand themselves, and later their own children. Pauline's mother may have had the best of motives for scolding her daughter—to help Pauline learn better habits. Like many mothers, she saw herself as teaching and correcting her daughter, but her scolding felt like criticism to the child. Pauline, being an exceptional person, went on to achieve a master's degree in self-criticism.

"I'm going to blow it this weekend, I just know it!" Pauline complained to me. "We're going out to dinner with friends on Friday night to a great restaurant that makes the best ribs, and I know I'm going to have them. Saturday evening there's a big party, and I'm going to want to have four or five drinks. They'll have chips and dips and some kind of chocolate dessert that I love. Then, on Sunday, we're having my in-laws over for a brunch of bagels, lox, and cream cheese. There's no way I can possibly stay on my diet."

She was right. With an all-or-nothing approach, all Pauline could do was fail. She wanted to do everything perfectly so she wouldn't be criticized, and out of her fear of criticism she became an extremist. She had come to me for help in reducing her weight and cholesterol, and though she knew her high-fat diet added to both, she was dismayed to learn that alcohol affected her cholesterol as well. Since our bodies burn sugars before fats, and since alcohol is a quickly assimilated form of sugar, it's difficult to reduce cholesterol—which is a fat—as long as you drink.

Pauline knew she was willing to go to the party without drinking or to go to dinner or be at her brunch without eating fats. We began by looking in advance at each meal for viable alternatives. My goal was to help Pauline see that she could make some progress even if she ate some fats and had a few drinks. And any progress was a step forward.

"What other foods will be available at dinner besides ribs?" I asked her.

"French fries and cole slaw," she quickly replied.

I temporarily put aside the subject of the ribs, knowing it was the food she most wanted. "Could you get a baked potato instead of the fries?" I questioned, wanting to know what options existed.

"Sure, I probably could," Pauline said. "But what about all the butter and sour cream I usually put on it? What's the difference, if I just exchange one fat for another?"

"You could put some of the cole slaw on your potato," I suggested, "or eat a bite of one, then a little of the other. Or even use half the amount of butter than you usually use, and pass on the sour cream. It would be better than having butter with sour cream or having french fries. Would that work for you?"

She thought it would, and she was willing to consider other options through which she could feel good about the taste of the foods she was eating and still succeed at making progress, instead of writing the meal off in advance as a failure. The restaurant served a large platter that contained both chicken and ribs. Pauline was willing to order this combination and to take the skin off the chicken, as long as she could also eat some of the ribs so that she wouldn't feel deprived. I knew deprivation wouldn't work for long. Her best choice, I felt, was to eat "better than" she would have on her own.

That weekend, Pauline began her "better than" approach. Each choice she made was a little better than the one she would have made before we met. She had two drinks instead of three or four at the party. She was not only satisfied, but she was also extremely pleased at her accomplishment. She put only a film of cream cheese on her bagel instead of piling it on, and she enjoyed the family brunch. In the past she had gained a pound or two after weekend parties with family and friends. At the end of this weekend she had actually lost half a pound. Pauline felt victorious.

Over the months she reduced her intake of fats and alcohol even further. Pauline is now one of those rare individuals who can eat a little bit of something for the taste, then leave the rest. Instead of having her usual full order of spareribs at a Chinese restaurant, she ate one from her husband's order. She had one drink at a party. She took a few of her daughter's french fries and was satisfied. She ate two teaspoons of ice cream every single day. In nine months, Pauline's cholesterol count went from 252 to 170, and she lost forty-eight pounds.

When all-or-nothing won't work, use the "better than" approach. I remind myself and my patients of this option daily. On the wall behind my chair in my office, facing my patients so they can't miss it, is a framed message embroidered for me by a former patient. It contains the advice she found most helpful: **"Forget perfection. Aim for excellence."**

Every week I see at least one new patient who, like Pauline, is sensitive and capable and wants approval and recognition. Often, such a person goes to the opposite extreme and becomes immobile if she is unable to succeed. The embroidered saying is a valuable reminder for the perfectionist part of these patients, the part that causes them to simply stop trying.

You don't have to eat perfectly all the time. Just eat well as often as you can, and do a little better as soon as you are able. Aim for excellence, and leave your need for perfection behind. When you do, you also leave your guarantee of failure behind. I often look at the beautiful plaque on my wall and silently thank the woman who was moved to make it for me. When I look closely, I can see the imperfections in the stitching—what a beautiful reminder of the truth it contains!

Perhaps being a perfectionist works in other areas of your life, and perhaps not. In any event, it usually backfires in the area of eating patterns. An all-or-nothing approach is one of the best excuses you can create for failing, in eating or in anything else. At some point you're likely to slip. If you think of this slip as a failure, you only reinforce your ability to fail. In time, you've created the perfect excuse to stop working on your overeating: you can't possibly succeed 100 percent of the time.

When you slip off your diet or eating program, whether deliberately or unconsciously, you may feel you've failed for the day, the weekend, or the week. You haven't. You're using your momentary error as an excuse to overeat. Time is arbitrary. It's an endless succession of events we mark for our convenience by units of measurement called minutes, hours, days, and weeks. Time, as we live it, is only *now*. You can only succeed in the moment, although you can look back at past successes. And you can only fail, or slip, in the moment, not for an arbitrary unit of measurement called a day or a week.

If you were to spill a glass of water on yourself in the morning, it would be foolish to deny yourself any more liquids for the rest of the day. You would only be using the accident as an excuse to avoid liquids or to punish yourself. It's the same with eating: when you eat something you didn't intend to eat, the worst you can do is slip in the moment. There is no way of extending this moment into the future, except in your mind. Moments don't extend. Look at what you did, forgive yourself, and move on to the next moment.

If you learned something about yourself—that you sometimes eat unconsciously, that you overeat when you're under stress, that you crave a particular food and can't seem to stop with just a little—what took place in the moment was certainly not a failure, but a lesson that taught you more about yourself and your relationship to food. Don't punish yourself; instead, appreciate the lesson you've learned. Share this thought with your child and encourage her to appreciate the lessons she learns that lead to her self-improvement, rather than being disappointed or angry with herself for not doing something perfectly. We make mistakes as we learn. That's part of learning.

You may feel it's easier to recognize a single error, and to forgive yourself for it, than it is with a series of lapses, but look at the multiple times you've slipped as an opportunity to practice forgiveness. Most likely you haven't been very forgiving with yourself, and your child may be equally hard on herself.

Celebrations and holidays give all of us an opportunity to observe our eating patterns and to learn important lessons, including that of being gentle with ourselves. In some months there may be so many celebrations that you write off a whole block of time, using it as an excuse to overeat. During the month of December there are numerous occasions for slipping. You may be in the habit of giving up the first time you break down and indulge in a food or drink you've sworn off "forever." The new year is only weeks away, you may rationalize, separated from Christmas and Hanukkah by a series of parties, and you can begin fresh with a resolution to return to your better eating program soon enough. In the back of your mind, you know that this year's resolutions won't last any longer than last year's did. If you find your life filled with celebrations, each one filled with irresistible foods, the suggestions in Chapter 25 for enjoying these events without feeling deprived or emerging as a failure can help you.

Instead of trying to be perfect in your eating habits, begin to slowly improve your diet and gradually change your eating habits. You may not be able to eat perfectly, but you can succeed in eating "better than" you have in the past. In time, you can even eat extremely well! This approach worked for Pauline. She is still eating "better than" she has in the past, although there are times when she slips back into her old patterns. She continues to improve slowly, and by seeing her improvements she knows she will never again be back where she began: feeling like a failure and feeling overwhelmed by her inability to eat perfectly.

If you criticize your child when she makes mistakes rather than encouraging her to see the good in what she's done and do better next time, point out what you see instead of criticizing her and let her know she can either learn from her mistakes or become defeated by them. Demonstrate how this is done by doing it first yourself. Be her role model.

TAKING ACTION

1. **Affirmation:** I am good and capable, and I keep improving.

2. **Look at your critical side:** How do you feel when you are criticized? Would you rather have an imperfection pointed out to you once and then dropped, or repeated over and over? Does the tone of voice used and the manner in which the criticism is given affect the way you feel about it?

   Pay attention for one week to whether or not you criticize yourself, your friends, your co-workers or your children. When you criticize someone, look for that fault in yourself. What are you really upset about? With whom are you upset?

Take a one-day inventory: Write down each critical remark you made in that day, and how you felt afterward. What could you have said or done differently? When you act differently, does it feel more or less effective?

Share with your child any of this list that pertains to her. Talk together about new ways you can use to correct her. Bring a little gentleness and humor into the situations—for example, "Was there a reason for your not cleaning up your room, like hiding an alien from another planet underneath that pile of laundry in the corner? You know I like to meet all your friends!" If this doesn't come easily to you, you could simply say, "Please clean your room." Either would be easier for your daughter to hear and respond to than "I told you to clean up your room!! You're the laziest person I've ever known. Can't you even keep your clothes in your own room picked up??" Be more gentle and lighthearted with yourself, as well. *Stop criticizing yourself.*

3. **The Gold Star Exercise:** This exercise is designed to reinforce your successes and de-emphasize your failures. When one of my patients has had an exceptional week and has succeeded in overcoming a difficult pattern in her eating program, I reach into my desk for a gold star and paste it in her food diary or on the back of her hand! Gold stars bring back pleasant memories of having done well in elementary school. They tell us we've excelled; they make us feel good inside. The little girl inside us responds to them at any age. This exercise is designed to help you concentrate on your successes with food rather than focusing on failures.

Keep a diary of everything you eat for a week. Don't look back at anything you've written until the week is over. At the end of the week, sit down with your diary and a package of gold stars. Paste a gold star next to everything you ate or drank that was part of your intended program: drinking plenty of water, eating vegetables, having chicken without the skin. Don't do anything about the times you slipped. You've been hard on yourself long enough. Now it's time to take a gentler approach and look at the positive things you do.

Look back at your diary and see how many gold stars you have. Keep the diary for another week, and aim for the stars. Give yourself credit for each little success that takes you a step closer to your goal. See where you've slipped, and think about how you could turn similar situations into gold-star opportunities in the future. Accentuate the positive, and the negative will be eventually eliminated.

You can use the Gold Star Exercise with your daughter if she is old enough to keep a diary and go over it with you. Don't compete with your daughter to see who can get more gold stars. Compete only with yourself, from one week to the next. Try for a "better than" approach with yourself. Your goal is not to be "better than" your daughter, nor is hers to be "better than" you.

4. **Forgiveness Meditation:** There is nothing more powerful than forgiveness. It comes from love, the most powerful force there is. If you feel powerless over food at times, use this force to help you heal yourself.

Be kind to yourself. Be gentle and loving. When you are angry or disappointed with yourself for the way you're eating use this Forgiveness Meditation. Record it on a cassette tape, and play it back to yourself every chance you have until you can accept the words and forgiveness has become a natural part of you. Speak slowly, and leave enough blank time after any questions for you to answer them mentally when you listen to the tape. If you would like to change some of this meditation, feel free to do so. Use your own words, your own example, to help you change.

To do the meditation, begin by sitting quietly in a relaxed, comfortable position. Take a few slow, deep breaths. Allow your worries to melt away as you look at a recent time when food temporarily took control of your life. For a few moments, detach yourself from your emotions surrounding this incident and become an observer.

Mentally move outside your body and visualize yourself as you were the last time you ate uncontrollably or ate a food you'd been trying to avoid. What was going on? Did you feel lonely, angry, worthless, unhappy? Did you eat for emotional reasons, or did you have a physical craving you couldn't resist? Look at your actions as if you were looking not at yourself, but at someone else whom you love very deeply. This person has felt helpless and trapped, but she is working to move beyond her past habits and gain new information that will help her to learn new patterns.

Visualize her as being weighted down with heavy bags of guilt, depression, anger, and self-hatred that are tied to her clothing. She can hardly move. Each time she judges herself, another bag of heavy emotions appears and makes it more difficult for her to budge. Help her to free herself from these judgments. Show her how easy it is to move about without the bags. Now mentally pick up a pair of scissors and cut the strings that attach these bags to her clothing. The scissors are so sharp they can easily cut through any material. Use them to cut through the bags, allowing the emotions inside to spill out and vanish.

Now this person is lighter. She is free to move to the next time in her life where she will be given an opportunity to look at her patterns with food. She is no longer weighted down by the emotions that accompanied her old patterns. She can move more easily and change her actions without the distractions of guilt or other emotions. She can create new patterns in which she feels comfortable with food, patterns in which choices are effortless.

Tell her you understand how hard she has struggled. Take her by the hands, hold her in your arms, and let her know you are there to love and support her. The past is gone. She can let the emotions from all the yesterdays disappear. Give her your love to replace her negativity. There is no room for both. Fill her heart with your forgiveness. Tell her you forgive her for holding on to her anger, for judging herself, for feeling she was unlovable. You know she did the best she could with the information she had. You are helping her find new information.

Now blend into her once more. You are no longer the observer. You are the person who sat down a few moments ago, only now you are lighter. Feel the lightness inside you. The bags of guilt and disappointment are gone. There is no need for your guilt, your anger, or your hurt. You are working to change your habits and find solutions to your cravings. Each day, you move closer to your goal of freedom with food. You are a very wonderful person to love yourself enough to work with yourself in this way.

Take a deep breath and feel the love that accompanies the forgiveness in your heart. Forgive yourself for having been harsh with yourself in the past, for not having known the power of gentleness and love. You did the best you could. Now you know more, and you are moving closer and closer to feeling comfortable around all foods. Take in another breath as you slowly open your eyes, and continue your day refreshed and centered in your love.

13

LEARNING TO PACE YOURSELF:

The Solution to Eating for the Past or Future

As we saw in the last chapter, someone who procrastinates may be so immobilized by the fear of being criticized for making the wrong decision that she puts off planning meals ahead of time. She thinks a great deal about herself and what other people think of her. On the other hand, someone who eats a large meal for a past one she missed or for a meal that she anticipates missing later often doesn't think of herself at all. This is another example of denial. In her view, her job, her family, her projects, and her friends are all more important than she is.

Some people eat a larger breakfast if their busy schedule doesn't include time for lunch. Others eat more than they either want or need at lunch just in case dinner is delayed and they have no time for a snack. Many people skip breakfast or lunch, only to stuff themselves at the next meal because they're extremely hungry.

If you are compensating by overeating to avoid the possibility of being hungry later on in the day or because you skipped a meal earlier, you're putting yourself last and making yourself less important than what you do. And you're teaching your children to do the same. You haven't learned to pace yourself and plan ahead, and as a result you may often feel overfull or bloated, and you may be gaining unnecessary weight.

News flash! Skipping meals may help you gain weight!!

Missing meals doesn't necessarily help you lose weight. If you skip meals, your body may hold on to extra calories to guard against starvation. This is a survival tactic your ancestors' bodies adopted generations ago because of their exposure to floods, wars, poor crop production, and outright famines. If you have a "survivor's body," it doesn't know you plan to eat dinner. It just knows you're not eating breakfast or lunch, so it's holding on to every calorie it can, storing it away in your fat cells, to protect you from famine. Don't fool yourself into thinking you're doing yourself a favor by eating a large meal and skipping another.

A growing number of women skip meals because they feel they simply have no time to eat three meals a day. "I don't have time for breakfast," Darlene complained to me. "I have to be out of the house before seven to get to work on time. By lunchtime, I'm starved. I know that's why I overeat, but I have no choice. Sometimes I work right through lunch, then I stuff myself at dinner and eat afterward until I go to sleep."

Darlene might not have time to prepare eggs and toast or even to sit down to a bowl of cereal before she leaves for work, but somewhere in the early-morning hours she has time to take care of her nutritional needs before she starts work, even if this means eating only a piece of fruit or a healthful muffin. If she doesn't do this, she is denying herself good health and energy by making her work more important than her health.

Actually, it can take only an additional fifteen minutes to fix and eat a simple breakfast without wolfing it down. Isn't your physical and emotional health worth your getting up fifteen minutes early? If you have a family, you have an additional reason for taking care of yourself by eating breakfast. When you tell your children how important it is for them to start the day with breakfast and then ignore your own advice, you're giving them a confusing double message.

Although she is not yet twenty-five, Darlene holds an important position with a large company. Her many responsibilities force her to begin work at seven-thirty, sometimes work through lunch, and often leave after seven at night. She came to me complaining of fatigue, weight gain, and more colds and flus than she'd ever had before. Whenever she became too sick to work, her duties at the office piled up, and she dreaded going back. Her prestigious job had become a nightmare, and Darlene felt trapped.

"When was the last time you went out to eat with friends?" I asked her.

"A few months ago I went out to lunch with some girlfriends from work," she recalled.

"What about dinner dates?" I questioned, wondering why such an attractive young woman was limiting her eating out to having a rare lunch with colleagues.

"I'm too tired," Darlene confessed. "I just make a huge dinner for myself after work because by then I'm starved, and then I climb into bed with a book or watch a little television. On weekends I relax, sleep late, and eat whatever I feel like—my favorites are pepperoni pizza and hamburger with fries. I do chores around the apartment and as little else as possible to get ready to face all the work that I know will be waiting on my desk Monday morning."

Here was a talented, responsible, beautiful woman who had barely enough energy to get through a busy workweek, and who overate at dinner to make up both for a missed lunch and for a lack of companionship. These should have been some of the best years of her life, and yet she felt tired and depressed. Where was the fun? And where had her attitude about sacrificing her life for her job come from?

Darlene grew up in a family that culturally put a great deal of value on the work ethic. It was instilled in her at an early age that a person's job comes first and that it is important to excel in one's job, not just to be adequate. Darlene never gave her other options a second thought. She was trained from childhood by her family to work, and to work hard. She was never taught to take care of herself or to put herself before her job. Darlene was the perfect employee, but she was an exhausted, unsatisfied woman who had no idea why she felt as she did.

Her denial was a composite of the attitudes of her self-sacrificing mother and her work-oriented father. Darlene rarely thought about herself unless she was too sick or too exhausted to work at her usual pace. When that happened, she felt guilty for not being able to meet the standards her parents had set for themselves and for her.

"What would you like to do with your life?" I asked Darlene in one of our sessions. "Do you want to stay with this company and eventually get promoted into an executive position?"

"Absolutely not," she replied with no hesitation. "If you think I'm overworked, you should see what my boss and the other executives have to do!"

"Then why in the world are you sacrificing your life for this job? You skip meals because there's no time to eat, then you overeat once, and sometimes twice, a day. Your missed meals and overeating are making you tired and run-down. You have no fuel for energy, no fuel to feed your brain so you can think clearly. My guess is that some of your decisions, especially those you make in the afternoons, are sometimes not your best." Darlene nodded at my observation. I continued, "You indulge in all kinds of junk foods on weekends because this is one of the only pleasures you have in a life empty of friends and recreation."

"Where do I begin?" Darlene asked, finally realizing that she had been giving up her life and health for a job she didn't even want to keep for very long.

"You begin at the beginning, with breakfast," I suggested. "Then you continue with lunch and dinner. You find or make time for three meals a day and an occasional snack, if you need it. You think ahead, you prepare ahead, but you never *eat* ahead. In other words, don't overeat just because you don't know when you're going to have your next meal. Don't overeat because you didn't take time for a meal earlier and now you are overly hungry. If you skip a meal because you're not hungry, perhaps having a snack before your next meal would suffice as a compromise. Live in the present, and eat in the present."

Eating for the past or the future may not be just the result of poor planning but may also come from the belief that the work you do is of primary importance in your life. You figure that since you're invincible and will survive just about anything, you can skip a meal with little consequence. Not necessarily true. You are not your work; you are not what you do. Your health is primary. Without it, you can't work as effectively, and you may not be able to work at all for periods of time—as Darlene found when she had repeated bouts of the flu.

When you are hungry, weak, or tired, or can't think clearly, it may be because you have skipped a meal. If you can find five minutes to take a bathroom break, you can take the same amount of time, or more, to eat.

Years ago, a friend of mine surprised me by saying, "I like selfish people."

Thinking I may have misunderstood, I asked her to elaborate.

"I don't mean those who don't think of others," she explained. "I mean people who take care of themselves. Then I don't have to take care of them. I can if I *want* to, but I don't *have* to. They're not dependent on people; they're self-sufficient."

Become a little more selfish—or self-sufficient, if you will. Take care of yourself so others don't have to take care of you. Take care of your body so it will support the other work you choose to do. By doing so, you present a powerful role model for your daughter. Teach her how to take care of herself, too. Show her how you can create satisfaction and joy out of any work you do when you have the energy, enthusiasm, and strength to complete it without feeling depleted at the end of the day.

Eat in the present. Make time for yourself and plan ahead when necessary by bringing food with you when you have a busy day scheduled and don't know where you can grab a quick meal. Don't take yourself for granted, even if other people do. See your value. Take care of your body. When you make yourself more important than your activities, you can usually find enough time to eat the meal you thought you'd have to skip. Remember, you're teaching your child she's important and needs to take care of herself, too.

Is it difficult for you to plan ahead for yourself? Do you find there's just not enough time to take care of everyone and everything in your life and still have time for yourself? You set an example for your daughter and everyone around you simply by eating three times a day, no matter what. You may also avoid the crankiness, fatigue, and unclear thinking that can come from a drop in blood sugar when you miss meals.

Take care of yourself so you can be there for the people in your life. When you make yourself healthier by consistently nourishing your body, and happier by keeping yourself clearheaded and energetic, you can also take better care of others. Value yourself for all you do. Teach your children you are not "just" a mother—there is no such thing. You are a loving caretaker who often takes on a number of additional tasks, but none is as important as that of demonstrating and teaching love. Love yourself enough to plan ahead and eat regularly. Love your children enough to teach them this lesson.

TAKING ACTION

1. **Affirmation:** I am taking care of myself first, because I have value.

2. **Schedule your meals:** Become aware of your past negative eating patterns and how missing meals has led to overeating. Begin by thinking ahead and looking at your day. Make a schedule and write in the times of your meals. Whether you work at home or at an outside job, set aside time for three meals at equal intervals. When that is impossible, have a small nutritious snack—such as a piece of fruit, a muffin, some vegetables, a piece of whole-grain bread, or some crackers—to keep from becoming too hungry later on. Write in the times for your snacks if you feel that having a little food between meals will keep you from overeating at your next meal, and do your best to eat at these times.

3. **Prepare food ahead of time:** Make a large salad and one main dish on the weekend that will tide you over for some lunches or dinners during the week. Even if this food is not enough for every meal, it will get you into the habit of eating better foods during the workweek.

Freeze some of the meals in individual portions (zip-lock bags work well). Take one out of the freezer each morning for that night's dinner, or pop it into the microwave, if you have one, when you get home at night. Some foods can be cooked ahead, including these: beans, stews, chili (made with lean ground turkey rather than fattier beef), pasta with marinara sauce filled with vegetables, hearty soups with vegetables and barley or brown rice, packages of precooked brown rice or millet, broiled chicken breasts, and sliced turkey for sandwiches or main meals.

4. **Help your child plan meals:** Talk with your child about the importance of putting herself and her health first by eating regularly. Let her know that by taking care of her body's needs she becomes more grown-up and responsible. Sit down with her and help her plan times to eat, just as you did for yourself. If you have difficulty doing this, work with a psychotherapist who will help you find the time, or a nutritionist who can give you specific information on healthy meals.

14

LEARNING HOW TO
MAKE CHOICES:

The Solution to Being Overdisciplined

An overly disciplined child eats whatever she is given, whether she likes it or not or is hungry or full. She often behaves herself to get attention and praise or to avoid the anger of her mother or grandmother, or of some other person. She may, in fact, be the model child. Children certainly need discipline, but they also need to learn how to make choices and how to learn from them. They need to learn which foods to eat and how much, so they can avoid overeating or eating an unbalanced diet.

When you feed your child the foods you want her to have and leave no room for her to make her own choices, she may miss this important lesson and have difficulty later in choosing the proper foods and amounts herself. She may also have a difficult time making other choices in her life. This can lead to her either taking the easy way out or not choosing at all. Remember, the attitudes and decisions you make around food are often mirrored in other aspects of your life. If it is difficult for you to stop eating when you're full or to select nutritious foods, you may not trust your ability to make good choices at work or at home.

It was dinnertime, and nine-year-old Audrey's plate was filled with hot dogs and Tater Tots. She didn't particularly like this meal, and once again there was too much food, but she had to eat everything on her plate before she could have dessert—the only part of the meal she liked.

Often she ate so much that she came close to being sick, but she pushed herself past her stomach's limits and stuffed herself to get to the chocolate cookies. "If you're too full to finish your meal, you're too full for dessert," her mother would say. She always piled too much food on Audrey's plate. Audrey tried to reason with her, but her mother never listened. Since dessert was her favorite part of the meal, she overate daily.

Her little stomach was often so full that she could feel it pushing against her ribs. She felt a familiar dull pain, but she knew it would eventually go away. Her tummy was bloated because she had eaten too quickly in an attempt to finish all the awful Tater Tots; when she swallowed them almost whole, she couldn't taste them as much. Audrey was used to this discomfort. She knew from past experience that she would have room for some cookies without actually becoming sick. The sweetness of the cookies filled her mouth with pleasure. For a few minutes her pain was masked by the delicious taste of chocolate.

Because Audrey was never allowed to choose the amount of food that felt comfortable to her, and because she had to eat everything on her plate before eating the part of the meal she liked best, she grew up eating the same size portions she had been given as a child. Overeating was familiar and predictable; Audrey's stomach *always* hurt after a meal. Today, Audrey still doesn't know what it feels like to eat and feel comfortable at the same time. She stuffs herself to the point of familiar discomfort and looks for dessert whether she really wants it or not.

Some children are not given the opportunity to choose the amount of food that feels comfortable to them. They are taught to overeat, and their overeating becomes a negative pattern. Others are not allowed to choose the kinds of foods they want, and they grow up not listening to their bodies' needs. They, too, tend to follow the patterns they learned at home, continuing to eat the foods they grew up on, even when they know better. This can lead to confusion surrounding shopping for foods, preparing meals, and enjoying food or feeling comfortable around it.

Your body has different needs at different stages of your life. The amount of energy from calories needed by a child at play is more than that needed by an adult working at a sedentary job. As we age, it becomes more important for us to eat smaller quantities of foods. These foods must be rich in nutrients; while we require fewer calories, we need just as many vitamins and minerals as ever, and perhaps even more. Peanut-butter-and-jelly sandwiches will no longer work as a dietary staple. In fact, we're finding that children don't need as much fats as we once thought. Even children don't do as well on nut-butter and sugar sandwiches as they will on tuna, turkey or veggie-burgers. And since your energy output as an adult is less than when you were an active child, you can't get away with eating as many sweets without gaining weight or putting your health at risk.

Your body has innate wisdom. Listen to it!

One important reason we should allow our children to choose some of the foods they eat and how much they want is that they can learn to listen to their bodies at a young age. This is a vital lesson, because it can help them to become and stay healthy and energetic. Inside each of us lives our body's wisdom. It has a quiet voice that tells us when we've eaten enough, a voice that can prevent us from overeating if we pay attention. You may be ignoring this voice. Perhaps you haven't heard it since you were a child.

This inner wisdom can also let us know at times what nutrients we need in order to be healthy by informing us of the different foods we need as our requirements change. It may communicate with us by placing the image, thought, or name of a food containing the vitamins and minerals we need at any given time in our mind. Then we find ourselves thinking of a particular food without knowing why. I don't mean a craving for something like chocolate or coffee, which can be a signal of an imbalance. Instead, I'm referring, for example, to a desire for more red meat than usual just before you learn you're anemic. Or, you may feel tired and know that nothing would satisfy you like a piece of fresh fruit; feeling more wide awake after eating is a clue that your blood sugar may have been low.

When large portions of food are placed before you during your formative years and you are told you must finish them, you do not listen to this inner voice of wisdom. As a result, you don't learn the difference between being full and being overfull. You may develop a pattern of learned overeating—a negative pattern that can lead to overweight, digestive problems, and unhappiness. Perhaps the saddest part is your being unaware of this pattern because all you have known is being forced to eat too much at each meal.

If your child stuffs herself, she may be imitating you or following your instructions to eat everything on her plate. Do you listen to your body and stop eating when it tells you that you've had enough? If you believe there is no small voice inside you giving you this information, you are mistaken. There is a mechanism in each of us that performs this task constantly.

As we discussed in Chapter 10, when you eat, your taste buds send a signal to your stomach to produce hydrochloric acid, a substance that begins to break down food in one of the first stages of digestion. After your stomach is full, it sends a message to your brain that no more food is needed. If you don't hear this signal, or if you eat too quickly for the signal to be transmitted, you may eat too much. It takes about fifteen minutes for your stomach to tell your brain that no more food is required—an excellent reason to chew well and eat slowly. When we ignore this voice, we overeat. In time, this overeating becomes our norm, and we don't know how to eat less.

The first step for Audrey was awareness. She began by paying attention to how long she felt uncomfortable whenever she overate. She realized that she did not enjoy life as much when she felt too full. She felt guilty for overeating. The pain in her stomach was a constant reminder of her transgression. She became angry with herself when she was too bloated to fit comfortably into her clothes. Most important, Audrey saw that by remaining stuck in this pattern of overeating she was throwing away hours of her life every day, wasting days of her life every month. Much of her time was spent feeling bad physically and emotionally. Each time she overate she reinforced her ability to fail, and she saw herself as a failure. Food was running her life.

After she realized how much time she spent feeling stuffed, guilty, or angry with herself, Audrey was ready to experiment with choosing nutritious foods and incorporating them into her meals. While she had learned to select healthful foods rather than foods with empty calories or too much fat, she tended to buy too many of them at once and overeat. **The Grocery-List Exercise** at the end of this chapter helped her learn to buy just a few foods at a time.

Some children are fed fast foods, TV dinners, and junk foods daily and grow into adults who don't know anything about proper nutrition or healthful meals. Some rebel against their past by eating whatever they want just because there's no one to tell them what to do. When we begin to listen to our bodies, the advice we hear can be startling.

Children who are fed healthful foods and who are given the opportunity to choose one food over another pay more attention to what their bodies need. They instinctively eat foods that provide them with important nutrients. These children are often healthier than children who eat whatever is placed in front of them.

If you were never taught to make choices when you were a child; if you were a model child and followed your mother's instructions to eat everything, even when it was too much; and if you don't know how to choose healthy foods or reasonable amounts, it's not too late to make changes.

TAKING ACTION

1. **Affirmation:** I feel good eating the foods my body wants in the amount it needs.

2. **Inner-Voice Exercise:** To help you make better choices about the kinds of foods and the amounts your body needs, write down a selection of several possible foods for a meal. Even if it feels a little foolish, ask your body which one it wants. Look at each food one at a time and ask yourself: Will this help my body? Will it hurt my body? How much can I have now?

Next, circle whatever food on your list immediately comes to mind without your thinking about it first, and write down the amount that has popped into your mind. Now, for the first time, give your selection some thought. Did you pick this food because you prefer its taste or texture, or did something inside you seem to push you toward this food for no apparent reason? If you picked a food without knowing why, just because you "felt like it," you may have heard your body's inner wisdom.

Perhaps your body was telling you it needed more vitamin A, and that's why a salad came to mind. It may have wanted more energy, so you chose something starchy, such as spaghetti or a piece of fruit. Consider the possibility that your body may have actually communicated with you, and repeat this exercise at another time. Practice it until you feel comfortable trusting and following your inner voice.

3. **Share it with your child:** Repeat the Inner-Voice exercise with your child, and let her pick a food from your list without thinking about it first. Talk with her about her reasons for making her choice. Often, children have an easier time listening to their inner voices than adults do, because no one has told them they can't do it or that the voice doesn't exist. Encourage your daughter to ask herself what her body wants, not just her taste buds.

    Talk with her about the foods she usually eats. With which ones does she feel satisfied after eating? Which ones leave her hungry for something she may not even be able to describe? How does her stomach feel after she eats various foods? Does she feel better after eating a particular food, or does she feel a little tired? Sleepiness after eating may suggest a food sensitivity, especially if the food is one you often crave (see Chapter 21).

4. Teach yourself how to make choices at the grocery store without buying too much food by practicing the **Grocery-List Exercise:** Drive to the grocery store when you are not hungry. Leave your money in the glove compartment of your car before going into the store. Bring a paper and pencil with you, and make a list of all the healthful foods you want to buy. When you have finished

your list, return to your car and make a new list, choosing three items from your original list. Tear up the old list and get your money from the glove compartment. Then go back into the store and buy only enough of those items on your new list for one moderate-sized meal.

By limiting your choices, you limit your ability to overeat. If it is necessary for you to shop daily for a while to avoid bringing too much food home, do this. It is time well invested in your healing. When you feel comfortable shopping for a few days, or a week, without overeating or feeling confused, ease into this new pattern.

5. If you're stuck, get more help: If you dislike grocery shopping, dread any contact with food, or dislike preparing meals for yourself or your family, take a look at the underlying reasons. You may believe there are only a limited number of foods you can eat that will feel safe to you. Talk with a psychotherapist about whatever is in the way of your taking better care of yourself. Perhaps additional information about nutrition would dispel some of these beliefs and give you more foods from which to choose. Begin by reading Chapters 23 and 24, then look to other books to get the information you need.

   You may be afraid of having cooking disasters because your mother never taught you how to cook. Ask a friend to teach you how to prepare a few simple, tasty dishes, or take a cooking class. Face your fears by reeducating yourself so that you can pass on a healthy relationship with food to your children.

15

FINDING SECURITY
WITHIN YOURSELF:

The Solution to Feeling Lonely
or Abandoned

When there is no one in your life you can count on, when you feel abandoned and totally alone, food is usually available. It fills the void temporarily, and anything seems better than the pain of feeling isolated. When this feeling of being alone in the world occurs repeatedly in childhood, the result is often a negative eating pattern in an attempt to fill the emptiness. Even though it is impossible to fill an emotional emptiness with something physical like food, a full stomach gives a message of satiety that is comforting.

Whether a feeling of abandonment originates in a child's mind or in reality, the result is the same, and food is a familiar response. It is difficult to change this response without first understanding what it is and where it originated. Food is a substitute for real security, which is inside us waiting to be found. Until you stop denying your real feelings and realize that you eat when you feel lonely or abandoned, you may be unable to find this security or help your children find theirs.

I am always surprised to find so many people in my nutritional practice who grew up feeling abandoned by their families, and who knew loneliness by its first name and turned to the only "friend" who was there—food. When I was a child and felt consumed daily by a feeling of isolation, I thought I was the only one. Even though I now know better, I do tend to think we are in the minority—but perhaps we're not.

My childhood was a little unusual in that I had no friends. I grew up alone and lonely, with no one to confide in or with whom I could share intimate thoughts. The ache of isolation was a daily specter that visited me and drove me to escape into a world of fantasies, where I lived from the time I was a very young child until the day I went away to college at seventeen. In these fantasies I was loved and admired, I was beautiful, I was talented, and I was always thin. When I awoke from them to go to school or to join the family for dinner, I found myself still "pleasingly plump" and alone.

Whenever I couldn't find an escape through fantasies or books, I could find a different kind of satisfaction through food. Even if there were no people in my life I could count on, food would never desert me. The more lonely I felt, the more I ate. The more I ate, the more I was reminded of my loneliness.

Accompanying my feelings of isolation was a feeling of abandonment. My first conscious experience of this feeling was when I was three years old, and my father temporarily lost me in New York City's vast Pennsylvania Station when he went over to a newsstand. I remember his telling me to stand by a post and not move, and that he would be right back. But after what seemed like a very long time (but was, in fact, less than three minutes), I wandered off into the crowd. My father found me hours later in a police station, where I was crying loudly because I wanted the ice cream cone being offered me but had been instructed by my parents never to accept anything from a stranger. Ever since that singular incident, whenever I feel abandoned or upset I want ice cream.

Recognized or hidden, many eating disorders involve feelings of abandonment. Alice's overeating pattern began with more than one abandonment incident. One by one, everyone in her family left— some physically, some emotionally. Alice grew up with a father who had been orphaned at a young age and who worked obsessively, sometimes for twenty hours a day. Eventually, he divorced Alice's mother and left the family completely. Alice's mother then took her two children and moved in with her parents.

The only family activity Alice can remember was that of sitting around at dinner. The family never did anything together except eat. Then and now, food means family to Alice. In her mind, when everyone got up from the table, the family disappeared. The longer she ate, the longer the family would exist.

As a young child, Alice felt that her grandfather, an alcoholic, gave double messages: "I'm here for you," and "I'm not here." He was always around with money and groceries, but he wasn't there emotionally. His "I love you" rang hollow in Alice's ears, and she never felt close to him.

Alice's mother had to work to support her family, so the grandmother did the cooking. She, too, was an alcoholic. She also suffered from arthritis, which worsened to the point where she was unable to do much of anything. She retreated into her illness, and Alice and her brother were left on their own. Alice remembers the chill of isolation she felt while standing in front of the refrigerator at night, eating cold leftovers.

Alice didn't ask much of her mother. In fact, she tried to please her mother in any way she could, afraid that she, too, would leave. By the time Alice was twelve she was fending for herself: her father had left, her grandfather had died, her grandmother was too ill to do much, and her mother was working full-time.

Alice's mother didn't eat breakfast and didn't have time to prepare it for her children, so they learned to fix cereal for themselves in the morning. Much of it was sugar-coated and tasted like candy; Alice remembers feeling alone in the morning and eating as many as five bowls of cereal at a sitting. After school she would eat cereal again, along with other snacks. Her cereal bowl became her symbol of security.

Alice's mother had stopped packing lunches for her, and she didn't like the school lunches. She spent her lunch money on sugary snacks—sweet rolls, coffee cake, and chocolate milk—and she isolated herself at lunchtime from her classmates. Her after-school snacks, too, were always sweets—more sugared cereal, cinnamon toast, or peanut butter and jelly—and were always too much.

It is not unusual for us to associate sweets with feelings of comfort that alleviate feelings of abandonment. In fact, this association is explained in other cultures, like that of the Chinese, where various tastes are identified with specific emotions. In China, sweets are seen as being connected to low self-esteem, a feeling that can grow out of loneliness. This explanation fits Alice's behavior of overeating sweet foods to compensate for feelings of abandonment and loneliness.

Often, Alice would suddenly become very hungry late at night, even when she had eaten a large dinner. She would eat large quantities of toast or often another complete meal. She thought she was hungry for food, but now sees that what she was hungry for was attention. When she announced she was hungry at night, her grandmother would fix a meal for her and take care of her. Her grandmother could comfortably take care of her granddaughter's hunger, but she could not easily show any other form of affection.

Alice's daughter has already learned some of her mother's negative eating patterns, and asks for food at night at times when she cannot possibly be hungry for food. Alice is now teaching her the difference between physical and emotional hunger—an important lesson for both mother and daughter. If the hunger is emotional, Alice gives her daughter emotional "food": a hug, a story, a quiet talk with no one else around. If it is physical hunger, Alice gives her a piece of fruit rather than a complete meal.

TAKING ACTION

1. **Affirmation:** I am safe. I am secure. I am loved and comforted.

   Feel a blanket of warmth surround you as you say this affirmation throughout the day. See yourself content and filled. When you touch the love inside yourself, you are not alone.

2. Fill yourself with love, using the **Loving-Heart Exercise** in Chapter 3. Repeat this exercise until you feel enough love. Is there ever enough? Yes, there is, and you deserve to feel it.

3. **Share some of your background with your child.** Let her know that you, too, feel insecure or lonely at times. Let her see your vulnerable areas, and allow her to teach you just as you continue to teach her. If you feel uncomfortable playing games because as a child you never played them, for example, let her teach you how to play.

4. **"Heart Food":** When your child is hungry, ask her whether she wants food for her stomach because it's empty, or food for her heart. Talk about the difference between the two with her, and make a list of "heart food" that you can give her, or yourself, when that's where you feel empty. Heart food can be a hug, a game played together, reading an uplifting book, time spent in nature. For you it can be quiet time spent with your child, your loved one, a phone conversation with a friend, or fresh flowers to remind you of the beauty in the world.

5. **Healing the abandonment:** Some feelings of abandonment can't simply be recognized and let go. Remember that when you're stuck looking at an emotional roadblock, psychotherapists have been trained to not only help you see them, but remove them . . . permanently. EMDR (Eye Movement Desensitization and Reprocessing) is a new non-intrusive technique used by some psychotherapists and psychiatrists to rapidly facilitate the healing of trauma. If you are looking for short-term therapy for specific issues, like abandonment, you may want to find someone who uses EMDR (see Resources section).

16

LEARNING TO ENJOY YOURSELF:

The Solution to Being Bored

Eating can give you something to do when you're bored. When you're bored you may actually be denying that something else is going on you're not looking at. Or you may overeat because you like the taste of the foods you're eating so much that you don't want to stop eating them. The sensation may be so satisfying that you're willing to feel overfull just to continue, even though you think you can stop whenever you want to. Some people have a sensual relationship with food. Particular tastes evoke such strong pleasure responses for them that they want the sensation to go on and on.

There are those who complain that a boring diet contributes to their overeating. When they grow tired of how the foods they eat taste, they binge on others just for the taste and variety. And the foods they eat at these times are often high in fat, sodium, or sugar. There are enough healthy ways to add interesting tastes to your diet to make this reason obsolete. Many cookbooks emphasizing healthy foods contain delicious recipes. While it's true that a few may be even more boring than your present diet, a variety of cookbooks exist to help you spruce up your meals (see Resources section).

Different tastes can stimulate your taste buds when your life seems bland and uninteresting, when your life at home or at work seems dull, or when you lack stimulating companionship. There is a difference between boredom that comes from a lack of variety and boredom that comes from an underlying sadness that you're not addressing. Food can seem like a satisfactory escape, because it's often easier to lose yourself in pleasurable tastes and sensations than to identify the reason for your boredom or to get out of your lethargy and risk doing something different, something that might be frightening or uncomfortable (for example, going to a meeting where you could make new friends, or becoming involved in a project that interests you).

Joanna felt bored. But in fact, she was lonely. Today was her day to spend with Daddy, and they were visiting her aunt and uncle instead of going for a walk in the park and looking at the ducks and flowers. Joanna sat on a big chair in the living room, watching the three adults talk and talk. It seemed as if she had been there for hours. She began to swing her legs up and down rhythmically. Maybe she could pretend she was at the playground on the big kids' swing. She was running out of things to pretend.

"Here, Joanna, have some candy," her aunt said, thrusting a box of mints at the child. "And stop swinging your legs. You could fall or break the chair!" She set the candy down on a table next to the child and hurried back to the conversation.

What a fusspot! Joanna thought. She didn't see how she could possibly break the chair. It was too big to tip over and she was too short to kick it, but she was grateful to her aunt for the candy. At least it gave her something to do. She unwrapped a piece and began to chew it slowly.

Sweetness flooded her mouth and slid down her throat. For a few moments her world was all sugar and peppermint, and Joanna forgot about being bored. Her aunt's house seemed to disappear, and she was living in a world of sweetness. The second piece tasted delicious, too, and she waited for the mint to melt all by itself, without chewing it. Eating candy became a game, and she ate one piece after another, even after it had stopped tasting so good. Even after her head hurt a little.

There were times at home when she would wander through the house aimlessly, looking for something interesting to do, and her mother would hand her some cookies or potato chips to keep her busy. When there was nothing to do, Joanna discovered, you could always eat. Whenever she was bored, she reached for food.

As she grew older, Joanna discovered she could lose herself in the salty crunch of fried chicken and potato chips, the sweetness of ice cream and cookies, or the spiciness of the little red cinnamon candies that made her mouth burn with a curiously appealing taste. She was drawn to the taste and sensation of certain foods, and she would eat until their flavors erased her boredom. Food became the solution to her problem, although in fact it was only a temporary diversion.

It was also the solution she offered her daughter, Linda. When Linda was a baby, Joanna gave her bottles of juice to stop her from crying; later, she gave her other sweets when she was upset. Eventually, Joanna handed food to Linda whenever the child was bored. It never occurred to her to ask her daughter how she felt or what she might want to do, since her own mother had never asked *her*.

After Joanna and I talked about her pattern of boredom bingeing, she saw that eating when she was bored hadn't solved anything for her. After she ate, she was still bored, and she often had a stomachache or a headache to boot.

"Now I realize I was turning to food because I didn't know what I was feeling at times," she confessed to me one afternoon. "And when I did know what I was feeling, I had no one to talk to about how I felt, no one to help me figure out what I wanted to do. My mother was too busy to help me understand what I was feeling or offer any real solutions. Besides," she continued, "now that I think about it, my grandmother always pushes food at my mother and me when we visit her, and the three of us have nothing much to say to one another. Maybe relieving boredom with food is all my mother knows how to do."

With this new understanding, Joanna began to act differently toward her daughter. Instead of ignoring Linda or encouraging her to eat when she was bored, Joanna began to talk with her whenever she saw her reaching for food out of boredom. "Linda, you're eating because you're bored," she would tell her, identifying the problem for the child. "Don't eat now. You don't eat when you're bored—you find something to do." She took the time to talk with her daughter about whatever was on her mind or to help her find an activity to absorb her interest.

"What happened when you identified Linda's overeating as a distraction from her boredom?" I asked Joanna several months later.

"It backfired," she laughed. "Linda caught me eating leftovers in the kitchen the other night after dinner and said, 'You don't have to do that, Mom. You're just bored.' The worst part of it was, she was right! I taught her too well. We decided I wouldn't be bored if we played a game of Scrabble together—and, incidentally, she beat me!"

If you eat when you're bored or if you overeat when you're bored with particular foods, you are asking food to take on a role it was not intended to have. Food is a combination of chemicals designed to nourish you, to give you health and energy you need to find fulfillment in other areas of your life. It is not meant to serve as a means of escape from feelings or your primary form of entertainment, although you may be using it in these ways. Its purpose is not to be the focus of pleasure in your life, although it can certainly taste delicious and is something to enjoy.

You may be passing this erroneous meaning along to your daughter. Is she primarily interested in eating "fun foods" or fast foods that taste especially salty, spicy, or sweet, or is she content with ordinary foods like baked chicken, vegetables, and potatoes? Does she eat when she's bored? It may be time for both of you to look to other areas of your lives for interest and excitement.

Being bored can be a self-indulgent state, and eating to relieve boredom or to have the sensation of a particular taste is a self-centered response. You become absorbed in your feelings, your apathy, your taste buds, and, eventually, your guilt. When this happens, it's time to get out of yourself and do something for someone else. Take the attention off yourself and put it somewhere else. The most important thing to realize when you're bored is that it's time to take action!

TAKING ACTION

1. **Affirmation:** Doing something for myself and others keeps me busy and fulfills me.

2. **The Promised-Project List:** Identify your boredom, and do something you enjoy doing besides eating. Make a list of projects you've promised yourself you'd get to eventually but never seem to have time for, along with the materials you need for each one. Check off all the projects on this list for which you already have everything you need, and arrange the list in order of the projects you most want to get done.

   Keep this list in a handy place so you can add to it easily, and refer to it when you're bored. Even if you don't feel like doing any of the projects, start one of the first three anyway, and work at it for an hour. Divert your attention from yourself, and see if your boredom leaves as you become involved with your activity. If after an hour you are still bored, realize that you have done an hour's worth of work on a project you very much wanted to do. Any accomplishment you have made with the project is still much "better than" eating, isn't it? Take a look at whether or not you have been covering up your feelings. If so, address them now.

   Just as it's all right to be hungry and not eat, it's all right to be bored. If you're bored long enough without diverting your attention by eating, you are likely to find something to do that's "better than" being bored, even if it isn't the ideal solution.

3. **Help someone:** Offer to help a friend, or call a retirement home or church group to volunteer a few hours of your time. Do something for someone else; you might pick up a few groceries for a neighbor who is unable to get to the market. When you give your time and love to another person, you are filling more places inside you than food can reach.

4. **Eat different foods:** If you find that your meals are boring, get out of your cooking and eating rut and add new dishes. The addition of an Oriental sauce can turn sautéed vegetables into a dish

as tasty as one you might get at a Chinese restaurant. A bit of curry powder can liven up rice, lentil soup, or chicken with vegetables. Look through some ethnic cookbooks for one or two simple recipes you can add to your repertoire, and prepare them. It may be time to explore specialty markets or sections of the supermarket you usually pass by. Remember, if you're stuck and can't take this step on your own, a nutritionist or a class on food preparation may be a simple way through your block. Tasty foods can be very easy to make.

Prepare a meal you particularly enjoy but rarely make any more because you're too busy. Make extra, and invite a friend over for dinner or freeze the leftovers for times when you're too busy to cook.

chapter

17

LEARNING TO
EXPRESS YOURSELF:

The Solution to Swallowing Anger
and Other Emotions

Some people eat when they don't feel comfortable or safe in talking about their feelings, or when they can't identify their uncomfortable feelings. They push down their emotions with food, even though they may not be aware that this is what they're doing. Covering up feelings is a form of denial that often leads to continued negative eating patterns like overeating or bingeing.

While some people can't contain or express their happiness and sedate themselves with food to keep from bursting with joy, it is far more common to cover up anger or unhappiness with food. Unfortunately, the anger and unhappiness don't disappear; they just become buried under layers of bread, ice cream, or other foods, where they ferment and grow.

If you are swallowing anger, unhappiness, or other emotions along with the extra food you eat, don't fool yourself. The emotions you are attempting to avoid are affecting your life negatively, and they will filter through any facade you may put in front of them. You may pretend to be content and forgiving, but people around you can see when you're not. The anger or unhappiness won't leave simply because you pretend it isn't there or decide not to face it. It becomes part of you and muddies your decisions and relationships, guaranteeing continued unhappiness. Until you change your response, you may also be teaching your children how to be unhappy.

Judy was angry with her mother for not allowing her to stay out late with her friends. This was the second time her mother had changed her mind about Judy's curfew. Judy felt like hitting her and screaming at her, but she couldn't even tell her mother how she felt. If only her mother hadn't changed her mind at the last minute! Now Judy would be embarrassed to tell her friends she couldn't go, and they were all counting on it.

She took a loaf of French bread from the bread box and tore off a large chunk. In her imagination, she was ripping and tearing into her mother. She didn't care about its taste as much as the mindless chewing and swallowing. In time she became unconscious of the world around her and forgot her anger and disappointment. Tearing off pieces of bread and stuffing them into her mouth was soothing. She ate the whole loaf.

Judy knew her overeating was just covering up her anger, but it satisfied her. Finally, she felt too stuffed to move. What else could she do? Her mother would never allow anyone to get angry. Once before, when Judy had been upset and had tried to explain how she felt, her mother had threatened her, saying, "Don't raise your voice to me, young lady! You're heading for a *real* punishment if you don't watch out. How would you like to be grounded for two weeks?" So Judy stuffed down her anger with food.

Like Judy, you may have found that suppressing emotions with food gives you some temporary satisfaction and has become a negative habit. And, like her, you may have noticed that eating does not eliminate your anger; it only keeps you from dealing with it temporarily. The anger will surface again, perhaps inappropriately. When you cover up your anger, you're not hiding it from your friends and family—and certainly not from your daughter or other children.

Children are particularly perceptive. They are little creatures walking around with receptive antennae that pick up all unspoken emotions. As a very young child, Judy learned not only that food is love, as we saw in Chapter 1, but how to stuff her anger from her mother. There were countless times when her mother would look sternly at her without saying a word.

"What's wrong, Mom?" Judy asked.

"Nothing!" her mother would snap. "Nothing at all." But she would then stomp through the house, cleaning or straightening up with a vengeance. Then she'd march into the kitchen, grab a bag of potato chips or cookies, and go to her room and close the door. When she finally emerged, she was calmer. Judy never knew whether her mother was angry with her or with someone or something else. She only knew that her mother was angry, and food sedated her.

The taste of food can also temporarily cover up feelings of unhappiness. You might turn to favorite foods your mother gave you when you were sad as a child, or you may eat sweets because your parents gave you candy and ice cream when they didn't know any other way to help you feel better. If this is what they did, they probably learned it from their own parents.

Some disappointments, and some catastrophes, occur in all of our lives. We can eat to avoid feeling pain—or we can face the problems, talk about them with friends or a therapist, work through our feelings, and grow from our experiences. We can become more sensitive, more compassionate, and more understanding by feeling our feelings instead of deadening them.

Many people overeat to cover up each disappointment and unhappiness from daily incidents in their lives: having an argument, dealing with job or money problems, getting a dent in the car, not being able to find anything to wear to an important function, or finding that the supermarket has run out of the laundry detergent that's on sale.

When you overeat to cover up these daily disappointments, you are using them as an excuse to eat, and you are reinforcing a habit that has become more and more difficult to break with time. Recognize and feel your disappointment. Do what you can about it: change whatever you can, and accept whatever you can't change. Feel your unhappiness, and understand that it will pass. Find other ways to soothe yourself when you're unhappy besides eating.

We are fortunate to be living in an age of self-exploration. Many of us are discovering that we have similar feelings, and that these are easier to handle when we talk about them and recognize them as part of life. We are beginning to share our feelings more openly with others. Some people find support groups are safe places for talking about feelings they can't yet share with friends and family. Other people find the quickest way to learn how to express themselves is in therapy with a trained psychotherapist. Choose whatever works for you, but find someone, or a group of someones, and begin working on your self-expression.

Unhappiness is an emotion every one of us experiences. We can't effectively pretend it's not there. It's important to recognize that feelings of unhappiness will eventually pass. (If they do not, we may be clinically depressed, and professional help is needed. For nutritional insights on depression, see Chapter 22.) If you use food in an attempt to erase the unpleasant feelings caused by little disappointments, take a look at those disappointments. We all feel disappointed at times. Don't give these minor hurts the power to ruin your day, let alone your life. You are not perfect, other people are not perfect, and life is neither perfect nor fair. That's the reality. The challenge, and the gift we give ourselves, is to find an appropriate way to handle problems.

Look at the power you have given an incident or a person in your life. That is your own power, which you have given away. Take it back by recognizing the imperfections in all things, and choose to be content or happy in spite of those imperfections. Change what you can to make things better when you can, but accept the fact that life isn't perfect. *Don't let unexpressed emotions run or ruin your life.*

In the past, you may not have been able to look at your feelings and express them. Chances are that your mother kept her own feelings buried inside. She may not have been aware of what she was doing and of how it could affect you. But you're not your mother, and right now you have an advantage over her. You can become more aware of how and why you're using food as a distraction, and you can share your discoveries with your children.

TAKING ACTION

1. **Affirmation:** My mother did the best she could. I am responsible for only my own happiness. I am the happy, healthy, balanced person I always wanted to be.

You may remember this as Lola's affirmation from Chapter 2. If you like, modify it to suit your particular needs, or write a different one if you prefer.

2. **Feel stuck? Take a hike!** When you are feeling uncomfortable with any emotion—joy, anger, sadness, and so on—do something physical before reaching for food. Take a brisk walk or jog around the block; clean a closet; mop the floor. Whatever you choose to do, make it the most vigorously physical activity you can at that moment. Walking up and down a flight of stairs or walking around in circles in the rest room at work for five or ten minutes will do when no other options are available.

3. **Identify your emotion:** Pay attention to how you feel when you eat to cover up your feelings. Are you eating mindlessly to sedate yourself? Are you pretending to destroy someone instead of tearing into a piece of food? Begin by admitting that you are angry or unhappy. Then find a safe way to express your feelings.

   Feel it: Anger is an emotion we all feel at times. There is nothing wrong with it, or with you for feeling angry, even if you have never been allowed to express it. It is all right for you to be angry. This feeling is just an acknowledgment of imperfection—another person's or your own. Give yourself permission to be imperfect, to make mistakes. Give yourself permission to be angry or unhappy, to feel whatever it is you feel.

   Talk about it: If you can, tell the person who angered you or triggered your unhappiness what you have experienced. Don't put any blame on him or her; just say how you feel. No one else can *make* you angry or upset; no one but you is responsible for your unhappiness. Explain to the other person how his or her words or actions affected you: "When you said, or did, this, I felt (upset, angry, hurt, sad), and I want to tell you why."

   Don't be afraid of talking about how you were affected by someone's words or actions. They are your feelings, and no one can argue that you didn't feel them. There may be other ways to handle them in the future, but your feelings are your own, and you are entitled to them.

   Write about it: If it's not possible to talk to the person because he or she is unavailable or doesn't want to hear what you have to say, or if you don't feel safe in expressing yourself, write down your feelings. Pretend the person is sitting in front of you, willing to listen without becoming angry or defensive and willing to talk.

Write down a dialogue between the two of you in which you talk openly about your feelings, without fear of reprisal. Tell the other person what you would like from him or her in the future. Can you remove blame so that you can voice your needs more easily and be heard less defensively? Perhaps your calm tone will be enough. Forgive this person for any words or actions that contributed to your pain.

4. **The Anger and Resentment Letter:** When you are not ready to forgive yourself or another person for your anger, hurt, or unhappiness, when you are spitting mad and want only to injure and destroy, write your feelings down. In this way you can get this venom out of yourself so that it will not cause you physical and emotional damage. On paper, say whatever's on your mind, no matter how nasty or cruel. Don't leave anything out. Write down every little detail that's bothering you, that keeps you angry or unhappy.

    When you are finished, read the letter out loud. Hear your words, and feel the pain. Then burn the letter, and let go of your suffering. Forgive the person who caused your pain. Forgive yourself as well, for causing pain or for holding on to it. There is nothing you have done and nothing that has been done to you that cannot be forgiven. Use the Forgiveness Meditation in Chapter 12 to help you release the emotions causing you so much anguish.

5. **Take an anger workshop:** There are workshops to help people express their anger in many large cities. Small towns often have psychotherapists who have been trained in releasing anger. Find someone—or some group—that can help you move through your anger into your peaceful center. Even if you haven't felt this peaceful place in years, it's still there.

PART FOUR

Physiological Answers
to Physiological Problems

You may overeat for emotional or physiological reasons, or for a combination of both. Until now, we have discussed only some of the emotional ones. As a nutritionist I focus on nutritional imbalances, and I usually find one or more physiological reasons for eating disorders among my patients. These physiological problems most often take the form of cravings—for starches, sugar, chocolate, or other specific foods—and they are frequently the result of nutrient deficiencies, food sensitivities, and early-childhood addictions to sugar. Craving certain foods and eating when depressed can be corrected by making specific dietary changes and increasing particular nutrients.

Frequently, depression is closely connected with a person's diet. Many people eat when they're depressed and are depressed in turn because of the choice of foods they eat. The foods they often eat when they're depressed are exactly those foods that keep them feeling depressed. Until they change their body's biochemistry, all they can do is take medications that either mask their depression or chemically correct some of the imbalances a different diet could improve.

Some people believe they are powerless over food and must stay on a rigid diet for the rest of their lives. I say this is not necessarily true. Rigid diets are not only difficult to maintain consistently, but they can also be just Band-Aids—that is, they can often mask a problem and make it manageable, but they solve nothing.

You can certainly keep your cravings under control with a strict diet that forbids starches, sugars, or other foods, but you are not correcting the deficiency that causes you to have these particular cravings in the first place. In addition, many of these diets are unbalanced and contribute to further nutrient deficiencies, causing a new set of problems and reinforcing the belief that you are helpless to resist a piece of chocolate or a loaf of bread.

Physiological cravings can stem from a deficiency or an addiction. The deficiency is one that your body is either trying to overcome by restoring your biochemistry (for example, if you crave chocolate, which is very high in magnesium, when you have a slight magnesium deficiency), or one that your body is perpetuating (for instance, if you eat a lot of candy to raise your blood-sugar level to normal, causing another blood-sugar drop and driving you to eat even more sweets).

An addiction may be caused by a food sensitivity or allergy. Sensitivities to foods can often be overcome by avoiding these foods completely for a few months or more, then eating less of them. But if you have a true allergy to any food, you may need to eliminate it permanently. The good news is that more people have sensitivities than allergies, so it's likely that you will not have to eliminate any foods forever.

When nutritional deficiencies and food addictions are corrected, you may be able to eat all of the foods that you now feel helpless to resist. It's possible that you won't want them any more, but they won't be forbidden. If it is necessary for you to avoid them, you will be able to do it more easily. Either way, you will be free from your food obsession; you will be in control.

For now, I ask you to keep an open mind and consider the

possibility that some of your eating disorders may come from phys-iological imbalances. When you feel out of control with food, it is difficult to feel in charge of your life. Once you restore your body's biochemical balance, you will be more in control of all aspects of your life, not just food. There are no Taking Action sections in the next chapters, because each chapter is itself a program for solving the identified problem.

If your eating disorder can be caused by a physiological imbal-ance, so can your child's. The following chapters are designed to give you the information you need to take to a doctor who can monitor your child's nutritional program. Although the nutrient therapy mentioned is safe, you cannot be too cautious with your child's health or your own. Therefore, *always* seek professional assistance in diagnosing a problem and monitoring any program.

18

FEELING SATISFIED
WITH STARCHES:

The Amino-Acid Solution to
Carbohydrate Bingeing

Julie was almost finished with her second baked potato. She had already eaten half a loaf of bread, and she wasn't through eating. "Next," she thought, "I'll have some cookies."

Her stomach was so full she didn't know how she would manage anything else. "I don't understand it," she said to herself, feeling desperate. "There's no room for cookies, but I have to eat them. They don't even taste good any more. It seems like no matter how much I eat, I'm never satisfied."

Julie's craving is not an isolated case. Many people can't seem to eat enough carbohydrates. They stuff themselves with sugars and starches, waiting to feel satisfied, but the feeling of satiety never comes. No matter how much they eat, they keep wanting more. These people are convinced they are powerless over food. Certainly, that is how they feel. I am convinced that many of them have an amino acid deficiency of tryptophan. This particular amino acid plays an important role in our feeling satisfied after eating. To understand the part tryptophan plays, let's look at the mechanisms of hunger and satiety.

THE PHYSIOLOGY OF HUNGER AND SATIETY

Hunger and satiety seem to be controlled in part by two separate sections of the hypothalamus, a tiny gland at the base of the brain that helps regulate numerous body functions. While the functions of the brain are extremely complex, we can take a simplified look at some of the ways a number of researchers believe the brain works in relation to appetite control.

Glucose—a component of carbohydrates—fuels the brain. When we have enough glucose, the hunger center in the hypothalamus tells us it has enough fuel, so it's not necessary for us to eat. The result: we are not hungry.

The hypothalamus contains sensitive cells that receive physical or chemical messages called satiety signals. These signals include the feeling of fullness, or the recognition and identification by our cells of the amounts of proteins and fats in our stomach and small intestines. The cells in the hypothalamus then send their own messages, letting us know whether or not we're hungry and what kinds of foods we want to eat.

Messages of satiety and hunger are sent from your brain through your body's electrical circuitry by neurotransmitters, substances that transmit information between nerve endings in the brain. Two of them in particular, serotonin and norepinephrine, are important in regulating satiety by increasing serotonin production.

Serotonin sends a message that you are satisfied; norepinephrine tells you you're hungry. So, if you're an overeater, you want to be certain that you have enough serotonin to shut off your hunger signals after you eat a moderate meal.

Carbohydrates affect the amount of tryptophan available to the brain. When you eat more carbohydrates, you have more tryptophan available; when you eat fewer carbohydrates, you have less available tryptophan. Less tryptophan means less serotonin. Less serotonin means that your body will ask for more carbohydrates to increase serotonin and shut off the hunger signal. A diet high in complex carbohydrates with a little protein helps you feel satisfied; a diet high in protein and low in carbohydrates doesn't. *If you are on a high-protein, low-carbohydrate diet, you may keep craving carbohydrates because your brain is not producing enough serotonin to turn off this signal!*

Some people cannot utilize either refined sugar, fruit sugar (fructose), or both. Now there is a way to determine your body's individual ability or inability to handle sugars (including carbohydrate metabolism—how quickly your body takes starches and turns them into sugars) through a new patented vitamin blood test through SpectraCell Laboratories. See the Resources section for more information.

FEELING POWERLESS OVER FOOD

Some people have lower serotonin production than normal, so their brains do not signal that they're satisfied. Even with painfully overfilled stomachs, these women keep craving carbohydrates, as their bodies desperately try to get more tryptophan into their brains.

Low serotonin production, which can leave you feeling out of control with sugars or starches, can be genetic in origin or can result from high-protein diets, obesity, or antidepressant drugs.

Genetics

Julie put a third loaf of French bread in her shopping cart. It was no use trying to fool herself; she was just like her mother. They both ate more bread than anyone else she knew. Julie remembered being amazed as a child watching her mother work her way through a loaf of bread. It didn't even matter what she put on it—butter, jam, peanut butter . . . or nothing at all. Now Julie was doing the same thing, and no matter how hard she tried, she couldn't stop.

If you were born with low tryptophan levels or with the inability to utilize tryptophan effectively, you may not be producing enough serotonin to stop craving foods, especially carbohydrates. If your mother can't seem to get enough carbohydrates, even when she's full, you may have inherited her overeating problem. Chances are that your child will have the same problem.

You may respond to amino-acid therapy very well. This might

require your taking supplementation on a daily basis. Look for a doctor who can confirm or rule out your suspicion, since you and your children don't want to take any substance if you don't need it. Also, at this time, tryptophan is a prescription item and not an inexpensive one, at that. But if you need it, it may be worth feeling in control with food should your doctor find it necessary and you find it affordable.

High-Protein Diets

Connie is on a strict high-protein diet to lose weight. She must eat protein at each meal; sometimes she eats it by itself, sometimes with vegetables. Connie can never have starches and sugars on this program. She's relieved. She knows exactly what to eat, and none of the allowed foods make her want to binge. All the foods she usually craves are forbidden. No potatoes, no bread, no cookies, no candy. Not even a piece of fruit.

She has been on this program for more than six months and has consistently lost weight, and she's willing to stay on the program forever. She will do anything to lose weight and not be ruled by her cravings. Because all of her changes have been gradual ones, Connie is not aware that she is not as strong as she once was. Strength was never as much of an issue with her as appearance, and when she moved to a new apartment and found that the boxes containing her belongings seemed especially heavy, she dismissed this as a result of her being tired. But it wasn't. Some of her weight loss is muscle loss.

There are times when Connie's memory slips into a crevice and temporarily disappears. This, too, is unlike her, but again she rationalizes it as being due to work pressures. The truth is, her high-protein diet is not giving her brain enough fuel.

For the first time in years, Connie's body is beginning to have a shape. She is heavy, but she is no longer obese. If she knew there was a connection between her diet and these symptoms, she would still gladly make the trade. To her, the weight loss is worth being a little less strong and having a slightly faulty memory.

Unfortunately, her high-protein diet is also rather high in fats. She eats great quantities of beef, pork, and cheese. Since chicken skin is not forbidden, she eats this, too. Connie's high-fat diet is putting her at risk for heart disease, breast cancer, and colon cancer. Her high-protein diet may also contribute to kidney problems, for proteins have many more waste products that must be eliminated by the kidneys than carbohydrates do. Because she doesn't know any other way to free herself from carbohydrate cravings, Connie is playing Russian roulette with her health.

In addition to low serotonin production, there are three other primary reasons to avoid a high-protein diet: muscle loss, excessive calcium loss, and rapid weight gain when the diet is relaxed.

No matter how large or small you are, your brain needs a minimum of 120 to 140 grams of glucose every day. Body fat is not a good source for this fuel; fat is stored in your cells in the form of triglycerides, only 5 to 10 percent of which can be converted to glucose. Carbohydrates, however, are an excellent source, and one that will help in serotonin production to keep you from feeling hungry.

When your diet consists of protein with no carbohydrates, your body will take glucose from the only source left: your muscles. And because muscle protein can only produce at most 57 percent of the necessary glucose, you need almost twice as much protein as carbohydrates to get enough glucose to fuel your brain.

Using protein alone for fuel, your brain will use up 200 grams of muscle protein every day, since muscle is only 20 percent protein. You are giving up a lot of muscle for a little brain power, and you risk stripping your muscle tissues and having less physical stamina. If you accompany this diet with exercise, you will build strength, but you will still lose muscle, since the brain needs it for fuel.

A high-protein diet will also result in excessive calcium loss— something few women who want to avoid osteoporosis can afford. For a reason that has not yet been explained, it is impossible to stay in calcium balance with a diet of this kind. You will always lose more calcium than you take in, *no matter how much calcium this is*. If your diet is excessively high in protein, you are *increasing* your risk of osteoporosis.

A few people have died in the past from the effects of high-protein diets. Even if nothing terrible happens to you, you are very likely to regain much of your original weight quickly as soon as you go back to eating normally. The reason for this is that if your diet was suddenly cut to a lower amount of calories, your body learned to adapt by functioning more efficiently. It still knows how to function with fewer calories, even when you begin adding more calories back in. These extra calories—the difference between the amount you are now eating and the amount you consumed on your diet—are likely to be stored as fat.

Many people are looking for quick results with weight-loss programs and so are turning to high-protein, low-carbohydrate diets. If your daughter is currently on such a program, show her this section so she can see what she is doing and why. Help her to find another solution. No one wants to be thin and sick; the goal for all of us is weight loss and long-term good health.

The Obesity Treadmill

Jean had ended her dinner of meat, potatoes, and vegetables with two pieces of her mother's homemade apple-cinnamon pie, and she still wanted more. "I don't understand it," she thought. "I used to be able to eat much smaller portions and feel perfectly satisfied when I was thinner. Now I can never seem to get enough."

She reached over to the fruit bowl and picked up a banana. "At least fruit is good for me," she rationalized as she peeled it and took a bite. But the banana wasn't enough, either. Feeling driven by her hunger, Jean went into the kitchen for another snack and then joined her parents in the den with an unopened bag of potato chips and a magazine. By the end of the evening she had finished the bag. If it hadn't been so late, she would have looked for something else.

Even when she was stuffed and felt uncomfortable, Jean kept eating. She was waiting for a feeling of satisfaction she remembered having had when she was sixty pounds lighter, but it never came.

And it never will, until Jean loses enough weight so that her body can become sensitive to insulin once more and signal her to stop eating. Since the cells in our bodies can't communicate through a language of words, they have another language: sensitivity. Some are sensitive to particular substances, such as glucose, fats, and insulin. When they become insensitive, there is a breakdown in communications.

The fat cells we are born with are designed to receive information throughout our lives as to how much energy we need. Insulin—a substance needed to move sugar into our cells—is one important part of this information network. As we age, or if we overload our systems by eating too much fatty foods or sugars, the network ceases to work effectively. When insulin is no longer effective in allowing glucose to be taken up into our cells and used as energy, diabetes can result. By merely changing their diets, some diabetics can avoid the need to take extra insulin.

As a person becomes fatter, her muscle cells, which are usually sensitive to higher levels of insulin, become less sensitive to it. Just as we can get used to living in a noisy neighborhood and eventually don't even hear the noises around us, our cells learn not to pay attention to the message insulin is trying to deliver: "Take in some of the amino acids from the bloodstream so I can get enough tryptophan to the brain to shut off the hunger signals. This body has enough food for now."

When amino acids from carbohydrate meals don't get into muscle cells, your body acts as though you've eaten a high-protein meal. Larger amounts of amino acids get into the brain, lowering the amount of tryptophan, and they do not allow enough tryptophan in to produce serotonin. The result is a continued feeling of hunger.

Jean can restore some of her cell sensitivity by losing fat weight through proper dieting and exercise, and she may be able to break her overeating cycle with amino-acid therapy. Tryptophan may enable her to eat less by taking away her craving for carbohydrates. Once she is eating less, she will be able to lose weight more easily, and her cells can regain their sensitivity to insulin.

If you (or your child) are greatly overweight and have difficulty feeling satisfied after eating a moderate-sized meal, your body may not be giving that satiety signal to your brain. Talk with your doctor about amino-acid therapy to help you lose weight, and see if your body will then be able to function properly.

Antidepressants: A Vicious Cycle

Before Lois was put on medication for her depression, she had no problems with food. She would eat medium-sized meals three times a day, and that was that. But ever since her doctor put her on antidepressants, she has been unable to feel satisfied with the same amounts. Her depression is better, but she is unhappy about eating so much and gaining weight.

Lois thinks there may be a connection between her weight gain and the antidepressant, but she is too afraid of being taken off her medication to mention this to her doctor. This is unfortunate, for the doctor may be one of those who is well aware of the possible physiological effects of this medication and so could help Lois if he knew of her problem.

Some physicians treat patients for depression with antidepressant drugs. While there may be excellent reasons for taking these drugs, some of them lower serotonin levels. When this happens, a patient often gains weight after being on drug therapy because her brain does not register satiety. Some physicians counteract this antidepressant effect by also giving their patients tryptophan. After a while, antidepressants may not even be necessary; tryptophan could be enough.

If you or your child is clinically depressed, you may want to discuss with your doctor any options for increasing serotonin production.

THE AMINO-ACID PROGRAM

If you are afraid of adding carbohydrates back into your diet because you believe they caused some of your problems, you can begin with amino-acid therapy. First, increase your serotonin production with tryptophan. When you feel satisfied with eating less or you no longer crave carbohydrates, you can bring them back into your eating program and reduce your protein.

Amino-acid therapy is not the answer for everyone, since a lack of serotonin isn't always the problem. You may crave carbohydrates because you miss meals or because you have food allergies or sensitivities (discussed in Chapter 21); an overgrowth of *Candida albicans*, a yeast or fungus that needs carbohydrates to live and flourish (addressed in Chapter 19); or a psychological craving.

For others, however, amino-acid therapy could be the "miracle" they have been waiting for. If you are bulimic, have a very strong carbohydrate craving, are obese, or are on a high-protein diet or modified fast, you would do well to consider this program. If you are a depressed overeater, you may be a candidate for tryptophan therapy, because depression is often an indication of a serotonin deficiency.

Research has shown that tryptophan therapy has mild to moderate success. For some people, tryptophan will take enough of an edge off their carbohydrate cravings to allow them to succeed in eating smaller amounts of food in a well-balanced diet. You may have to exert an effort, but you could find that you are no longer powerless over food.

In an article published in *Advances in Therapy* in 1987, J. Christopher Caston, M.D., talks about the successful results obtained with tryptophan in treating obesity and depression. Numerous other researchers have made similar discoveries over the past ten years. Dr. Caston relates a case history of a woman on a 1500-calorie diet who was unable to lose weight until she took tryptophan four times a day. Her diet remained the same; the only difference was the tryptophan. For some people, both diet and tryptophan are necessary, however, tryptophan can only prescribed by a doctor.

Tryptophan requires good amounts of vitamin B6 to help it get past the liver, where most of the amino acid is used. This vitamin is also needed for an important enzyme involved in converting tryptophan to serotonin. The active form of vitamin B6—the form in which it can accompany tryptophan and help convert it to serotonin—is called pyridoxyl 5-phosphate, or P5P. The usual form of B6 you will find in vitamins is the inactive form, called pyridoxine. If your body is inefficient in effectively converting pyridoxine into P5P, then the amino acids dependent upon active B6 (such as tryptophan) can't be used. For this reason, the most *effective form of vitamin B6 to use with tryptophan is P5P.*

It is always wise to take all the B vitamins in a supplement rather than taking one or more separately. For this reason, you should take a good-quality multivitamin-and-mineral supplement each day. Again, for best absorption, use one that is powdered in capsules.

Use the least amount you need to get results, and stay with this amount, rather than increasing it.

1. *Under your doctor's supervision*, 500 to 1000 milligrams of 1-tryptophan with four ounces of diluted fruit juice, taken one hour before each meal and once before bedtime, on an empty stomach. The simple sugars in the fruit juice will activate the tryptophan more rapidly and get it into your bloodstream.

2. 5 to 10 milligrams of pyridoxyl 5-phosphate (P5P), taken four times a day (with the tryptophan).

3. A multivitamin-and-mineral supplement, taken at least once a day, with meals.

Research has shown side effects in individuals who have taken more than 3000 milligrams of tryptophan all at once in the morning. With 500 to 1000 milligrams, it is unlikely that you would have any. However, the side effects reported in people who have taken very large doses of tryptophan include nausea, sedation, diarrhea, and muscle spasms in the legs. If you get any side effects, stop taking the tryptophan and call your doctor. There have been no side effects reported with P5P, and in any case, you will be taking it in small doses.

Tryptophan should not be taken if you are pregnant, have diabetes or a family history of diabetes, have a bladder irritation, or have ever had cancer or lupus. It has also been known at times to aggravate bronchial asthma. Tryptophan is contraindicated for anyone currently on such drugs as MAO inhibitors, Prozac (fluoxetine hydrochloride), tranquilizers, or antipsychotics. If you are currently taking *any* medication at all, be sure to let your doctor know before you begin this medically-supervised program.

You may want to eat protein once a day, at midday, and have carbohydrates for breakfast and dinner to help your body produce more serotonin. At night, a time when you may have overeaten carbohydrates in the past, you will now have more serotonin from taking tryptophan with P5P and from eating grains and vegetables at dinner. More information on this kind of dietary program is found in Chapter 24.

Foods Containing Tryptophan

If your doctor won't prescribe tryptophan or you can't afford it (your cost could be as much as $75 to $150/month) there are certain foods that are natural sources of tryptophan that will help solve your carbohydrate-craving. It may just take longer.

One food high in tryptophan is chocolate (1 oz of milk chocolate has 120 mg). Perhaps this is one reason why so many people claim they really do feel better—more content—after eating it. This is not a reason or excuse to run out and stock up on chocolate bars or brownies. Because in addition to the tryptophan, chocolate also gives us a clue about another missing nutrient—magnesium—which is discussed in depth in Chapter 20. As much as your body may need both tryptophan and magnesium, it doesn't need or want the sugar and fat contained in chocolate—especially the amount you'd need daily to raise serotonin levels.

Let's look for healthier foods high in tryptophan which you can increase in your diet. And when you increase them, be sure to add B6 and more magnesium (see Chapter 20). I'm listing foods many people would be willing to eat (as opposed to jack mackeral and pork pancreas), along with the amount of tryptophan they contain. Because you may need 500 mg three or four times daily, I'm only listing foods with a minimum of 250 mg. Since soy products have been associated with lowering a woman's risk of breast cancer, you may want to emphasize soy protein as you raise your tryptophan through the foods you eat.

Tuna fish: 3 oz countains over 250 mg of tryptophan

Red snapper: 3 oz contains 250 mg

Soy flour, defatted: 1 cup contains 683 mg

Soy nuts, dry roasted: ½ cup contains 495 mg

Tempeh (a soy product found in health food stores): ½ cup contains 234 mg

Tofu, firm: ½ cup contains 310 mg

Soybeans, boiled (add to soups and stews): 1 cup contains 416 mg

Chicken, light meat without skin: 3.5 oz contains 325 mg

Ground beef, extra lean: 3.5 oz contains over 300 mg

Beans: 1 cup of most beans contains from 175 to 225 mg, making them an excellent low-fat food to eat along with other high-tryptophan foods.

19

GETTING UNHOOKED
FROM SUGAR:

Diets for Low Blood Sugar
and *Candida*

There are a number of physiological reasons for why we crave sugars in any form. Two of the most common ones are low blood sugar and an overgrowth of a yeast that grows in all our bodies, *Candida albicans*. We may crave these sugars in their various forms: white sugar, honey, large quantities of fruit or fruit juice, malted barley extract, dried fruit, and a substance that enters our bloodstream quickly without needing to be digested—alcohol.

LOW BLOOD SUGAR:
THE PROBLEM

When you are hungry, it is often because your blood-sugar level is low. This is a normal occurrence, and your glucose level is restored by eating. Hypoglycemia, on the other hand, is a condition in which your cells are constantly low in fuel because of an abnormal glucose metabolism.

Your brain needs glucose, a form of sugar, to function and think clearly; your muscles use glucose for fuel; and your body burns glucose as a form of heat. Carbohydrates are its primary source. Glucose is transported into your cells with the help of insulin, a hormone produced in the pancreas, which is secreted when blood-sugar levels rise.

When you eat a lot of sugar in any form, insulin is released to carry the sugar into your cells and muscles. The more sugar there is in your blood, the more insulin is released. When too much insulin is released, the glucose is removed so efficiently from your blood that its level drops. Your thinking can become foggy; you may feel weak, dizzy, depressed, or anxious; you may have headaches; or you may feel tired—and you then crave sugar to raise your glucose levels to normal.

Alcohol does not need to be digested. It is released immediately into the bloodstream. Since refined white sugar and honey are digested rapidly, they also make their way quickly. Other sugars, refined grains (such as white flour), potatoes, fruit juices, and whole fruit come next. However, the glucose from beans or from whole grains, such as brown rice and cornmeal, is released very slowly and steadily. And proteins take a long time before they become glucose.

You can see that eating a lot of sugars and refined carbohydrates can cause high levels of sugar in the bloodstream and may result in the release of too much insulin. Excess insulin may also be released if the pancreas is not functioning properly. To determine whether or not your body can handle refined sugar or fructose may be as simple as having a newly-formulated blood test through SpectraCell Laboratories (see Resources section for additional information).

Whether or not you take this test, have been diagnosed by your doctor as being clinically hypoglycemic (through the administration of a six-hour glucose-tolerance test), or simply have low-blood-sugar symptoms is unimportant. The symptoms are uncomfortable, and the solutions are the same.

If you periodically crave sugar, and you suspect that at least some of this craving is physiological, you may have been born with—or have created—hypoglycemia. Look to your background to see if your diet may have contributed to this condition. It may have begun in infancy, and it could even have emotional origins.

The Creation of a Problem

Linda, Joanna's baby, is crying again, and Joanna feels like screaming. Linda's diapers are dry, and she has been fed. Joanna has no idea what's wrong. She is in the middle of preparing dinner and can't stop to hold the baby, but even when she does Linda often cries. The sound of her baby crying for no apparent reason gives Joanna a large knot in the pit of her stomach. She feels helpless and frustrated, reaches for a bottle with fruit juice, and pops the nipple in Linda's tiny mouth. The baby stops crying.

Although Joanna can't identify the problem, she has found a solution. As Linda grows, whenever she fusses she is given something sweet. Whether it's fruit juice or candy, Linda calms down when she tastes the sweetness. She has learned that this is what she gets when she's upset.

Linda continues associating food with relief from anxiety, since no one tries to help her identify the source of her anxiety or to address it directly. It never occurs to Joanna to do so. She has learned how to stop her daughter's anxiety, and she reinforces the sugar-as-pacifier solution by feeding her rather than asking her what's wrong. When Linda is a teenager and is anxious about schoolwork or relationships, her mother takes her out for ice cream. She knows it calms her.

Because Joanna has always been thin and was given sweets by her mother to keep her from being bored, she sees nothing wrong with eating a lot of cookies and ice cream. These are the foods she turns to when she's bored. Linda has learned to do the same, even though she has a tendency to gain weight more easily than her mother.

It becomes more and more difficult for Linda to stop eating sugar, even when she makes a deliberate effort. She is constantly fighting her weight problem, but whenever the diet she's on feels frustrating or events in her life seem too difficult to handle, she automatically turns to cookies, candy, and other sweets. By this time, her binge foods have altered her body's chemistry.

When Linda is calm from bingeing on sugars and is able to stop eating sweets she frequently becomes tired and weak, feels disoriented, and is unable to think clearly. There have been times when she has almost blacked out for no apparent reason. At these times, only sugar makes her feel better physically.

Over the years Linda has slowly altered her body's insulin response to sugar, creating hypoglycemia. She uses sweets for more than relieving anxiety. She has created a monster and is caught in a physical and emotional cycle she doesn't understand. By not understanding where her need for sugar originated, why she uses it as she does, or what she has done to her body by abusing it, she has become trapped.

We learn to use sugar to pacify ourselves when that is what we are given as children to keep us quiet. We continue this pattern throughout our lives, turning to sweets to calm ourselves instead of voicing our pain and expressing our feelings. Some of us eat a lot of chocolate, high in tryptophan, when we're unhappy or upset, which triggers our brain's release of the feel-good chemical seratonin. This may create another negative pattern, a physiological response, which is even more difficult to break. Both patterns can begin with our mothers.

If your mother was not there for you emotionally when you were young, you may still ache for the part of her you miss. But sugar is not a substitute for your mother. If you have created a physiological craving for sugar by misusing it, it may take more than recognizing what you've done to change this pattern.

Most people have this kind of low blood sugar, called reactive hypoglycemia. They have an adverse reaction to sugar, honey, and other foods that turn into sugar rapidly, like potatoes. They often feel tired a few hours after meals, have low energy in the afternoon and tire easily.

The amount of these substances required to create a blood-sugar imbalance varies from person to person, with the exception of people who smoke marijuana, and alcoholics. I have found that every one of my patients who has smoked marijuana for six months or more on a daily basis suffers from low-blood-sugar symptoms. And a number of doctors, nutritionists, and medical researchers believe that nearly all alcoholics, recovered or active, are hypoglycemic.

The Problem Inherited

Low blood sugar may be inherited from one or both of your parents. You may have been born with a genetic inability to properly metabolize sugars. In his book *Mental and Elemental Nutrients*, Dr. Carl Pfeiffer suggests that 95 percent of all alcoholics have this type of low blood sugar, called functional hypoglycemia. If one or both of your parents were heavy drinkers when you were conceived, you may have been born with hypoglycemia.

When low blood sugar has been inherited, it is even more difficult to recognize, because your response to sugar has been consistently sensitive all your life. It has become normal for you. For example, it is only now, as an adult, that Inge can see that she was probably born with an inability to handle sugar.

Inge's grandfather had diabetes, and she believes that all of her brothers and sisters had some mild form of blood-sugar disorder. As soon as they came home from school, they would run for the refrigerator, even before putting down their schoolbags, and stuff themselves with cold potatoes.

Inge remembers often feeling weak and shaky as a child. Nothing would make her feel better except sweets and starches. Now she often attends meetings where doughnuts and sweet rolls are available. She finds it easy to avoid them until the meeting is over and she is feeling shaky. After she eats three of them as quickly as she can, she feels better.

Inge's childhood was filled with good, healthful foods. Her family had a farm and grew much of their produce. It was not her diet that led her into bouts of sugar craving; hers was an inherited weakness. Inge watches her diet carefully, but when she skips a meal or waits too long before eating she often gets a low-blood-sugar attack. Then nothing will do but to stuff herself with large quantities of food.

If you find that you crave sweets even when you don't need them for emotional reasons, and you have some symptoms that are similar to Linda's or Inge's, you may have altered your body's chemistry or you may have inherited an altered biochemical response to sugar. Have your doctor check your fasting glucose level to see whether or not it's normal. Even if it is, you may still have a subclinical hypoglycemia. By this, I mean that you may not have the condition itself, but just symptoms that may be leading toward it and causing sugar cravings. An even more accurate blood test is a *fasting glycohemoglobin*. If it is low, you probably have low blood sugar. If it is on the low side of normal, you may have symptoms without the label. These symptoms can often be eliminated through diet and a little nutritional supplementation.

In my practice as a nutritionist, I have seen many people whose blood-glucose levels were in the low ranges of normal but who continued to have low-blood-sugar symptoms until they changed their eating habits. Their doctors had told them that their blood-sugar levels were normal, or that there is no such thing as hypoglycemia. Some doctors believe that hypoglycemia, along with premenstrual syndrome and *Candida albicans*, doesn't exist. But these problems are not imaginary; they are very real.

Even when there is not enough evidence with laboratory testing to show that you are clinically hypoglycemic, a sugar craving that remains even after you have stopped bingeing with sweets to relieve anxiety may be eliminated through supplementation and a change in diet.

THE SOLUTION TO LOW BLOOD SUGAR

Whether you were born with an inability to utilize sugars efficiently or have created this condition by overeating sweets or drinking too much alcohol, you can usually repair much of the damage through proper nutrition and supplementation. The most common nutrients missing in adequate amounts in someone with low blood sugar are chromium and the amino acid l-glutamine.

A medical-doctor colleague of mine once asked me, "What do you do for physical sugar cravings if chromium and l-glutamine don't work?"

"They always do," I replied—and I might have added, "when accompanied by a proper diet, eating every four hours, and eliminating alcohol and refined sugars while the body is repairing."

Remember that everything is temporary. When you avoid certain foods, like candy and desserts, you are giving your body a chance to repair itself. Once it is stronger and more balanced, you may find you can handle small amounts of sugar and alcohol. Or you may decide that you feel better without them. If you stop your supplementation too early or go off your program for an occasional food or drink that can affect your blood-sugar regulation, you may temporarily feel worse than you did before you began. Just use that experience to help you do what so many people claim is impossible: heal yourself.

Diet

Keep a four-day food diary listing all the foods you eat. Underline all foods with refined sugar or honey, since honey turns to sugar more quickly than fruit sugars. Circle all complex carbohydrates (grains, beans, starchy vegetables like potatoes and yams). Modify your diet to include a portion of complex carbohydrates every four hours. Reduce the simple sugars. If at the end of this week you are eating simple sugars more than once a day, take the next step and eliminate them entirely for a while.

Now it's time to eliminate all refined sugar and honey. Not to worry. You can substitute with fruit-juice sweetened foods. Muffins, cereals, cookies, and jams sweetened with fruit sugars are now available in many supermarkets and all health food stores.

To keep your blood-sugar levels normal, you may need a diet high in complex carbohydrates, especially whole grains and beans. As you will see in Chapter 23, these are not forbidden foods. In fact, they are low in fat and high in nutrition, and they contribute to weight loss rather than weight gain. When you physically crave sugar, you may need complex carbohydrates in small quantities throughout the day.

Every four hours, eat something to help stabilize your blood sugar. The best foods to choose from are fresh fruit in moderation, lentils, beans, brown rice, whole-wheat pasta, and whole-grain, sugar-free muffins (corn, wheat, or oat bran). Use the following guide to help you choose foods for each meal that will keep your glucose levels from dropping too rapidly.

Breakfast. Foods made with whole grains will give you a good start in the morning and will last until your mid-morning snack. Some suggestions include a sugar-free whole-grain cereal (hot or cold), with a small piece of fresh fruit or a half cup of berries as sweetener, one or two pieces of whole-grain toast with a little fruit-juice-sweetened jam, or a whole-grain muffin made without refined sugar or honey.

Mid-morning Snack. A small piece of fruit, a few carrot sticks, some baked corn chips, or a few whole-grain crackers.

Lunch. Protein takes several hours to be digested. You will get more energy from your protein if you eat it at midday rather than at night. Have a serving of a protein food with vegetables. Some possibilities include a salad with chicken, turkey, or beans; a chicken breast with raw vegetables; a vegetable omelette; stir-fried vegetables and chicken with a little rice; or a turkey sandwich and cole slaw.

Mid-afternoon Snack. Before your blood-sugar level drops, causing you to crave an afternoon sweet, have a small piece of fruit, a few whole-grain crackers, some baked corn chips, a cup of air-popped popcorn, or a small fruit-juice-sweetened muffin.

Dinner. To avoid craving sugars at night, eat more whole grains and pasta for dinner, and less animal protein. Some examples would be spaghetti with tomato sauce and vegetables; a bowl of lentil soup or bean soup with whole-grain bread and a small salad; tortillas, rice, beans and vegetables; or brown rice and steamed or stir-fried vegetables. When you have protein, keep the amounts low. Concentrate on the starches.

Evening Snack. Try a small bowl of popcorn without butter, a small piece of fruit, a muffin, baked corn chips or a few crackers.

Eat no more than two small pieces of fresh fruit a day, and for now avoid fruit juices containing high concentrations of fruit sugar.

You may want to use dietary methods alone to help correct your child's low blood sugar. The correct diet is a powerful tool by itself. But when a person's blood-sugar levels have been low for many years, supplementation is one of the most rapid means of repair. I have seen remarkable results achieved through the combination of proper diet and supplementation.

Supplements

Chromium. Chromium is an essential micronutrient found in a number of foods, including brewer's yeast. It is needed for the proper functioning of insulin and thus helps maintain normal glucose tolerance. When it is lacking in sufficient quantities, you could have anything from slight hypoglycemic symptoms to symptoms so severe they mimic diabetes. Since chromium is abnormally low in our soil and is eliminated from grains when they are refined, our diets are often low in chromium.

One of chromium's effects is to stimulate enzymes involved in glucose metabolism. Insufficient chromium can upset the function of insulin. In addition to adding whole grains to your diet, adding chromium supplements for a month or two will often help you break your physiological sugar craving.

Chromium is a mineral that can be toxic in large amounts. Researchers at the Linus Pauling Institute of Science and Medicine have found that a safe form of the mineral, called glucose tolerance factor (GTF), is an organic form of chromium that helps normalize glucose tolerance more effectively and without toxicity. Chromium picolinate is also safe and easily absorbed.

You may want to check with your doctor first, but I have found that 200 micrograms of GTF chromium taken three times a day with meals for two to six months, or two tablespoons of brewer's yeast taken daily, can help eliminate sugar cravings in many people. In my practice I find that the best results are achieved with chromium tablets or drops rather than brewer's yeast.

In the past year, a large newspaper ran an article saying that chromium was toxic in laboratory animals. And it was. These animals were given 1,200,000 mcg before it caused damage to their cells. If you were to take 200 mcg three times a day, you'd be taking 2,000 mcg less than the smallest amount that would damage hamster cells in a laboratory. That newspaper article worried people unnecessarily.

L-glutamine. L-glutamine is an amino acid, and all amino acids are components of protein. Individual amino acids have been used to enhance a variety of body functions. For example, tryptophan has been used successfully to help a person sleep and to reduce depression. One of l-glutamine's many uses has been to take away the craving for sugar, including alcohol.

I first used l-glutamine with Eleanor, an alcoholic who came to me for nutritional support as she worked with her psychotherapist to understand the psychological reasons for her drinking. When she came to see me she had reduced her alcohol consumption from a half gallon or more to a quart of wine a day, with the help of therapy. She was unable to drink less than that.

I had read medical reports suggesting that l-glutamine could be helpful in eliminating alcohol cravings, and I put Eleanor on my program of chromium and l-glutamine, along with a diet that would help correct her low-blood-sugar problem. Within two weeks she had reduced her intake of alcohol to one glass of wine a day. She didn't crave it anymore; this one glass was a psychological crutch, and she stopped drinking completely the day she went to her first Alcoholics Anonymous meeting.

After Eleanor, I was inspired to suggest l-glutamine to anyone who was physically addicted to sugar. I reasoned that since alcohol enters the bloodstream rapidly, like a predigested sugar, l-glutamine might also alleviate physiological sugar cravings that came from a source other than alcohol. It worked beautifully.

My preference is to use 500-milligram capsules of l-glutamine, rather than tablets, which may or may not dissolve quickly in the stomach. I give my patients 1500 milligrams of this amino acid once a day when they crave sugar. L-glutamine is taken between meals with a little diluted fruit juice, which enhances its absorption. You may need to take it for a period of two weeks to three months. It's not necessary to take it forever.

All amino acids need magnesium and vitamin B6 to be utilized. Be sure you're taking a multi-vitamin with minerals and are on a diet with plenty of whole grains and beans to give yourself sufficient amounts of these nutrients.

THE SOLUTION TO A
CANDIDA ALBICANS OVERGROWTH

"Friday night, at last!" Eva thinks as she walks out of the office toward her car. All of her friends are busy tonight, so she won't be meeting any of them for a few drinks to begin the weekend. "A few drinks," she smiles to herself. "It's never only a few." Meeting friends for drinks at the end of the work week is Ritual One. Eva shifts her thoughts into Ritual Two and heads her car in the direction of the supermarket. "This is even better than drinks."

She will do her weekend grocery shopping later. This is her Friday night quick stop. She drives into the parking lot of the same market every time and picks up a small shopping basket. She doesn't want the foods she buys to stand out in a large shopping cart. Her heart begins to beat faster as she walks briskly past the cereals and stops in front of the cake-mix section. "It's here," she breathes with relief as she grabs a box of her favorite brownie mix.

The next stop is the icing. It, too, must be a certain brand. Eva's face is flushed with excitement. "This is better than a date." With her last item, a large double bag of cheese-flavored chips, she heads over to the fast checkout line.

A little later, at home, Eva takes the hot brownies out of the oven and spreads a thick layer of chocolate icing over them. Careful not to burn her fingers, she gently eases a large slice out of the pan. She stands by the sink and eats the first piece. The rest are carefully arranged on a clear glass plate etched with flowers that her grandmother gave her when she moved into her own apartment. She carries the plate and a bowl of chips over to her favorite chair and arranges them on either side of her. With a deep sigh, she begins eating.

After Eva has eaten all the brownies she can, she reached for the salty chips. She finds that alternating sweet and salty foods enables her to eat more sweets. Finally stuffed, she carries the plate with the few remaining brownies into the kitchen and covers them with tin foil. She will have them the next morning for breakfast. "This is better than being with friends. This way, I have something to look forward to in the morning!"

The next day she wakes up feeling a little foggy. "Uh-oh," she thinks. "It looks like this is going to be another spacey Saturday." She tries to remember what she had intended to do over the weekend, but her thoughts keep slipping past her and disappearing. Eva's friends often tease her and call her an airhead. Sometimes she is, she will admit, but there are times when her thoughts are clear and crisp. But it's not often enough, she muses.

For years, Eva has begun her weekends with one of two rituals: drinking or eating brownies. She enjoys both, but not the consequences, and she is unhappy that her weight has climbed to an all-time high. Conscious of her appearance and wanting to look as pretty as her younger sister—her mother's favorite—she has tried to diet several times, but never with lasting results. The problem isn't just Friday nights. Eva can't stay away from sugar during the rest of the week either. She has a craving that doesn't leave until she has fed it with cookies or a drink.

After a number of unsuccessful diets, Eva finally decided to try acupuncture. She had heard it could help with controlling one's appetite. Her acupuncturist was dismayed at the amount of sugar Eva ate and drank. "Give me a chance to help you," she urged Eva one afternoon. "Stay away from sugar completely for three or four months, and let me help you get results." But Eva couldn't do it.

"I think you may have *Candida*," her acupuncturist finally said, explaining to Eva that a sugar-eating yeast could be at the root of her weight problem. "I think that's why you're so spacey, and why you can't stop eating sugar. If you're having trouble staying off sugar, I'd like you to see a nutritionist."

Eventually, Eva came to me. As we traced back to find the cause of a possible *Candida* overgrowth, she remembered having taken a lot of antibiotics fifteen years earlier. She had not, however, followed up this treatment by taking *Acidophilus*, a supplement that restores the helpful intestinal bacteria that keep *Candida* in check. In addition, Eva was taking birth-control pills, which altered her hormonal balance and provided an environment that encouraged the proliferation of the yeast. While she had always eaten sugar, her troubles really began after she had taken the antibiotics and begun to use birth-control pills. To confirm the presence of an overgrowth of *Candida*, Eva had a blood test through ImmunoDiagnostic Laboratories (see Resources section for more information).

Just understanding about her overgrowth of *Candida* and the role it played in her sugar cravings and weight problem was not enough to stop Eva from drinking alcohol or eating sweets. The day I said to her, "When you love yourself as much as I love you, you'll take care of yourself and stop eating sugar," something inside her changed. At that point she was able to begin eating properly and eliminating the excessive *Candida*.

Eva doesn't think about her weight anymore. She loves pampering herself by buying healthy foods and fixing them for herself. While she may slip at times and have a drink or eat sugar, she always returns to her anti-*Candida* diet. She is slowly getting her yeast overgrowth under control, and her mind is clear more often than it is foggy.

Just What is Candida?

Because there are dozens and dozens of symptoms associated with an overgrowth of this organism, *Candida* is the name many people give to health problems they cannot otherwise explain. Sometimes a yeast overgrowth does exist, and sugar cravings are a common indication.

All of us have a yeast, *Candida albicans*, in our intestinal tracts. We cannot eliminate it entirely, and in fact there is no reason to do so. This organism lives quite happily in our bodies without causing any problems, unless there is an overgrowth.

Stress, lowered immunity, hormonal changes, sugar, and long-term antibiotic use can all contribute to an overabundance of *Candida*. Since sugar feeds this yeast, women with an overgrowth of *Candida albicans* often crave sugars. If you or your child crave sugars of any kind, and you cannot attribute this craving to any other physical problem or to your emotions, it may be due to an overgrowth of *Candida*. In the past five years, it has become very popular for health care practitioners to attribute many symptoms to this overgrowth. I have not found this to be the case and prefer using laboratory tests to help diagnose this problem.

Acidophilus is a bacteria in our intestines that normally helps keep *Candida* in check. If we feed the *Candida* by overeating sugar, or if we kill off some of the *Acidophilus* with antibiotics, we can upset the balance of these organisms and create a *Candida* overgrowth. Women know this overgrowth as *Monilia*, or, simply, a vaginal yeast infection. (In babies, it is called thrush, and it appears as a white, patchy fungus in the mouth.)

In a small percentage of women, this yeast proliferates to such a degree that it works its way through its natural barrier in the intestines and gets into the bloodstream. If it is permitted to continue growing, it can travel to various organs and cause additional problems, including headaches, depression, indigestion, food sensitivities, disorientation, PMS, extreme fatigue, and sensitivity to odors such as gasoline and perfume. This form of overgrowth is called *Polysystemic candidiasis*. It is this form that can be diagnosed through laboratory tests.

Both forms of *Candida albicans* are normally treated with antifungal medications, including fluconozol, nystatin, mycostatin, and nyzerol. Some women find that such medications do not eliminate their overgrowth. Few doctors tell them to stop feeding the yeast by temporarily eliminating sugars from their diets—precisely those foods they crave.

Under ordinary circumstances, when the flora in your intestines is in a balanced ratio, sugar will not cause an overgrowth problem. But when this delicate balance has been upset, a high-sugar diet can encourage its growth. You may want to change your diet to see if this diminishes or eliminates your sugar craving. If you have *Candida* symptoms, the diet can only be beneficial.

For a few weeks, or even a few months, you may need to eliminate all foods containing sugar. Even large quantities of fruit, which contains fructose, and milk, which contains lactose, can feed *Candida*.

One popular misconception is that women with a *Candida* overgrowth must also stop eating all foods that contain yeast. This belief originated when several medical doctors who were allergy specialists discovered that *Candida albicans* was the missing link for some of their patients who did not recover on an allergy program alone. If you are allergic to yeast and have *Candida*, you will have to eliminate not only sugars but also foods that contain yeast. Similarly, if you are allergic to chicken, you should eliminate chicken to free your immune system to fight the *Candida*. Stop eating whatever you're allergic to. Otherwise, the solution is simple: just eliminate sugars, repopulate your intestinal tract with helpful bacteria like *Acidophilus*, and take some form of antifungal to kill off the overgrowth.

Identifying a *Candida* Overgrowth

You may suspect you have an overgrowth of *Candida albicans* and be willing to go on a program to reduce its colonies. Or you may want to know more. If so, there are some laboratories that test blood for antibodies to *Candida*. The lab I use is IDL (ImmunoDiagnostic Laboratories), listed in the Resources section.

Whoever does the test should be looking for IgG, IgA, and IgM antibodies. If your IgM antibodies are above normal, or if either of the others are very high, there is a good possibility that you have an overgrowth of *Candida*.

An Anti-*Candida* Program

Diet. When you understand that an organism that is causing problems is the reason for your sugar craving, it is easier to avoid sugar than to do so just because "it's not good for you." Think of it like this: somewhere in your body is a living organism that, like you, wants to live and thrive. You may need clothes, money, shelter, and food to live; all it needs is sugar. Whenever you crave sugar, this troublesome organism is asking to be kept alive. Whenever you say no, you deprive it of its nourishment and lead it closer to extinction. Don't feed your *Candida*.

The following foods contain too much sugar for an anti-*Candida* diet: sugar, honey, maltose, malted rice syrup, barley malt, molasses, fruit juice, dried fruit, and dairy products (because they contain the milk sugar, lactose). Potatoes turn into sugar quickly and feed *Candida*; eliminate them for now. However, all kinds of pasta, both whole wheat and regular, turn into sugar slowly and so they are fine.

Small amounts of fresh fruits low in sugar, like berries, and very small quantities of milk in cereal are permitted, except in extremely uncomfortable or persistent cases.

Foods and beverages with artificial sweeteners may help you through your initial cravings as you eliminate sugars from your diet, although these have been found to contribute to sugar cravings in a number of people. If they work for you, use them temporarily. They are "better than" sugars of any kind when you want to eliminate a *Candida* overgrowth. But whole, fresh foods are always preferable to artificial or manufactured ones, which may cause problems we don't even know about yet. As your *Candida* diminishes, so will your sugar craving. You won't need a substitute.

An anti-*Candida* diet is too high in protein for you to stay on indefinitely. Use it only until your overgrowth is under control, and then replace some of the proteins with complex carbohydrates. For now, concentrate on eating plenty of vegetables, with a few servings of chicken, fish, tofu, or beans each day. Small quantities of carbo-hydrates in the form of whole grains will round out your diet.

In the following sample diet to control *Candida* overgrowth, *choose one food from each category:*

Breakfast: Eggs or vegetable omelette; oatmeal or other whole-grain cereal, hot or cold, with ¼ cup milk and half a chopped apple or ½ cup unsweetened berries; whole-grain toast with almond butter

Lunch: Salad with chicken, tuna, or beans; lentil, split-pea, or bean soup with a small salad; leftover vegetables with protein (chicken, turkey, fish, meat, or beans)

Dinner: Stir-fried vegetables with chicken; ½ cup cooked brown rice, with chicken, fish, or meat; ½ cup cooked brown rice, 1 cup cooked beans, and a salad or cooked vegetables; spaghetti or other pasta with tomato sauce and cooked vegetables or salad; Chinese food (not deep-fried) without sugar or rice

Snacks: A few raw nuts; one of the following fruits (keep to only one of these a day): apple, pear, orange, $1/2$ cup unsweetened berries; 1 cup plain popcorn; 1 or 2 (only) puffed-rice cakes

Eva finds herself slipping off her diet when she gets bored with the foods she's eating. To avoid this boredom, you can concentrate on changing the tastes of these basic foods with various spices and sauces—for example, curry, garlic, tomato sauce, soy sauce, and other flavorings without sugar. You may want to write out a menu plan to keep you from eating the same foods over and over. Buy different vegetables at the market for variety, and check cookbooks for new recipes. Several *Candida* cookbooks are listed in the Resources section of this book.

Supplementation

There are two types of supplementation recommended for killing off *Candida* organisms: *Acidophilus* and antifungals.

Acidophilus. Give your intestinal tract more of the organisms that help keep *Candida* in check: *Acidophilus.* Your own colonies of *Acidophilus* may have been depleted by antibiotics. The most powerful form of this supplement is a powder, found in the refrigerated section of health-food stores. The brand I have found consistently more potent is made by Natren (800) 992-3323 ext. 114.

The powder should be mixed in room-temperature water. Liquid, tablets, or capsules are not as potent and may need to be taken for a longer period of time than the powder. Taking a half-teaspoon of powdered *Acidophilus* morning and night (on an empty stomach) for two weeks to six months will usually reestablish the intestinal flora.

Antifungals. Caprylic acid, a fatty acid found in coconuts, is a powerful and safe non-prescription antifungal used for eliminating excessive *Candida albicans*. It can be found in a number of supplements sold in health-food stores. Several doctors with whom I work find it more effective than Nizoral (ketoconazole), Mycostatin (nystatin), and other drugs. The brand we believe most effective is called

Capricin, but other caprylic-acid formulas, such as *Yeast Fighter*, also work well. Use them as directed, but begin using antifungals gradually and work up to a full dose. Some people eliminate their overgrowth in a few months; others need to take these antifungals along with *Acidophilus* for a year or more.

Another milder antifungal is Pau d'Arco tea. Made from the bark of a tree, this tea will also help keep *Candida* under control. If you want to begin with something mild but effective, try drinking a few cups of this tea every day while following a sugar-free diet.

When you begin killing off *Candida* overgrowth with antifungals, you may experience what is called "the die-off effect." As the yeast dies, some of your initial symptoms may return briefly and may be acute. They usually leave within a few days. Lower your antifungal dosage to remain comfortable, but use a little every day if you possibly can. Your symptoms will leave, and so will your sugar cravings.

A sugar-free diet and *Acidophilus* supplementation is safe for people of any age, and it may be an appropriate program for your child if her sugar cravings began after she took antibiotics for more than two or three weeks. Explain to her how a *Candida* overgrowth can contribute to her sugar cravings, and help her stay on an anti-*Candida* diet for a few weeks by suggesting or preparing foods that do not contribute to its growth.

20

OVERCOMING CHOCOLATE CRAVINGS:

The Magnesium Solution

There used to be a curious gathering of people yearly in Los Angeles. Thousands of people who did not know they had magnesium deficiencies met in a large hall. The aroma in the hall filled them with anticipation, excitement, and sometimes guilt. They mingled for hours, looking at and sampling foods that identified their deficiency, yet none of them knew this. They were simply people enjoying themselves at an annual Chocolate Convention.

Millions of people have an irresistible urge to eat chocolate. When this urge overcomes them, no other taste but chocolate will do. Many women experience this daily or weekly, while others feel drawn to candy counters and bakery stores by an invisible force once a month, just before their menstrual periods. Although they may feel this force twelve times a year for twenty or thirty years, some do not see a connection between their monthly chocolate cravings and their menstrual cycles. In fact, few people—men or women—see a correlation between craving the specific taste of chocolate with anything at all. But craving chocolate is often simply a sign of a magnesium deficiency.

Joyce frequently grabs a container of yogurt for breakfast before she rushes out the door in the morning on workdays or between doing loads of laundry and cleaning up the kitchen on weekends. She has a salad for lunch, with cottage cheese and a cola drink. For dinner she makes hamburgers, serving them with green beans and a seasoned white rice or enriched macaroni-and-cheese dish, since these are foods her children will eat. For dessert, or later in the evening, she joins her family for a dish of ice cream. After all, she thinks, her diet is low enough in fats. What's the problem? If this is an isolated day, there is no problem. But if this daily diet is typical for Joyce—and it is—then there is a definite problem.

Every month before her period begins, Joyce craves chocolate. It's an obsession she can't control. All month she is able to eat sensibly, but right before menstruating, she goes wild. She eats whole boxes of chocolate-chip cookies, and she indulges in candy bars and other chocolate snacks that don't call out to her as loudly once she begins to menstruate. In addition, she becomes cranky and flies off the handle at insignificant things. She can't help it, she tells her husband and friends; she has PMS. But Joyce *can* help it.

If you have monthly chocolate binges, then you know they can lead to your eating uncontrollably for up to two weeks a month—half your life! This is because hormones released before your menses also cause increased magnesium excretion, and your body often lacks enough of this mineral. In a desperate attempt to regain lost stores of magnesium, your body turns to craving chocolate.

One ounce of baking chocolate contains more than 81 milligrams of magnesium—as much as in a pound of steak. In fact, cocoa powder has more than twice as much magnesium as nuts, the food next highest in this mineral. Some other foods high in magnesium include whole grains, such as millet, wild rice, brown rice, corn meal, and wheat bran. These are often unknown or deliberately excluded from diets by women who are watching their weight and who believe, erroneously, that eating grains will make them fat.

This obsession with weight may help to create magnesium-deficient "chocoholics," since an increase in dairy products upsets the balance of calcium and magnesium. The amount of calcium you and your daughter eat affects your magnesium levels as much as the amount of magnesium-rich foods you eat. Our diets are often too high in calcium and too low in magnesium to give us the proper 2:1 ratio (two parts calcium to one part magnesium). When we eat a diet low or lacking in whole grains, and when we allow our children to avoid these foods while eating large quantities of dairy foods, we are encouraging magnesium deficiencies.

Yogurt, cottage cheese, milk, and ice cream have nine times as much calcium as magnesium. If you have been eating a lot of dairy products but few or no whole grains, you may have upset your calcium/magnesium ratio. To bring yourself back into balance, you would have to eat three cups of brown rice daily if you have yogurt for breakfast or ice cream for dessert. *Ten* cups of white rice would be needed, since white rice, like white flour, has been stripped of much of its magnesium.

Nuts and pumpkin seeds are also high in magnesium, but they are too high in fats to be eaten in great quantities. The answer to overcoming chocolate cravings is to eat more whole grains, such as brown rice and whole-wheat breads and cereals, and fewer dairy products.

THE CALCIUM MYTH AND OSTEOPOROSIS

If you or your children have a chocolate craving, it may be merely a symptom of a mineral deficiency that can greatly affect other areas of your lives besides your waistlines. With growing media and advertising attention on the role of calcium in the prevention of osteoporosis (brittle bones in aging women), little has been said about magnesium, which helps your body utilize calcium and move it from the bloodstream to your bones.

Calcium is currently being advertised as "the woman's mineral." It's being sold as a supplement that prevents osteoporosis, but there is still much debate as to whether or not it is absorbed into your bones to make them strong. Meanwhile, it is the most heavily advertised and widely sold mineral in the country. But calcium doesn't work alone; your body needs magnesium for many functions, including calcium absorption. The answer is not to take more calcium—although that's still what many doctors advise—but to have a diet *lower in calcium* and *higher in magnesium*, along with taking a magnesium supplement.

A change of this nature would help protect women against osteoporosis, according to Dr. Guy E. Abraham. And he may be right. Consider this. The countries whose populations have the highest calcium intake (the United States, Great Britain, and Sweden) have the highest incidence of osteoporosis, while those in which the calcium intake is lowest (Asian and African countries) have the lowest incidence of this condition. The key lies in calcium *absorption and utilization,* not in the amount of calcium you eat. When your diet is balanced and contains more magnesium than calcium, you will absorb a larger proportion of calcium, so you can eat foods that contain *less* calcium and still have enough in your tissues. Since whole grains and legumes contain both magnesium and calcium, they will help you achieve the balance you need to overcome your chocolate cravings.

Phosphorus is a mineral that blocks calcium absorption. All meat, which contains from ten to twenty times as much phosphorus as calcium, cheese, or cola, causes the body to *excrete* rather than absorb calcium. Caffeine and large amounts of sugar or alcohol will do the same. In addition to dietary factors, smoking cigarettes also causes calcium excretion.

Other Magnesium-Deficiency Problems

Absorbed but unutilized calcium often gets deposited in the joints, where it results in arthritis, or in arteries, where it causes atherosclerosis. Heart disease is the number one killer of post-menopausal women—women who are taking high amounts of calcium.

My concern is that more women are giving themselves unnecessary arthritis and heart disease, and this concern is shared by a growing number of medical doctors and researchers. This issue has already been reported in medical journals. Other health problems related to magnesium deficiencies include kidney-stone formation, muscle cramping, and soft-tissue calcification (arthritis). If you're a chocoholic, take a look to see whether there is any correlation between your craving and your present state of health.

THE CHOCOLATE CRAVER'S RECOVERY PROGRAM

Joyce's severe premenstrual symptoms had been reduced from two weeks of her feeling crazed and possessed to a few days of moodiness. We were both delighted with the progress she'd made. "I'm not eating chocolate much anymore," she mentioned, as an aside. "I don't care about it as much as I used to. In the past, I just *had* to have chocolate. Now it's easy to resist."

I hadn't known Joyce had been hooked on chocolate. She had never mentioned it to me, and she'd forgotten to write it in her food diary. Joyce's monthly craving for chocolate had become so much a part of her life that she had taken it for granted. After it was gone, she became aware of how much it had affected her.

"I remember making a conscious effort not to buy candy, even though I knew my period was due in a few days and the craving for chocolate would soon be gone," Joyce told me. "But on those days when I was able to avoid it, I'd end up in bed unable to sleep. I couldn't get the taste of chocolate out of my mind. I'd get out of bed, get dressed, and drive to the nearest store to get my chocolate fix. Once I had to drive for nearly an hour before I found a store that was still open!"

"Why didn't you keep a little chocolate in the house? It would have been simpler."

Joyce smiled. "I always thought I could overcome the urge. As soon as the craving left, I felt so strong, so sure of myself, that I couldn't imagine not being able to take control and resist it the next time. But I was always wrong."

By using a diet and supplementation high in magnesium and low in calcium to offset the imbalance you have created, you may be able to eliminate your chocolate cravings within a few months. By using diet alone, it could take much longer.

The easiest way to help your daughter eliminate a craving for chocolate is to first eliminate your own. When she sees you can take chocolate or leave it alone, she may be willing to try this program for herself. If she is overweight and struggling to lose extra pounds, her chocolate craving is only adding to her problem. Help her find the motivation she needs to try this program for a month or two. Children and young adults often respond to it more quickly than older people do.

Diet

Eliminate dairy products temporarily, with the exception of small amounts, such as a little milk on your cereal or some grated cheese on pasta. Use dairy products as condiments rather than primary ingredients. Spaghetti with marinara sauce would be better than macaroni and cheese, for example. Instead of including cheese on sandwiches, add more lettuce and tomato for moisture and flavor.

Bring whole grains into your diet. They're filling, satisfying, and low in fats. Eat whole-grain cereals, toast, or muffins for breakfast, and use brown rice and whole-wheat pasta for dinner instead of foods made with white, "enriched" flour. Put some garbanzo beans or kidney beans in your salads instead of cheese for added bulk that's low in fat.

Drink something besides milk. Cow's milk is food for baby cows, not for adult humans. We are the only animals on the planet that drink milk after we're weaned—and another animal's milk, at that. If you love and crave milk, yogurt, ice cream, and cheese, you may have an allergy or sensitivity to dairy foods. Read Chapter 21 on food allergies and sensitivities to learn how to break free of your cravings for foods that may be bringing you to a state of nutritional imbalance.

Children can absorb calcium from their food more easily than adults can. Therefore, it's not necessary to eliminate dairy products from your daughter's diet unless she has a lactose intolerance and has difficulty digesting them. If she eats excessive amounts, however, some of the dairy products in her diet can be reduced. More important, add whole grains, even if it means mixing brown rice with white rice or whole grain spaghetti with enriched pasta. Make her sandwiches with whole-wheat bread and help her slowly adapt her taste buds to a diet higher in whole grains.

Many cereals in health-food stores, and a few found in supermarkets, are not only tasty but also contain magnesium-rich whole grains. Read the labels carefully to separate refined, "enriched" cereals from those that contain the whole grain—and don't forget the old standby, oatmeal. You can cook it in a little apple juice for moisture and sweetness, eliminating the need for milk.

You and your children can add magnesium to your diets by eating homemade corn muffins, bran muffins, or oat-bran muffins for breakfast or snacks. Sweeten them with apple juice or honey, using a smaller amount of sweetener than the recipe calls for to help keep the sugar content low and guard against excessive calcium excretion. If you have a cookie jar for the family, keep it filled with low-sugar oatmeal cookies.

Magnesium Supplementation

If you are taking a multivitamin/mineral—an excellent idea in today's world, where our soil often lacks important trace minerals and our diets are not always comprised of nutritious foods—make sure that it has *at least* as much magnesium as calcium. If you have frequent chocolate cravings, take one that has *twice* as much magnesium as calcium. In combination with a supportive diet, these vitamins have been found to eliminate chocolate cravings along with emotional premenstrual symptoms including depression.

There is still controversy among many medical doctors concerning the amount of calcium necessary to guard against osteoporosis. To help you understand another point of view, and why you may *not* need 1500 milligrams of calcium a day (the daily amount recommended by many doctors for women), you might want to read Dr. Guy E. Abraham's article "The Calcium Controversy," published in the *Journal of Applied Nutrition* in June 1985. (You can obtain a copy by writing to: Dr. Guy E. Abraham, P.O. Box 3378, Torrance, CA 90510.

If you prefer taking more calcium than the amount found in some of these formulas, *you can simply add magnesium to your present supplement.* The ratio that works for my patients is twice as much magnesium as calcium. Magnesium is safe to take in large amounts; its only side effect is loose stools, so if you experience this symptom, simply cut back on the amount you take.

The PMS multivitamins on the market are safe for your daughter to take if she is menstruating, and they will provide her with extra magnesium. If she is not yet menstruating, concentrate on supporting her diet with magnesium-rich whole grains and beans.

In a few months, you may find that chocolate has loosened its hold on you, no longer pushing you into candy stores or ice cream parlors or forcing you to say yes when you're asked whether or not you want dessert. If chocolate doesn't taste as good to you as it used to, it you don't *have* to have it, don't simply eat it out of habit. Create a new, positive eating habit. Find other tastes you enjoy, and let chocolate have a more appropriate place in your life: something you choose occasionally, not something that chooses you.

21

ELIMINATING ALLERGIES
AND FOOD SENSITIVITIES:

The Rotation-Diet Solution
to Food Cravings

Some people would have called Bonnie's diet boring, but not Bonnie. She really loved the foods she ate. Every morning she had one or two large bowls of oatmeal and a glass of milk. Her lunches varied between salads and sandwiches, always accompanied by a glass or two of milk. And more often than not, she had granola for dinner. It was easy to fix, and she craved it.

When Bonnie first came to see me, she complained of being tired and irritable. She could understand feeling anxious just before her menses, but not throughout the month. No matter how long she slept she woke up every morning so tired she felt drugged, and although she felt a surge of energy after breakfast, by the time she was ready for dinner Bonnie could hardly drag herself to fix her bowl of cereal. Afterward she felt better for a little while, but in a few hours it was time for sleep and the cycle would begin again.

Blood tests revealed no abnormalities; Bonnie's blood-sugar levels were not responsible for her fatigue. I suspected that her premenstrual anxiety was coming from drinking so much milk, resulting in low magnesium levels, so I asked her to stop for a while. Perhaps this would affect her energy as well.

"I couldn't do that!" she exclaimed. "I love milk, and I always have. Besides, I feel so much better after I drink it. It picks me up more than a cup of coffee. Do anything, but don't ask me to stop drinking milk," she pleaded.

"Thank you, Bonnie," I sighed. "You may have just identified your problem. You may be craving milk and the oats in your two cereals as well because of a sensitivity to them. If I'm right, you're going to feel tired and tense as long as you continue to eat these foods. My suggestion is that you stop eating dairy products and oats for a few weeks, and see what happens."

It was not easy to persuade Bonnie to change her routine. In fact, it took several months of getting nowhere before she finally agreed. Then, for two weeks, she ate toast, bran muffins, or oat-free cereals with soy milk for breakfast; drank iced tea with her lunch; and forced herself to fix something for dinner other than cereal. At times she was too tired to make anything more than a frozen dinner, but she completely avoided all dairy foods and oats.

"How are you feeling?" I asked her at the end of her two-week elimination diet.

"I can't believe it," she marveled. "For the first week I could hardly drag myself around. I almost drove to the market one night to get a quart of milk. I wanted it so badly I was shaking. Then I realized this was crazy! If I could possibly be allergic to milk and oats, it was foolish for me not to know it and get better. So I stayed away from them 100 percent, like you suggested, and by the middle of this week I had more energy and wasn't snapping at people as much. Even my friends commented on how nice I was."

"Now you get to eat a bowl of cereal," I instructed. "Have some oatmeal for breakfast tomorrow, and call me the next day with your results. If you're not sensitive to these foods, you'll be fine. If you are, you'll know it."

Bonnie reported that she had felt miserable the entire day after eating her cereal. She had a headache that lasted all morning, was depressed, and felt exhausted. What's more, she began craving milk and cereal more than ever before.

"I'm convinced," she admitted. "Get me off this stuff so I can feel good again."

Because Bonnie's diet lacked variety, I was concerned that she would create other sensitivities if we exchanged dairy products and oats for just one or two other foods. Bonnie added as many other foods as she could to her diet and went on a rotation diet (discussed later). On this diet she ate only those foods to which she was not sensitive, and she ate each one no more often than every four days. She did this for three months. After following her rotation diet, Bonnie was able to reintroduce both dairy foods and oats without further symptoms, but she has never gone back to eating as much of them as she once did.

If you have any allergies or sensitivities to food, alcohol, tobacco, or chemicals, there is a good chance that your body is not producing sufficient pancreatic enzymes to completely digest proteins, report William Philpott, M.D., and Dwight Kalita, Ph.D., in their impressive book *Brain Allergies*.

When proteins are not digested, protein molecules reach tissues through the bloodstream. These partially digested proteins are treated by your body as foreign invaders and trigger the production of antibodies. When you eat the same food again you get allergic symptoms, and suddenly your immune system is busy handling partially digested proteins instead of viruses and bacteria. While you're provoking allergic symptoms, you're also diverting your immune system from its primary job: keeping you free from disease. The result is often more colds and flus.

We often crave particular foods when we have an allergy or sensitivity to them. If you are addicted to one or more specific foods and can find no other explanation for your craving, you may have a food sensitivity or allergy. A sensitivity, which is the most common of the two, can occur when you eat the same food over and over.

You could have a reaction if you eat large quantities of a food in one day that you usually eat only occasionally. If you eat any food frequently, you may have developed an allergic type of addiction to it. These reactions can often be reversed by avoiding the offending food for three to twelve months. A true allergy, however, may be a permanent condition.

Some reasons for food sensitivities include a deficiency or dysfunction of your immune system or a lack of sufficient digestive enzymes. Poor digestion and absorption is one important cause, and one that you may be able to correct by developing better eating habits, following an elimination and rotation diet, or taking digestive enzymes.

IDENTIFYING YOUR PROBLEM: THE ELIMINATION DIET

Without knowing it, many people who are addicted to certain foods crave them because these foods provide temporary relief from such withdrawal symptoms as fatigue, anxiety, headaches, and irritability. An elimination diet can help pinpoint these foods.

Eliminating a suspected troublesome food, then eating it and watching for any reactions is a very old method of food-sensitivity testing. Hippocrates told the ancient Greeks that they would have severe reactions after eating foods they were allergic to following a fast. This is still one of the best methods of determining whether you have a food allergy or sensitivity.

Some of the more common food allergies and sensitivities involve all products made with cow's milk, eggs, wheat, corn, chocolate, citrus fruits, nuts, and shellfish. However, you can be sensitive to any food, especially if you eat it often. An allergy or sensitivity to wheat could be one reason you crave bread, cookies, muffins, and crackers. Someone who can't stop drinking milk and eating cheese or ice cream could be sensitive to dairy products. I have seen patients who are affected by eating bananas, chicken, and other foods.

You may create a food sensitivity by eating any food daily, or your sensitivity may have begun when you were a baby. Breast-fed infants have been found to react to foods eaten by their mothers, components of which are passed on to the babies in breast milk. If you are sensitive to any foods, it is very possible that if you breast-fed your daughter, she is now affected by those same foods.

I often ask my patients, "If you were on a desert island for two months, which three foods would you not want to be without?" The foods they list without hesitation are the foods I then ask them to eliminate for two to four weeks, usually with successful results.

Pick one or two substances you think may be responsible for your cravings and avoid them *completely* for two full weeks. If you slip and eat small amounts of the food or foods you're avoiding, you may be unable to get accurate information. Read all labels carefully. Wheat (otherwise known as "flour") and dairy products hide in many processed foods. You may not think that bread contains milk, but many varieties are made with nonfat dry milk.

At the end of two weeks, eat a small portion of the food you've been avoiding by itself and wait for any reactions. If you are sensitive to this food, you will likely experience symptoms within two to twenty-four hours. If you find that you still crave the food; feel tired, nauseated, or gassy or have indigestion; or are experiencing any other symptoms, eliminate this food from your diet for three months. If you feel nothing physically or emotionally, wait a day and eat a larger quantity. If you still experience no symptoms, you are probably not sensitive to that food.

You may be able to eat small portions after avoiding the food completely for three months. If not, repeat the process until you experience no symptoms after eating it. Remember, you will not necessarily need to avoid this food forever; it is often only a temporary elimination program.

Continue the elimination process with all the foods you crave, eliminating one or two every few weeks. When you know which foods provoke symptoms, eliminate them completely for two or three months before conducting your challenge again. Your cravings will gradually disappear, and you will feel infinitely better.

Some people can stop their cravings for certain foods simply by reducing the amounts they eat, while others cannot. Although complete elimination will likely help you solve your problem more completely, you may want to begin by using a more gradual approach, even if it means a little slower progress. This is your body, and your craving. Do the best you can, and improve upon your program as you are able to. Be gentle with yourself.

Don't feel bad if you discover that you are sensitive to your favorite foods. You won't be giving up anything but your symptoms. You're just exchanging some foods for others temporarily to get the results you're looking for. Only *you* are saying you cannot eat dairy products, wheat, eggs, or any other food for the time being. And remember that you can always return to your present diet if you are not ready to be on an elimination diet right now.

Just identifying your craving as coming from wheat, dairy foods, sugar, or anything else is an important first step. If you truly want to be free of your cravings, you will do more when you can. Use an affirmation to help you move from where you are to where you want to be.

If you have identified problem foods for yourself, help your children determine whether or not they have a sensitivity to any of them as well. Even young children may be able to benefit from this information. Many years ago, a patient of mine had a three-year-old daughter who was always getting colds and a stuffy nose that prevented her from sleeping well. When she wasn't rested, she was cranky and unhappy. After the mother realized her own dairy sensitivity, she took her daughter off dairy products. The child's cycle of colds stopped, and her stuffiness cleared up. The child even seemed to understand that cheese and ice cream made her sick and uncomfortable, and for a while she was happy, energetic, and free from colds.

But children have short attention spans, and one day the child begged her mother for pizza. "You may get a stuffy nose and not be able to sleep well," her mother cautioned. The little girl would not let up. She didn't care, she told her mother. She wanted pizza. With an admonition, her mother relented. "You can have the pizza," she told her daughter, "but I want you to pay attention if you get sick. Then you'll know why."

The next day the child was sick, cranky, and stuffed up. She understood that dairy foods made her sick, and she was then able to resist it even when she was with friends who were drinking milk or eating ice cream or pizza.

THE NEXT STEP: IMPROVED DIGESTION

Chewing Better

You can begin to improve your digestion simply by chewing your food more thoroughly, especially starches and sugars. While protein digestion begins in the stomach, the first stage of digestion for starches and sugars occurs in your mouth. For this reason, it's even more important to chew oatmeal or an apple completely than it is a piece of chicken.

Vegetables and beans contain starches and need to be chewed thoroughly. To be on the safe side, chew all of your food well, and eat slowly. It takes only fifteen to twenty minutes to eat a small, leisurely meal. You deserve to take this time for yourself, especially since it can help you feel better and enjoy life more. Tension reduces the production of gastric juices that help you digest your food. As difficult as it may be at first, relax while you eat.

Teach your children to chew well, and explain to them why they should chew even soft foods like mashed potatoes and applesauce. If any of you has had intestinal gas or stomachaches, see if the problem is eliminated when you eat more slowly and chew foods, especially starches, more thoroughly.

Drinking Less with Meals

Reduce the amounts of liquids you drink during and right after meals to four to six ounces. Some people dilute the digestive juices in their stomach with very large quantities of water or other beverages. One reason you may be thirsty whenever you eat comes from not drinking enough water during the day. Try to sip water in between meals, and have some water before you eat if you're thirsty, rather than drinking it with your food.

Cola drinks, high in phosphoric acid, can signal your stomach to produce less gastric acid, so avoid drinking colas with meals. You can reduce the amount you drink with meals more easily when you eat moist foods like vegetables along with denser, drier foods. Chew well, and you may not even need to drink with meals.

Some children take a swallow of milk or juice with every mouthful rather than getting moisture from chewing their food. This is an easy habit to begin, and a difficult one to break. Start by suggesting that your child doesn't drink when eating vegetables, and then encourage her to drink less with other foods.

Taking Pancreatic Enzymes

An inflammation of tissues caused by partially digested proteins often shows itself as weight gain. In addition to helping digest proteins, pancreatic enzymes are also anti-inflammatory agents. As a result, some people find that when they take enzymes to eliminate digestive problems, such as gassiness and bloating, they also lose weight quickly. If you have food allergies or sensitivities, you may need to take pancreatic enzymes for three to six months, and possibly longer.

You may want to check with your doctor before taking pancreatic enzymes. They are normally very safe to take, but they can irritate your stomach if you have an ulcer or pre-ulcerous condition.

A complete program of enzyme therapy, containing pancreatic enzymes and other digestive substances designed to help eliminate inflammation caused by allergic reactions, is described in detail in the book *Brain Allergies*, by doctors Philpott and Kalita. Again, consult with your doctor before beginning this complex program, which must be individualized for each person. Never give digestive enzymes or hydrochloric acid to a child without first talking with a doctor. While adults, who may have had problems for many more years, can benefit from additional support, children's bodies often respond without enzyme therapy.

The enzymes I use in my practice contain 400 to 600 milligrams of pure pancreatin. I have my patients take one or two tablets or capsules after each meal for two or three months, and more, if their symptoms warrant it. They may also be taken either before or during a meal. You can find good quality enzymes in all health-food stores.

THE ROTATION-DIET SOLUTION

Although the type of rotation diet used by allergists is complex and requires planning and patience, some people find it to be the only answer to their food addictions, and well worth any difficulties. All foods belong to groups, called food families. On a rotation diet, foods that provoke symptoms are eliminated, and other foods are eaten only every three to four days. Foods that are in the same food family are eaten no more than every other day. When you separate all fruits, vegetables, animal protein, nuts, and grains into food families and rotate them, mealtimes can at first seem very complex.

An example of rotating fowl would be as follows: eggs, chicken, turkey, and Cornish game hen all belong to the same food family. If you are allergic or sensitive to eggs, you would omit them from your diet. You could then eat *either* chicken, turkey, or Cornish game hen *every other day*, but not repeat an individual food more than once every three to four days. On Monday of one week, you might have some chicken. Tuesday, you would have nothing from this food group. On Wednesday, you could have either turkey or Cornish game hen, but not chicken. Thursday, you would again eat nothing from this group. On Friday, you could have some chicken.

In some cases, a modified rotation diet is sufficient. This would mean eating as wide a variety of foods as possible to prevent further food sensitivities, rotating them often, while eliminating some or all of the foods that cause symptoms. Try to avoid having the same food more than every three to four days whenever possible. If this is not always possible, keep the portions small to avoid sensitizing your body to them.

If the only grain you eat in pasta, cereals, and bread and other baked goods is wheat, buy wheat-free crackers (for example, rice cakes or Ry-Krisp), corn pasta, rice, and wheat-free cereals. Discover and try new grains, like millet, which has a mild, nutty flavor; triticale; buckwheat (kasha), which is not a variety of wheat; amaranth; and quinoa. You may need to look for some of these in a health-food store.

A modified plan might be the best solution for a child, unless her symptoms are so severe that they warrant a more rigid, restrictive diet. If your child is on a rotation diet, eat along with her, at least for the meals she eats at home. Make a game of the way she's eating. Teach her the food groups as you learn them, and work together to find foods and combinations that taste good to her. Emphasize how well she will feel.

Refer to the Resources section for books that contain complete descriptions of elimination and rotation diets. Such books include lists of foods by food family, which will be useful to you if you are undertaking this program.

22

ALLEVIATING DEPRESSION: CORRECTING CHEMICAL IMBALANCES

Magnesium Deficiency and PMS: Why You Get Anxious and Depressed Every Month

As a child, I remember stealing coins from my parents to buy chocolate candy. Chocolate was always my favorite flavor for any sweets. I never understood why my brother would choose vanilla ice cream when chocolate was available. It didn't make sense at the time. As I matured, I experienced the classic PMS symptoms associated with a magnesium deficiency: irritability, mood swings, anxiety, and depression. I was told this was normal and something to accept. It was a small price to pay for "being a woman."

My mother, who has had arthritis and premenstrual anxiety much of her life, loved chocolate as much as I did, and she ate chocolate bars almost every night. We had friendly fights over small layered squares of chocolate truffles whenever my father brought home a box of candy for special occasions. Creamy chocolate candy was the ultimate affordable treat in our family.

According to Guy E. Abraham, M.D., who has been researching PMS for more than twenty years, premenstrual mood swings, depression, and anxiety can be corrected with a diet and nutritional supplementation higher in magnesium than in calcium. I have found this to be true for the hundreds of women I have counseled for PMS in my nutritional practice over the years. By eating magnesium-rich foods and cutting down on foods high in calcium, and by taking vitamins and minerals that contain more magnesium than calcium until this imbalance has been corrected, these women have eliminated both PMS and chocolate cravings from their lives. I did the same, after twenty-one years of PMS and a lifetime of secretly eating chocolate in my room.

When chocolate cravings disappear, it is easier to maintain your correct weight and be healthy. A high-fat diet is an illness-promoting diet. You can't expect to keep your weight and health under control as long as you're eating large amounts of fats and sugars, which chocolate contains. Furthermore, your PMS symptoms affect the quality of your life and your relationships long after your period is over. What's more, you may be passing this premenstrual syndrome on to your daughter by feeding her the same foods low in magnesium and high in calcium. Suggestions for this diet as well as magnesium supplementation are given in Chapter 20.

In addition to a possible magnesium deficiency, women with PMS-related depression and anxiety have been shown to be clinically or marginally low in vitamin B6. A number of nutritional supplements contain higher levels of both magnesium and B6, based on some scientific studies using the original formula, Optivite, developed by Dr. Abraham, president of Optimox, Inc. However, Optivite is the only supplement with this formulation that has been tested in double-blind studies. While other similar formulas may work well, studies indicate this one is well-absorbed and reduces numerous PMS symptoms including mood swings, anxiety and depression.

More on the Depression/ Magnesium Connection

A study on depression published in 1993 indicated an association between the hypothalamus in the brain, the pituitary gland, and the thyroid gland which all influence the levels of magnesium in our bloodstream and brain. Magnesium, these doctors said, may affect the regulation of our moods. Their study showed a link between the severity of depression and low levels of magnesium. Dr. Melvyn Werbach, in his excellent book *Healing With Food* (HarperCollins 1995), points out that low dietary magnesium is common in industrialized countries as well as in people who are under stress. Why is this? Because we eat fewer beans and less whole grains—foods which are high in magnesium. And to watch our weight we limit or omit nuts, also high in magnesium. In addition, the stress in our lives causes our bodies to require more magnesium. This mineral helps muscles relax, and when you're tense, your muscles are, too.

Eating disorders are common in people who are depressed. A candy bar, rich dessert, or too much food in general is not an unusual way of coping with feeling blue or having the blahs. The answer is not to restrict your foods so much as achieving the biochemical balance that will eliminate your desire for eating—and overeating—them.

Depression and other Nutritional Factors

Hank's therapist sent him to me for a nutritional evaluation. He had been depressed most of his life, and therapy wasn't giving him the results he sought. When he first walked into my office, Hank couldn't even smile. He was unable to laugh at himself or see the bright side of anything. While he was aware of problems with his work and in his personal life, his depression was so deep-seated and of such a long duration that I felt it was at least partially biochemical. He was a classic example of the importance of addressing both the mind and the body. Hank had been to numerous therapists but had never looked at any possible nutritional deficiencies or at the foods he ate.

When Hank first came to see me, he was around fifty years old. Since his depression had been present most of his life, it was not due to a mid-life crisis, although some emotional components were evident. In addition to his depression, Hank had high cholesterol and weighed more than he felt he should with his regular exercise regime. His diet contained plenty of fat-free foods, most of them highly-refined (and low in magnesium) and high in sugar. Because they were "safe" foods, and because they tasted good and he had few aspects of his life that gave him pleasure, Hank overate these foods. Instead of eating one or two fat-free cookies, he methodically finished the whole box. At the same time, he ate few vegetables, whole grains or beans.

I revised his diet to include plenty of these missing foods, and gave him several nutrients: chromium to reduce his sugar cravings; an amino acid; and the B6 needed to activate all amino acids. These changes were enough for Hank to notice a slight change in his life-long depression. Over a period of a few months he ate less food, but since his meals contained a lot of brown rice, corn tortillas, beans, split pea soup and pasta, it was both filling and high in nutrients. He lost some of his extra weight and kept climbing steadily out of his depression. We ran a SpectraCell blood test (see Resources) to see which nutrients were still low and boosted his diet with them. The results were dramatic. His life-long depression continued to lift.

The depression Hank is left with now seems to be mostly caused by the emotional blocks in his life. He's now working on them with a no-nonsense therapist and is determined to get past his depression and get on with his life. Most importantly, he walks with a spring in his step, looks better, smiles easily and is able to enjoy his life. He has also stopped overeating.

As Hank demonstrated so obviously, not everyone who is depressed has PMS-associated depression. For those who have, magnesium could be just one part of a more complex dietary and supplementation program that often reduces, and may even eliminate, their depression. But it is important for you to know that the pharmaceutical drugs doctors so often prescribe are not necessarily the only answer. There are often a number of nutritional factors that contribute to this widespread problem which I suggest you consider.

Please do not stop taking any medications you have been given on your own. This should only be done under the supervision of a physician who is familiar with them. One reason is that you may need drug therapy. Another reason is that some drugs should be tapered off gradually while others can be stopped all at once. A medical doctor can tell you when and how to safely reduce and eliminate your medications.

Numerous patients of mine have stopped taking medications after correcting their nutritional imbalances. Most of them began by overlapping their drug therapy with a nutritional program. Then their doctors advised them of the best way to discontinue their particular medications.

Depression and Specific Nutrient Therapy

Often, nutrient therapy for depression begins with adding specific amino acids to increase serotonin and norepinephrine, two brain chemicals called neurotransmitters which allow messages to be communicated from one cell to another. Various neurotransmitters signal different messages. Seratonin and norephinephrine have been found to be depleted in the brains of a great many depressed people. While a number of antidepressant drugs only increase one or the other, when vitamins, minerals and amino acids are given they stimulate the production of both brain chemicals.

L-tryptophan:
Available by Prescription

Serotonin is produced with the help of a particular amino acid, l-tryptophan (now available through your doctor by prescription only). For many years, l-tryptophan was available over-the-counter and used successfully, without side effects, for more than twenty years. After a contaminated batch caused several deaths and a nerve disease, eosinophilia myalgia, it was taken off the market. Now it is a prescription item.

While all proteins, animal and vegetable, are made from amino acids, tryptophan is the least abundant amino acid found in food. In other words, if you increase foods high in l-tryptophan you're going to have to eat a tremendous quantity of them in order to affect serotonin levels. Still, if you have no other option, these foods may help and are worth trying. For information on foods high in l-tryptophan, begin with soy products and turkey, and see Chapter 18 for a list of additional foods.

L-tyrosine

Norepinephrine is produced with the help of l-phenylalanine (a non-prescription amino acid). But before this amino acid can be converted into norepinephrine it turns into tyrosine. Some health practitioners use l-phenylalanine for depressed patients, others use tyrosine.

In Dr. Priscilla Slagle's book, *The Way Up From Down*, she suggests taking 500 to 3500 mg of l-tyrosine on awakening and the same amount mid-afternoon. In my practice I have used 1000 to 3500 mg on awakening and mid-morning on an empty stomach. In all cases, both Dr. Slagle and I recommend beginning with a lowered amount for one week and gradually increasing as necessary. Results may occur within a week or two, or could take several months before you notice a change.

You would be wise to consult with a doctor trained in amino acid therapy rather than use amino acids yourself. They can help you understand which of the various amino acids is likely to work best for you, and they are aware of the necessity for taking sufficient quantities of nutritional co-factors (B6 and magnesium, for instance), without which amino acids can't work. They can also help you get results using the small quantities of nutrients. When we design our own programs, we often take more supplements than we need out of feelings of desperation. If you are interested in amino acid therapy for depression, please discuss this with your physician. For help in locating physicians who use alternative therapies to pharmaceuticals, see the Resources section.

L-glutamine

Another amino acid, l-glutamine, was given to depressed people in a study published in 1976. The researchers indicated that 200 to 1,000 mg a day clearly elevated moods in the study participants. Glutamine is the most abundant amino acid in our brains. It has been used to reduce a person's need for alcohol and sugar—both causative factors in some people who are depressed. Although there are many foods which contain small amounts of l-glutamine, this amino acid is destroyed by heat. Raw meat, fish, and eggs are highest in glutamine but *should not* be eaten in the raw state.

How safe is l-glutamine? Patients who are given this amino acid after surgery may be given from 20,000 to 40,000 mg a day. It is available both in health food stores and in a product called Vivonex, made by Sandoz laboratories (4.9 grams in every 1,000 calories of Vivonex). The most common side effect from taking too much l-glutamine is diarrhea. If you already have loose stools, you will want to look for another solution. If you don't, talk with your doctor about using l-glutamine for depression, especially if you crave alcohol or sugar.

Other Necessary Supplementation

All of these amino acids require large quantities of magnesium and B6 in order to work. Since other B vitamins including folic acid (containing folate—from dark green leafy vegetables), riboflavin, thiamine and B12 may also be low if you are depressed, a multivitamin with 800 mcg of folic acid and 50 mg of the other B vitamins could be an important addition to your supplement plan. Keep your diet high in foods that contain these nutrients: Whole grains, beans, fresh vegetables and small amounts of protein. Magnesium, to help counteract depression, is often needed in doses higher than those found in the majority of multiminerals: from 400 to 600 mg, or to bowel tolerance, is frequently recommended. Magnesium is safe to take. When taken in excess, it simply causes loose stools.

Other nutrients which may be depleted in people with depression include calcium, potassium, iron, zinc, and essential fatty acids. When possible, a laboratory test to assess your vitamin and mineral levels, like that of SpectraCell (see Resources), could be invaluable. At the very least, you will want to take a good quality multi-vitamin/mineral and eat a diet that is nutrient-dense, not one filled with empty calories. This can be a challenge, since the foods many people turn to when they're depressed are low-nutrient foods.

Eating and Depression

Some people overeat when they're depressed. They choose foods that remind them of their childhood like ice cream, mashed potatoes, or pudding. Or they eat unconsciously to feel full, since depression causes an empty feeling. Another reason for overeating may be due to the foods and beverages they choose. Some substances actually contribute to depression. If they make up a substantial part of your diet, you could be eating, drinking, or smoking yourself into a depressed state.

Caffeine (including colas), sugar, alcohol, and smoking have all been shown in medical studies to contribute to depression. If you are depressed, begin by eliminating caffeine (or reduce your intake to one cup a day), stop eating refined sugar, and keep away from all alcohol—at least for two weeks. If you notice an improvement, keep these substances out of your diet for another month. One patient of mine, Peggy, stopped her nightly glass of wine and all refined sugar only to discover she was no longer depressed at all! Whether or not this change is sufficient for you remains to be seen. It's certainly worth trying, and unlike medications, any side effects are beneficial.

Whole grains and beans should be increased, since they're high in B6, a vitamin commonly low in people who are depressed. Remember that any tryptophan that's present in the foods you eat needs adequate B6 before it can be converted into serotonin.

Essential fatty acids are necessary to make hormone-like substances called prostaglandins. Low quantities of prostaglandin E1 are often found in people who are depressed. They are also found to be low in women with menstrual cramps. These essential fatty acids must be uncooked. They are particularly high in flax seeds, which you can find at most health food stores. You can grind them in an electric seed grinder and add to cereal or sprinkle on salads. I use 3 tablespoons of ground flax seed a day. If you prefer, you can use 1 to 3 tablespoons of flax seed oil which you can find in any health food store.

Begin to eat a more healthy diet with plenty of vegetables, whole grains, beans, and as much soy protein as you can easily eat (for natural tryptophan). If beans give you gas, try eating small amounts of them, chew them well, and take a digestive enzyme like Beano with your food. Beano is found in pharmacies, supermarkets, and health food stores.

Exercise and Depression

Just as positive thoughts are nutrition for your mind, exercise is nutrition for your body. Numerous medical studies have shown a connection between inactivity and depression. Exercise causes physiological changes, like the stimulation of endorphins in the brain which lift our moods. Interestingly, unlike preventing heart disease, which requires at least twenty minutes of aerobic exercise, there may be no difference in whether a person does aerobic or nonaerobic exercise to counteract depression. Both seem to work well. This means you can take a brisk walk, use an exercise machine, lift weights, play tennis, or engage in any other regular physical activity.

If you are depressed, begin to integrate an exercise program into your daily schedule. Start with a ten-minute walk every day, or ten minutes on an exercise bike if you have one. Or ten minutes of walking up and down your stairs or around your home. Try to exercise every day, and make sure you do some form of exercise five times a week. You can eventually increase the time from ten minutes to half an hour. Suggestions for books on walking programs are given in the Resources section.

It would be a mistake for you to take expensive nutritional supplements without regular exercise. In fact, your first step in alleviating depression should begin with changing your diet and exercising. Wait a few weeks to see how you feel, and if additional measures seem to be necessary, begin a supplementation program.

PART FIVE

Your New Program

Rose realized very suddenly that she was standing in front of the kitchen pantry, stuffing chocolate-chip cookies into her mouth so rapidly that her mouth was dry and it was difficult for her to swallow. "How long have I been here?" she wondered, looking at the empty cookie box in her hand.

As a child, she used to sneak into the pantry for a few cookies whenever she felt anxious. Hiding from her father, who disliked heavy women, and from her mother, who ate whenever she was upset even though she had been overweight for years, Rose would return to the pantry over and over for two or three cookies at a time.

The top of the cookie box lay at her feet. "Oh, God," she thought, "I've eaten the whole box." Shame and guilt flooded her, and she felt as though she were eleven years old again. Somehow, whenever she visited her mother, she was always eleven or twelve.

Like Rose, you have probably found yourself eating without thinking at times. You may have been surprised to find yourself in a supermarket or convenience store reaching for your "comfort" foods or foods you crave, when you had actually intended to be somewhere else. Many of the ways we use food have become habit, and we are not always conscious of our negative eating habits. If you have not been aware of your own patterns, chances are that your daughter is not aware of hers. You are helping her to look at her issues and face them simply by moving into a new awareness and beginning to make changes for yourself.

Whether your negative eating habits initially began for emotional or physical reasons, they have been repeated so often that they have become automatic and part of you. The first step to overcoming them is to develop awareness. The second step is to reprogram yourself to replace old habits with new ones. This last part of the book will give you further help with that crucial second step.

Chapter 23 discusses why foods are neither good nor bad, and why none of them need be thought of as forbidden. This chapter explains how you can improve a nutritionally deficient diet without eating perfectly and still get good results. It defines the healthful, low-calorie foods you can incorporate into your diet, and it explains why these are important for your physical and emotional health.

Chapter 24 shows you how to design an eating program for yourself and your family that includes these tasty, nutritious foods and is designed to eliminate your cravings and restore your nutritional balance. Because all of us constantly face occasions that are celebrated with food—for example, birthdays, anniversaries, and holidays—Chapter 25 gives you tips on how to survive these occasions and stay on your own eating program most of the time with as much comfort as possible.

If you are still struggling with eating disorders, you may need more support and encouragement in your life, and so may your children. Many of us have not felt enough love and support. Chapter 26 addresses the issue of support, beginning with yourself and including those friends and family members who are able to be supportive. Because some of the people close to you may be contributing to your problem, you may need to look outside your immediate circle to people who can relate to you through their own personal experience.

Overeaters Anonymous, other Twelve-Step programs (such as

Alcoholics Anonymous, Al-Anon, and Incest Survivors), and support groups that focus on eating disorders all provide a comfortable setting where you can be yourself. In any of these groups you will see that you are not the only person with an eating problem. Meetings provide an opportunity for you to make friends with people who have similar issues, who will not minimize your feelings, and who will listen to you. If you decide to go to some of these meetings, you might invite your child to accompany you for moral support if she is a teenager or older. Expose her to some of the techniques that she might find valuable for herself.

While this book is designed to help you become aware of your negative eating patterns and take some steps to change them, it is not a replacement for therapy. A trained therapist who understands eating disorders can guide you through deeper areas of your life more skillfully than any book can do. In Chapter 26, a therapist explains how you can find and choose a psychological counselor, and I will show you what to look for when selecting a nutritional counselor. With this information, you have the tools you need to provide you with a mind–body solution to your overeating.

23

GOOD FOODS, BAD FOODS

N o matter what you've been told, no matter what you have come to believe, there is no such thing as a "good" or "bad" food. All food is a combination of chemicals that either support or inhibit cellular growth and function. Some foods work *for* you, while others work *against* you. This depends on the particular food, on how much of it you eat, and on what your body needs and can handle at the time. Nuts may give one person indigestion and gas, while for another person these nuts provide the essential fatty acids needed to prevent menstrual cramping and to support their immune system.

You're doing yourself a disservice and making your progress more difficult when you think of either your behavior or your food as being either good or bad. If this is the way you think, you have accepted a number of myths about various foods. Your erroneous beliefs about food may be contributing to your unhappiness, not alleviating it. Undoubtedly, you are also passing these beliefs along to your children. By understanding this, you can begin to change your negative patterns surrounding the foods you choose to eat.

THE MYTH OF FORBIDDEN FOODS

Eating bread and spaghetti will *not* make you fat—if you don't slather them with butter, oil, or pesto. Potatoes, rice, and beans with no added fats are *not* fattening; they are filling foods that can help you lose weight and become healthier at the same time. Unfortunately, misinformation leads many people to place these foods on forbidden-food lists.

Many of the foods you think of as forbidden are actually good for you. Unnecessarily high amounts of dietary fats, *not* starches, contribute to weight gain and ill health. Many fats are hidden in such foods as whole-milk dairy products, nuts, egg yolks, chocolate, and avocados. A high-carbohydrate diet is not only the healthiest way to eat for most people, but it also promotes weight loss.

Diets high in fats have been associated with numerous diseases, including heart disease, colon and breast cancer, and diverticulitis. Even the usually conservative American Heart Association and American Cancer Society are now advocating diets high in starches (complex carbohydrates) and low in fats. And many cultures that have no dairy foods in their diets do perfectly well without them. In fact, people in such cultures tend to have stronger bones and a lower incidence of heart disease than do people in our culture.

Most of us need the vitamins, minerals, and fiber found in a diet high in complex carbohydrates (starchy vegetables, whole grains, beans, and fresh fruit) with a little protein. However, some people tend to emphasize protein over starches, thinking that protein is "good" and starches are "bad."

We become confused when we hear mixed messages about food at home and school. We are told that potatoes are good for us because they're high in vitamin C; at the same time, our friends or family tell us they're bad for us because they contribute to weight gain. Eggs are a perfect food, we learn in school, but newspaper articles say they contribute to high cholesterol and should be eaten only occasionally. Spaghetti is fattening; spaghetti is not fattening. Sugar is "natural," and everything natural is "good"; but excessive sugar can lead to fatigue, osteoporosis, and tooth decay. No wonder you're confused!

Eventually, we come to our own conclusions based on our education, our own experience, and the experience of our parents and friends— or we make decisions based on our frustration at thinking that everything we like is bad for us. When you understand why you believe what you do and why your information may be inaccurate, it will be easier for you to change your beliefs and eat differently.

For now, think of no food as being forbidden. You may choose to eat less of something or even to omit it from your diet because it gives you a reaction you don't want. But you have permission to eat whatever you want, anyway. Interestingly, many people find that when a food is not forbidden, they don't want it as much.

Many of our myths surrounding forbidden foods begin in childhood. Your children may already believe some of these myths. As you get more information, share it with them to make their journey easier, and build a new foundation together based on your new knowledge.

INNOCENT BEGINNINGS

Many myths about foods begin in school, and the sad truth is that we have been educated by vested interest groups. So have our parents. For decades, the educational materials on nutrition in our schools were provided by the dairy, beef, wheat, egg, and sugar councils. In 1956, when the United States Department of Agriculture (USDA) initiated the Basic Four food groups (meat, dairy, grains, vegetables, and fruit) in our school programs to help support the agriculture industry, we were told to emphasize eggs, beef, and dairy products.

We learned that sugar was a low-calorie food we needed for energy, and we were not told to put a limit on ice cream, candy, and other sweets. We were taught at an early age that we needed a high-fat, high-sugar, high-protein diet in order to be healthy; enriched, refined foods like white flour were said to contain all the vitamins and minerals we needed. School lunches that included hot dogs, cheeseburgers, enriched macaroni and cheese, pudding, ice cream, and potato chips (and in which catsup was later considered a vegetable) supported these teachings. Nothing could be further from the truth.

In 1977, the Senate Select Committee on Nutrition and Human Needs published a report known as the *McGovern Report,* which advised us to eat less fat, sugar, salt, and cholesterol and to increase our intake of complex carbohydrates like rice, pasta, potatoes, and yams. Farm groups let out an uproar at this suggestion, and some agricultural industries disputed the report so vehemently that the USDA and the Department of Health, Education, and Welfare (HEW) waited two years before making any comments. Although the USDA and HEW finally agreed with the report, their two years of studies resulted in no recommendations for dietary change.

Most schools still teach the Basic Four food groups and serve overly fatty foods high in salt and sugar. School lunches still contain more than the American Heart Association's suggested 15 percent of dietary fats, with whole milk, cheese, beef, fried foods, and ice cream often served in the same large proportions as before. Children are not taught or fed healthier alternatives.

Why are we still teaching old information? The reason is that special-interest groups providing information to the schools argue that there is not enough proof that the foods they produce and advertise are harmful. In other areas where health is a concern but there is no association with vested interest groups, no burden of proof is necessary. Irrefutable proof takes time and a great deal of research. But health research is funded by pharmaceutical companies to prove that drugs are useful for medical problems, not by agricultural groups to show whether their products do or do not promote some of these same problems.

When we learn in school that particular foods are good for us and then hear or read somewhere else that they're not, it's easy to throw up our hands and say, "Forget it. If any food was *really* bad, it wouldn't be sold. I'm going to eat whatever I think is best. There's no way I can know, anyway." But there *are* ways you can know, and your health and happiness may depend on how much you learn and put into effect.

As I've pointed out, many of us have come to believe that we should not eat some of the very foods that would contribute to our health, keep us satisfied, and allow us to achieve and maintain our proper weight. You can learn which foods are supportive and which are not. Whole foods packed with vitamins, minerals, and other nutrients will help build your body; large quantities of refined foods lacking these nutrients or foods high in fats, artificial preservatives, and chemicals can weaken your body and lead to imbalances— including eating disorders.

A few years ago the Center for Science in the Public Interest (see Resources section) came out with a new, improved food pyramid, their Healthy Eating Pyramid. It emphasizes whole grains and gives a pictorial view of the foods to eat anytime, sometimes, or seldom. Even they have no forbidden foods on it! This kind of information can make it easier for you and your family to begin changing your diet with awareness.

CONFUSING "GOOD" WITH "BAD" FOODS

Julie was obsessed with her weight. She believed that all starchy foods would make her fat, and that all proteins and vegetables would help her to become thin. But even though she had stopped eating potatoes, rice, beans, and pasta years ago, she was unable to lose weight. The food diary she brought to me explained why. Julie was confused about the various effects different foods had on her.

"Why are you eating so many spareribs, chicken wings, and cheeseburgers?" I asked her. "You seem to eat meat at least twice a day, sometimes more. Why don't you eat some potatoes, beans, and other starches? They're nutritious, filling, and much lower in fats."

Julie looked surprised. "I thought starchy foods would make me fat, and that all proteins would have the opposite effect," she said. "That's the only reason I eat so many of them. I don't like plain, water-packed tuna fish with nothing on it, so I eat the proteins I like. Do you mean they're one of the reasons I haven't been able to lose weight?"

I nodded. Spareribs and chicken wings are protein with a considerable amount of fat. And it was the high fat content of Julie's diet that kept her from losing the weight she wanted to lose. A good serving of spareribs has as much fat as three cups of ice cream, two medium pizzas, or *eight* cups of canned pork and beans! The chicken wings had only slightly less fat.

"Sometimes I go on a diet and eat only 'good' foods," Julie continued. "Then I watch what I eat very carefully. I eat foods like low-fat yogurt, salads, and cottage cheese. They're okay, aren't they?" she asked.

"Would it surprise you to know that an eight ounce container of low-fat yogurt has almost four times as much fat as a whole can of kidney beans, and twice as much as a cup of brown rice?"

Julie's mouth dropped open in amazement. "Really?"

"Really," I answered. "The scoop of 2-percent fat cottage cheese you put on your salad is even higher in fat than the yogurt. You could put a third of a can of kidney or garbanzo beans on your salad instead and give yourself more satisfying starches without compromising your weight at all. In fact, you might even *lose* a little.

"Both rice and spaghetti with tomato sauce are extremely low in fat, and potatoes have almost none at all. Don't think of these foods as forbidden any longer. Like many people, you've been misinformed. Whole grains can help you get rid of your PMS, and other starches will fill you up while they slim you down. It looks like it's time for the brown-rice-and-pasta approach," I told her, smiling.

Within a few weeks of reducing her fats and incorporating bread, rice, beans, and potatoes (without butter or margarine) back into her meals, Julie began to lose weight.

"I never would have believed it was possible!" she exclaimed enthusiastically after two months of starchy, low-fat meals. "I can fit into clothes I couldn't wear for years, and I'm never hungry! Who would have thought you can lose weight by eating spaghetti three times a week and popcorn almost every night?"

Like Julie, you can help yourself lose weight and be healthier by eating more whole foods like brown rice, whole-grain breads and cereals, and fresh fruits and vegetables. Read the labels of all foods you buy, and limit processed foods, which contain hidden fats. Some crackers are low in fats, others high. Choose low-fat foods whenever possible.

If you want even more information, you and your daughter can look up the fat and calorie content of each food you eat in a book such as *Nutrition Almanac* (see Resources section), a trade paperback book containing easy-to-read food-composition tables. Begin eating more of those foods higher in nutrients and lower in fats.

GROWING UP ON NUTRITIONALLY DEFICIENT MEALS

Every meal was like the next when Audrey was a child. There was never a balanced meal of meat, vegetables, and starches. She didn't know that other people ate any differently. Her mother did, but the foods she prepared for her three children were more a direct result of her husband's strong dislikes than of her own ignorance. After a day's work he would often get into the bathtub with a bag of potato chips and a cola drink. This was his dinner. He never wanted much else. Sometimes he would opt for a peanut-butter-and-jelly sandwich on white bread, the only bread he would eat, but rarely a complete meal. When he took the family out for dinner, they ate his favorite greasy foods, like fried chicken or grilled-cheese sandwiches.

Audrey's mother had grown up eating more balanced meals. At one time she had loved to cook, but no more. She was angry and frustrated that her husband did not appreciate her cooking and refused the foods she liked and knew were healthful. Shortly after her marriage she rebelled and stopped fixing proper meals.

She raised her three children on the foods her husband liked because she claimed he had destroyed her interest and enjoyment in good food. Audrey was the casualty of her mother's frustration. She grew up on a diet of hot dogs, peanut-butter-and-jelly sandwiches, macaroni and cheese, hamburgers, instant mashed potatoes from a box, Tater Tots, and an occasional pork chop. The only vegetables she knew were asparagus, artichokes, tomatoes smeared with mayonnaise, or romaine lettuce with oil and vinegar and crumbled blue cheese—vestiges from her mother's past.

Audrey didn't taste a baked potato or eat a carrot until she went off to college. There, she found that even overcooked vegetables tasted better to her than most of the foods she had grown up eating. While her classmates complained about the cafeteria's institutional food, Audrey actually *liked* it, since to her it was an improvement over the way she had eaten as a child. Because she had been raised on junk foods and a limited variety of healthful foods, Audrey believed her diet was acceptable and normal until she learned better in college.

While Audrey's story may be an extreme example, many children are raised without being taught what to eat. A woman who has grown up with an unhealthful childhood diet rationalizes that if a meal of french fries, a grilled-cheese sandwich, and a milk shake was not good for her, her mother would not have given it to her. Often, her mother did not know any better. We integrate these confusing messages into our lives, and negative eating patterns are often the result.

A generation of young women who have experienced this kind of diet so lacking in good nutrition is emerging, and they're having babies. Many of these new mothers have never been taught to eat healthful foods. Their own mothers didn't cook for a variety of reasons. Some did not know how, while others were too busy, too tired, or too preoccupied. Most were uneducated in the importance of balanced meals and believed they were doing no wrong. Today's young mothers often come from families where meals consisted of fast foods, TV dinners, and snacks. Unless they learn differently, this is what they will feed and teach their children.

It is time for you to become better educated for your own sake first, and then for the sake of your family. Of the many educational publications available, the very best I have seen is the *Nutrition Action Newsletter*, a monthly publication from the consumer-advocate group Center for Science in the Public Interest (CSPI). I strongly suggest that you subscribe to this publication, which is one of the best bargains around and will provide you with accurate, eye-opening information. You can incorporate the recipes into your family's diet, and your children can use the articles for school projects. The center also offers other helpful publications. The address for CSPI is listed in the Resources section at the end of this book.

A "BETTER THAN" APPROACH

Naomi used to crave ice cream every once in a while. It wasn't a daily occurrence, sometimes not even weekly. But when it happened, Naomi would sometimes get out of bed in the middle of the night and drive to an all-night market. To her, ice cream was "bad," and she felt guilty whenever she ate it. The more she believed she couldn't have ice cream, the more she wanted it.

One day she decided she'd had enough of her midnight runs to the market. She bought a pint of her favorite flavor just to keep around for the next time she wanted it. Weeks went by. Occasionally Naomi would open the freezer and look at the ice cream carton; just knowing it was there was enough for her. When she finally decided to eat some, she decided not to feel guilty. To her surprise, Naomi found she could be satisfied with eating a little ice cream whenever she wanted it, and that's not very often any more.

There are many people who are *not* like Naomi. They can't keep ice cream, candy, desserts, cheese, or other foods they need to avoid in the house. If they did, they know they would eat it all obsessively, whether they really wanted it or not. If you feel you would go out of control with foods you want to reduce, stay away from them for now, but realize this might change as you work through your physiological and emotional reasons for eating these foods. As you change, your obsession with them may disappear, and you may find yourself actually feeling comfortable around them and able to resist them effortlessly.

Not all foods may be good for us, but some are less harmful than others. Some can contribute to health and weight problems if you eat them in large quantities but they may be perfectly acceptable when you eat small amounts occasionally.

Because eggs have been implicated in heart disease, some people have eliminated them from their diets. While one egg yolk contains almost as much cholesterol as a cup of heavy whipping cream, eating one or two eggs occasionally may be acceptable. For most of us, eggs are fine in moderation.

Sugar is another example of a substance more acceptable in small rather than large amounts. It won't add to your health, and, in fact, it uses up some B vitamins during digestion. Not surprisingly, foods that contain sugar are often low in these B vitamins. In large quantities, its harm might be miniscule.

It could be better for you to share a dessert once in a while or eat a little bit of a "forbidden food" than to think about such foods obsessively, allowing these thoughts to rule your life, or to wait until the urge overtakes you and then overeat them. You may find that you can be satisfied with small amounts of such foods.

Even if you never have a perfect diet, any improvement is "better than" the way you used to eat. Make small improvements and integrate them into your life, as you are able.

Speak with your children about improving their diet rather than trying to make it perfect. Demonstrate a "better than" approach, and be their role model. Be easy on yourself, and encourage them to do the same. Remember, forget perfection. Aim for excellence.

BEST FOODS

I consider the best diet to be one that guards against the major diseases—heart disease, diabetes, arthritis, and cancer—and I call it an anti-illness diet. I spoke about this in more detail in my first book, *The Nutrition Detective*, now out of print. Other books on nutrition, listed in the Resources section, have similar information. This kind of a diet can also help you bring your body's biochemistry into balance and eliminate some of your physical cravings for certain foods. A healthful diet is low in proteins and fats, and high in beans and grains. It gives you the raw materials you need for energy that lasts throughout the day, instead of letting you down in the afternoon or leaving you exhausted at night.

In Chapter 24, you will find a specific eating plan for you and your family. For now, it is enough to look beyond the myths of forbidden food to see some of the more supportive ingredients for your dietary plan. To leave you feeling satisfied after you eat, help you reach and maintain your proper weight, and support your health, the best foods (in order of importance) are:

1. **Whole grains and beans.** Brown rice; whole-wheat bread, cereals, crackers, and pasta; oatmeal; corn muffins and corn tortillas; millet; buckwheat or kasha; rye crackers; garbanzo beans; kidney beans; split peas; lentils; pinto beans; lima beans; black beans; soybeans; and so on. Include whole-grain muffins, cereals, pancakes, cookies, and crackers in your diet; use brown rice or millet and whole-grain pasta as part of main meals.

2. **Vegetables.** These should be raw, steamed, or lightly sautéed in small amounts of olive oil. Try to eat two or more good portions of vegetables a day. When you aim for two, you will usually get at least one. All vegetables, including potatoes, yams, and sweet potatoes, are a healthy part of a good dietary plan.

3. **Protein.** Foods containing low-fat animal protein, such as fish, skinned chicken or turkey, and low-fat or nonfat milk or yogurt, are preferable to foods such as shellfish, bacon, corned beef, ham, luncheon meat, hot dogs, and cream cheese—which are too high in saturated fat, cholesterol, or sodium to be healthful.

   You can get some or all of your protein from vegetable sources whether you're a vegetarian or just wanting to cut down on animal protein for an overall healthier diet. By combining beans or tofu with whole grains, you can create a complete protein that is often more filling, and usually lower in fats, than meat, chicken, or fish. What's more, it's not necessary to combine these foods at the same meal, but just to eat them during the same day.

   By the way, most tofu is nearly 50 percent fat. You can find a 1 percent fat tofu in boxes in health food stores and some supermarkets. The brand is Mori-Nu. Tofu can be used to make cream pies, eggless egg salad, and other delicious foods you may want to integrate into your eating program.

   One serving of protein a day is sufficient for most people, even for many athletes, who get much of their energy and strength from complex carbohydrates like grains and beans.

4. **Fruit.** Fresh fruit has more vitamins and minerals than canned fruit, which has been cooked. Similarly, whole fruit has more

nutrients and less sugar than fruit juice. In large quantities, fruit and fruit juice can upset the body's response to sugar and can lead to blood-sugar abnormalities and sugar cravings. Keep the quantities you eat low.

5. **Nuts, seeds, oils, butter, and other fats.** For good digestion and weight control, keep the amount of fats in your diet low, but don't omit fats entirely. You need some vegetable oils for a number of important functions, including eliminating menstrual cramps and supporting your immune system. Have a variety of fats: saturated (animal fats, found in butter and even in lean meats, like white-meat chicken), monounsaturated (found in olive oil), and polyunsaturated (other vegetable oils, especially safflower oil, flax seed oil, and walnuts which contain essential fatty acids). Your body needs a balance of all three. It especially needs the essential fatty acids found in flax seeds and walnuts.

24

HOW TO DESIGN
YOUR OWN EATING PLAN

This chapter is not about dieting. Its purpose, instead, is to offer you ideas that you can use in designing an eating program for yourself and your children. It is not a rigid plan. The intention is for you to listen to your body and eat more of what it wants, and to take a "better than" approach to the way you eat. This is the way to create a positive eating pattern resulting in good health.

LISTENING TO YOUR BODY

When you learn to listen to your body and hear its messages, you will be better able to choose those foods that make you feel energetic, clearheaded, light, and satisfied. Your body may speak to you in a whisper or with a quiet voice. It rarely speaks loudly, and it almost never shouts. That is usually the demanding voice of food cravings. Listening to your body requires attentiveness and caring, and you may find its messages surprising at times.

Bonnie was not in the habit of eating foods her body particularly wanted. She just ate whatever tasted good—mostly hamburgers, french fries, pizza, and doughnuts. Her only vegetables were an occasional side of cole slaw or a couple of tomato slices on her burgers. She had recently begun to listen to her inner messages and follow them.

"I've been eating an awful lot of broccoli lately," she announced to me at one of her sessions.

"That sounds fine," I replied.

"You don't understand," Bonnie insisted. "I mean a *lot* of broccoli! I had broccoli yesterday for lunch and dinner, and then I found myself eating a huge plate of it this morning for breakfast. I've *never* eaten vegetables in the morning before. It tasted so good! My husband couldn't stop laughing at me—there I was, sitting at breakfast with a cup of coffee and a bowl of broccoli!

"He was pretty surprised last night when I reached for more vegetables instead of a second helping of fried chicken, but broccoli for breakfast was something else again. I didn't even realize what I was doing. It tastes so good to me right now that I don't want anything else. When I get home this evening I'm going to make more. I can't get enough!"

I told her not to be concerned. Broccoli was high in vitamins A and C, potassium, and calcium. I wasn't surprised that after years of a high-protein, high-fat diet, her body was asking for something green. "Just go with it," I advised.

Two weeks later I asked Bonnie, "How's the broccoli kid?"

"What do you mean?"

"A couple of weeks ago you were eating broccoli as if it were about to disappear forever. Are you still eating it for breakfast?"

"Heavens, no!" Bonnie laughed. "That was strange, wasn't it? My broccoli phase only lasted a few days more. Now I eat it once in a while, along with other vegetables, but not daily. I never realized how good some vegetables can taste! My meals are more balanced, and I don't even have to think about eating more healthful foods. I just ask my body what it wants, and it actually *tells* me!

"But every once in a while my husband and I catch ourselves chuckling over the picture of me sitting at breakfast with my bowl of broccoli. What an experience."

Be watchful, listen to your body, and eat the foods it asks for. If it asks for a food you know is not beneficial, mentally separate the ingredients of that food and ask which is wanted. Someone on a nonfat diet may hear a voice asking for french fries when her body lacks essential fatty acids—oils that contribute to a healthy immune system. She could eat a salad sprinkled with some walnuts, rather than potatoes deep-fried in grease, and no longer hear suggestions for eating fats.

Encourage your children to do the same, and talk with them about the foods their bodies tell them it wants. Help them differentiate between hearing a clear message and listening to a craving that may signal an imbalance.

LEARNING WHICH FOODS ARE "BETTER THAN"

I give my patients who know very little about food the information on the following page to help them separate some of the less beneficial foods with a "better than" approach.

Make a photocopy of this list, and underline all the foods in both columns that you have been eating. Next, underline any foods in the Preferred Foods column that you would be willing to eat. If you don't like something in that column, don't eat it. Choose others from that category instead.

Make a sample menu plan in your notebook, using as many foods from the Preferred Foods list as possible and as few of those in the Foods to Avoid column as you can. Following is the formula I give my patients for planning meals, along with some sample ideas. Change and modify them to suit your taste. Include ethnic foods you enjoy, keeping them low in fats and sugars. Substitute whole grains for refined bread, pasta, cookies, and cereal whenever possible.

Breakfast: Grains—whole-grain bread or cereal. Use fruit-juice-sweetened jam on the bread, and fresh fruit with low-fat milk on your cereal.

FOODS TO AVOID

Sweetners: white or brown sugar, honey, corn syrup, all artificial sweeteners

Carbohydrates: white flour, "enriched" flour (found in bread, baked goods, cereals, pasta, pizza, and most cookies)

Vegetables: canned, deep-fried, or frozen

Fruit: canned, sugared fruit juices, and fruit drinks

Protein: cured, processed, smoked (luncheon meats, bacon, ham, sausage, hot dogs, bologna, corned beef, pastrami, smoked meats and fish), shellfish (crab, shrimp, lobster, etc.)

Nuts and Seeds: peanuts, smoked, dry-roasted, salted nuts and seeds

Fats: margarine, fried foods, saturated oils (cottonseed, palm kernel), hard shortenings, chocolate

Beverages: coffee, black tea, all colas, diet soda, fruit drinks with sugar, alcohol

PREFERRED FOODS

Sweetners: small amounts of pure maple syrup, concentrated pure fruit juices and syrups, jams sweetened with fruit juice

Carbohydrates: whole grains: brown rice, whole wheat, corn, oatmeal, rye, buckwheat, amaranth, quinoa, barley, millet; potatoes, yams, and sweet potatoes, winter squash, all beans and lentils

Vegetables: all kinds, raw, steamed, or stir-fried

Fruit: any raw, stewed, baked; small amounts of dried fruit

Protein: tofu and other soy products, fresh fish, chicken, turkey, Cornish game hen, eggs, small amounts of low-fat dairy products; lamb, beef, and pork in small quantities

Nuts and Seeds: raw, unsalted nuts and seeds—especially walnuts, tahini (sesame-seed butter), ground flax seeds (add to cereal)

Fats: olive, safflower, corn, canola, sesame oils; small amounts of butter; avocado

Beverages: pure water, herb tea, fruit juices diluted with water or mineral water, flavored and plain mineral water, coffee substitutes (Pero, Caffree, Postum), small amounts of water-processed decaffeinated coffee and tea

Lunch: Protein and vegetables—chicken or tuna salad, chicken breast and leftover vegetables, vegetable salad with garbanzo or kidney beans, turkey sandwich with raw carrots.

Dinner: Carbohydrates and vegetables, with occasional small amounts of protein for accent—stir-fry vegetables and rice or noodles; pasta with tomato sauce and vegetables; brown rice-stuffed winter squash with a side of green vegetables, and salad; hearty vegetable soup with whole-grain bread.

Snacks: Fresh fruit, whole-grain crackers or pretzels, plain popcorn, rice cakes with fruit-juice-sweetened jam, fruit-juice-sweetened cookies or quick breads, herb tea.

A "BETTER THAN" APPROACH

Focus on each small improvement you make, just as you did in the Gold Star Exercise in Chapter 12. If you did not do this exercise before, you may want to do so now. Focus your attention on what you *are* doing rather than on what you have not yet accomplished. Every step forward is a step in the direction you have chosen to go. Each improvement counts and propels you forward. It doesn't matter how long it takes. This is a journey of improvement. Enjoy it, and be patient with yourself.

Pauline was having a difficult time staying away from potato chips. She picked at them between meals and in the evening, only to find herself going through several bags every week. If she knew why she ate them, perhaps she could eat something else that would be better for her and just as satisfying.

"What's my favorite taste? Crunchy!" Pauline answered my question without even thinking. "I go for the crunch before a salty or sweet taste." I suggested she mix slices of water chestnuts into her vegetables, and snack on thin carrot curls soaked in ice water until they nearly snapped at her touch instead of the potato chips. It was a much better solution, and it worked for her. With fat-free potato chips available in many markets, Pauline could simply have switched from one kind to another.

Pauline had struggled with food most of her life. She had slipped off various food programs for years. Failure was more familiar to her than success. After she ate foods she considered "bad" or "forbidden," she felt guilty and depressed. Discouraged with herself, she turned to food for comfort, and the cycle began again.

Her diet improved, but not overnight, as she had hoped. It took nearly a year before she was eating the way she wanted to the majority of the time. But instead of concentrating on how badly she ate when she slipped and punishing herself for each little transgression, she began to focus on her improvements, giving herself credit for any progress she made. One day she looked at how she was eating and realized that she ate well more often than not.

Watch your progress as you begin this journey, and encourage your children to take it with you. Many people find that the entire family begins to eat better when they do and when more nutritious foods are in the home. Be gentle with yourself, and be gentle with your family.

Taking Action

1. **"Better than" white rice:** Mix a little brown rice in with the white rice. It's not perfect, but it's "better than" white rice alone. Mix whole-wheat spaghetti with regular pasta to get a more palatable blend. Add a little brown rice, barley, or beans to homemade soups. Disguise grains and vegetables with a tasty tomato sauce (add pureed vegetables to pasta sauce, for example).

2. **Cook ahead and freeze it:** If you have a microwave oven, fix larger quantities of foods and store them in individual zip-lock bags. Cooked rice, beans, and pasta are only a few of the foods that keep well in the freezer and can be heated in minutes. This allows you to eat whole grains and other healthful foods even when your family doesn't, without extra preparation.

3. **Salad-in-waiting:** Have your children help you make a large salad at the beginning of the week and put it in a plastic bag. Then, when any of you wants a salad, you won't have to first begin washing and chopping vegetables, or face a head of limp lettuce. While a few nutrients will be lost, you will still be getting far more than you would if you weren't eating as many vegetables. Bags of washed and cut carrots, cauliflower, green beans, broccoli, and celery make nutritious snacks that you're more likely to eat if they're already prepared. You can also steam or stir-fry them for a quick meal to accompany leftover rice and pasta.

4. **A half-baked idea:** Partially bake potatoes, sweet potatoes, or winter squash, and store them in the refrigerator. When you are ready to eat them, put them in the microwave or oven for the remainder of the cooking time.

5. **Fill your freezer:** Stock up on the most healthful frozen entrées you can find at the market for quick meals when there is no other alternative. Read labels carefully. When sugars and fats are mentioned, it may mean that the food contains more of them than you want. Not all "health" foods are healthful, but many are.

25

HOW TO SURVIVE HOLIDAYS AND OTHER CELEBRATIONS

The meanings various celebrations have for us and the foods we eat on these occasions are most often passed down from mother to child. We learn how to celebrate at home. We get permission to eat whatever we want and as much as we want on special days from watching our mothers and families do the same when we are young. We may even learn to prepare these foods by helping our mothers cook them. The importance that different holidays and celebrations hold for us begins in childhood, and it is hard to break our patterns of how we celebrate them and what foods we eat on these occasions.

Thanksgiving at Rose's house always meant a typical dinner of turkey and stuffing, but first the family gathered in the living room to catch up on family gossip and eat cheese and crackers, chopped-liver pâté, and raw vegetables with a dip of sour cream and onion. The food was the same every year, and so was the way Rose's mother ate. It looked to everyone else as though her mother were eating normally, because the portions she served herself were small, but Rose knew differently. She had watched her mother prepare holiday meals before.

Rose's mother always made more stuffing than the turkey would hold and baked the extra portion in a large casserole. By the time she served it to the family, she had put the stuffing into a much smaller serving dish. She had eaten the rest while she prepared other foods. She trimmed the cheeses "so they would look better," she once told Rose, and invariably selected a small silver dish in which to serve the chopped liver so that there would be some left over. "It shouldn't go to waste," she would say, guiltily, if anyone saw her eating the cheese trimmings or the extra pâté.

As her daughters cleared the table, Rose's mother picked at their plates, finishing any morsels that remained. She cleaned the turkey bones like a giant bird devouring its prey, sucking them until they sat on her plate like the skeletal remains of a long-dead carcass.

Like her mother, Rose learned to eat less in front of other people. She ate normally at dinner, but when all the relatives had left and her parents and sisters had retired to their rooms, Rose tiptoed into the kitchen. Careful not to make any noise, she opened the refrigerator and put a large portion of stuffing and thick slices of turkey on a double layer of paper towels that she could easily throw away. She closed the refrigerator door without a sound and crept back to her room. She, too, had become a closet eater.

Every year, numerous holidays, birthdays, dinners with friends, and other special occasions interrupt our eating routines. Each one provides us with another temptation or excuse to eat more sugars, more fats, greater quantities of food, and often to drink more alcohol than usual. Because it's a special occasion, we give ourselves permission to overeat meals that "don't count," except to our bodies. Most likely, your children are learning to do the same.

Eating has become more than nourishment; it is a social event that requires participation. Food has long been a sign of welcome, handed down from generation to generation in all cultures. When special foods are offered, they bring with them a warmth that goes beyond the ordinary greeting. If you decline to eat these offerings, particularly on special occasions, you run the risk of insulting your host or hostess—especially when that person is your mother.

Social pressures encourage us to overeat and to eat foods we normally avoid. At birthday parties or other gatherings, we are often surrounded by people who want to feel comfortable as they eat or drink too much. It becomes more and more difficult for us to resist extra food and drink when friends and family tug at us to join them. Somehow, when we all overeat or eat poorly, it becomes acceptable.

Each celebration may be associated with its own food or foods, and we'd feel as though we were missing something if we didn't eat them—a special cake or pie, turkey, potato salad, or a particular drink. It doesn't feel like a birthday party without cake and ice cream. To many people, Thanksgiving is not the same without turkey, stuffing, and pumpkin pie. A Fourth of July picnic has to have hot dogs, potato salad, ice cream and beer. Even sports events are minor celebrations (whether your team wins or loses) where peanuts, hot dogs, and beer are the order of the day.

Memories of celebrations and the foods that accompanied them may be some of the happiest moments from our childhood. They may even be the only pleasant memories to come out of a painful past. But there are people who remember holidays as being anxious times, and a familiar tendency is to overeat to sedate the tension.

Many of us have carried this habit over into our present lives, turning to familiar foods when family tensions bring up old feelings. You may be a competent woman capable of running a complex business or be a "supermom," but when you go to your parents' home you are likely to become the same little girl who ran to the cookie jar and refrigerator when your feelings were hurt.

Every Christmas from the time Lola was eleven years old, she binged on chocolates and other holiday food. Afterward, she dieted. It all began when her mother started working outside the home and had less time to devote to the family. She had always been busy taking care of them and making special holiday meals, but when her job began she became more difficult to be around. Everything had to be perfect, especially on holidays, and she hurried around the house filling it with Christmas decorations, tempting odors, and tension.

It was the middle of the afternoon on Christmas Day, when Lola was fifteen. She was used to the way her mother acted on holidays, but this year things were much worse. She had overheard her stepfather and her mother arguing just before he went out of town. If he was gone for good, Lola's mother was thinking of moving the family again. Lola couldn't bear this. They were always moving. After staying in this town for three years, she had finally been able to make real friends. The thought of leaving them added to the holiday tension.

Upset, she reached into the large box of chocolates her aunt and uncle always sent the family and began eating. It wasn't enough. Neither were the two candy canes that followed. The knot in her stomach was still there, and Lola looked around for something else to eat that might take it away. Something sweet. She wandered into the kitchen and decided to make some Christmas bread. Mixing and kneading it always soothed her, and right now she needed comfort.

Lola began to eat some of the raw dough, careful to save enough for a whole loaf. As soon as she took it out of the oven she cut herself a small piece. By the time the family had gathered in the living room and Lola had arranged the Christmas bread on a plate, she had eaten half of it. Although she is now in her forties, Lola still reaches for chocolate or anything that resembles Christmas bread when she is anxious during the holidays.

How can you celebrate without overeating if you still have the same feelings at holidays that you had when you were young? How can you stop reacting by reaching for the foods that comforted you then? How can you enjoy parties and stay on your program, no matter what is being served? You can do these things by *planning ahead* and *being watchful*; by *making a decision* not *to feel guilty if you slip*; by *making gradual improvements*; and by *being yourself*, even if it means feeling a little uncomfortable at times.

GIVING UP GUILT

When you revert to old patterns of eating at holidays or other celebrations, be gentle with yourself. Notice what you are eating, and enjoy the tastes. Pay particular attention to how you feel afterward. Most important, don't waste your time feeling guilty.

Guilt is the beginning of a negative eating cycle that is often followed by deprivation and bingeing. It is an emotion that gives you nothing but unnecessary pain. Give up your guilt, and you are on your way to giving up the rest of the cycle. As long as you continue to beat yourself over the head for whatever you ate or drank, you are unable to make any progress. As difficult as it may be at first, simply make note of what you did and move on. Get back on your program as soon as you can, and be as loving as possible with yourself.

"My eating's been a little erratic," Julie explained to me, looking a bit embarrassed. "I had a birthday last week, and I ate *everything*!" By her expression I could see she was not talking about a solitary incident. "For how many days?" I asked. As I suspected, Julie had used her birthday as an excuse to celebrate nonstop for more than a week. Friends had taken her to lunch and dinner during the week preceding the event, and there had been two parties over the weekend.

Her food diary was filled with notations of fried appetizers, rich entrées, and desserts, and with more alcohol each day than she had recently been drinking in an entire week. Previously, her diary had shown a gradual change from large quantities of fatty and sweet foods to smaller portions and more balanced meals. Julie had slipped back into her old pattern of bingeing on foods that caused her indigestion, fatigue, and weight gain—her original reasons for having sought nutritional counseling.

"Did you enjoy yourself, at least?" I asked her.

"Not really. I felt guilty most of the time, and I was so stuffed I could hardly move. And you wouldn't believe the gas! It took almost two days before I felt back to normal, and by that time I was having another birthday meal with a friend. I had forgotten how bad I used to feel. Oh," she continued, "I've also been tired a lot. Once, I had to drag myself to a birthday dinner. And another thing I noticed that really surprised me was that some of the foods I've always thought of as my favorites didn't even taste that good! But I ate them anyway, because it was my birthday."

Julie's guilt detracted from her ability to learn a valuable lesson: the foods and quantities she used to eat had given her the very symptoms she had been working to eliminate. Those foods no longer even tasted as good to her as they had in the past. She wasn't hooked on them anymore; she had just used her birthday as an excuse to slide back into old habits.

It was more important for Julie to backslide into old habits and become more aware of her reactions to food than it was for her to eat perfectly. If her eating was now flawless, she would never know how bad her previous diet had made her feel. Whenever you have a temporary relapse, think of it as a test. Watch yourself closely, and learn everything you can so you don't have to keep repeating the lesson. Teach your children the valuable lesson of learning from their imperfections rather than adding to a problem with guilt. In this way, your temporary lapse becomes a real blessing.

TAKING ACTION

1. **Stop the guilt:** Celebrate without guilt, and enjoy whatever you eat. Life is too short, and guilt is too immobilizing, for you to waste your time feeling guilty. Learn from any mistakes you make so that you can choose differently in the future. Think about the choices you could have made and be as conscious as you can the next time.

2. **A little *anything* is fine:** Eat and drink small portions of whatever you want. Don't fill up on soup and salad if what you really want is spareribs. Eat until you are satisfied, not stuffed. Enjoy in small quantities the party foods you know you're going to eat today, and get back on your program tomorrow.

3. **How do you feel?** Watch for any reactions from the foods you eat that have given you problems in the past. When you eliminate these foods, you may also eliminate the discomfort they cause. If you feel uncomfortable, write your feelings down in your notebook. Read what you've written as a reminder to yourself before you leave for your next party.

KEEPING SPECIAL OCCASIONS SPECIAL

"If you didn't feel good eating as you did, and the food wasn't as wonderful as you remembered, why did you continue?" I asked Julie.

"Because it was my birthday, and birthdays are special!"

Our birthdays *are* special to many of us. So are Thanksgiving, Christmas and Hanukkah, New Year's Eve and New Year's Day, and the birthdays and anniversaries of loved ones. And let's not forget Mother's Day, Father's Day, Easter, Passover, and the Fourth of July. If you are looking for an excuse to overeat and you have a large enough group of family and friends, you may be able to justify overeating almost every week of the year! And if you use these times as excuses, you will be diluting the specialness of these occasions.

What's so special about eating birthday cake four times in a week when you recently ate wedding cake and anniversary cake? When you eat them only now and then, their taste becomes more distinct. We are more apt to associate them with a particular event, and they become more special when we eat them less frequently. Have a small piece of birthday cake *once*, on your birthday if possible, and pass on desserts at other birthday celebrations. Or share a portion with another conscious friend.

TAKING ACTION

1. **Have a singular celebration:** Celebrate an occasion with one special meal or party, not several. Whenever possible, celebrate on the day of the event. If you feel you have to eat certain foods that are not the best for you, eat small portions. Drink in moderation. A celebration loses some of its luster if it is marred by feelings of being stuffed, depressed, or tired and hung over the next day.

2. **Cut back on sugars and alcohol:** If you celebrate more than once for any occasion, skip any dessert or alcohol after the first time. Explain to the people with you that their company and the meal

you are sharing with them are celebration enough. The people around you make an occasion more special than any foods.

3. **Find other ways to celebrate:** Celebrate with special activities, not always with food. Focus on an evening of playing games, with a light buffet dinner, or go to a play or to the movies. Or center a celebration around being outdoors—for example, taking a long walk in the country, going to the zoo, or having a picnic where the emphasis can be on playing Frisbee or softball rather than simply on eating. You are probably not the only person who would appreciate diffusing the focus on food.

4. **Always make at least one healthy dish:** When you prepare a special meal at your home, serve some low-fat, healthy foods along with your usual dishes. Potato salad made with fat-free mayo and dijon mustard, or a vegetable slaw with raw grated carrots, beets, and cabbage are tasty additions. Crisp baked potato slices can substitute for french fries. The possibilities are endless. Make certain you always have available enough of the kinds of food *you* want to eat. Watch what your friends eat. Not all of them may want overly rich foods to choose from. Showing yourself that you care about yourself is giving yourself a special gift.

5. **Change family celebrations:** Ask your child what she would like to do to celebrate a special occasion. Center a party for her around an activity, and serve foods she and her friends will like without overdoing the sweets and fats. Begin to de-emphasize junk foods so that her experience will be different from yours.

THE BEST IS OFTEN "BETTER THAN"

When holidays and other celebrations bring up associations of particular foods or tempt you to binge, you have other options besides either eating everything or having nothing. These are times to take the "better than" approach. Just because you have always stuffed yourself at a particular holiday doesn't mean you must continue the tradition.

Ever since she was a little girl, Judy overate on her birthday. It was the one day she was allowed to eat as much as she wanted, and she did. Her mother fixed her favorite, fried chicken, and there were always grandma's brownies along with the traditional birthday cake and ice cream.

By the time dessert was served, Judy felt so stuffed she could hardly move, but she had a large slice of cake with extra ice cream. After all, it was her birthday. She tried not to think about how awful she felt and concentrated instead on how good the food tasted. She adjusted to feeling bloated and overfull, and as soon as a small amount of discomfort left she filled the space with brownies.

Now Judy eats differently, not only on her birthday but on the day *after* as well, and she feels much more comfortable. She has realized that her favorite food from those birthday celebrations was her grandma's brownies, so every year on her birthday she goes to the best bakery in town and buys the largest brownie she can find. It may not be on the sugar-free, weight-loss eating program she has designed for herself, but it's "better than" going wild and stuffing herself.

"Better Than" Tips

1. Eating a little of anything is "better than" eating a lot of it.

2. Going off your program for one meal is "better than" doing it for a whole day.

3. Celebrating for a whole day is "better than" overeating for a few days or a week.

4. Celebrating for two days is "better than" overeating for a week.

5. Feeling good about yourself while you celebrate, as well as afterward, is *much* "better than" feeling the guilt you used to feel.

TRANSFORMING YOUR LONELINESS

For some people celebrations are lonely occasions, times when they overeat to forget their loneliness. Such occasions give them an opportunity to immerse themselves in the tastes and sensations of foods they know are not their best choices. Guilt mixed with loneliness creates depression. If celebrations and holidays make you depressed and bring up feelings of loneliness for you, it's time to change your pattern and do something completely different.

When a friend, Valerie, lived in a city more than an hour's drive from me, she invited me to a party she was giving. I didn't know too many of the people there; those I did know were sequestered in small groups, talking about subjects about which I knew little. Each group I approached continued with its conversation. I listened closely, trying to find something to say, but there was no opportunity to join in. I felt very isolated.

Old feelings of loneliness and of feeling out of place in the midst of people came back to me, and there was a familiar hole in the pit of my stomach. Whenever I had felt this emptiness in the past, I had stuffed it with food. The loneliness left while I was eating, but it always returned as soon as I stopped. Instead of just feeling out of place and alone, I then felt lonely, depressed, and sick to my stomach.

I had planned to stay the night at Valerie's since it was a long drive home, but the longer I stayed, the more uncomfortable I felt. I debated between staying and leaving. Undecided, I looked for Valerie and saw that she was having a wonderful time. So wonderful, in fact, that dirty dishes were piling up everywhere, the ice in the ice bucket had turned to water, and the platters of food on the buffet table were looking a bit sparse.

Rather than tell her that a little cleanup and replenishing were in order, I dug in. For an hour or so I gathered up the dirty dishes, washed some silverware, and restocked the food platters. When I was nearly through, Valerie's husband, Jack, wandered into the kitchen. "Oh, you don't have to do that, love," he said. Ah, but I did. It was the only way I could stay and feel comfortable. My alternative was to sit in a corner feeling isolated and depressed and eat, and I didn't want to do that.

Instead, I pretended I was a caterer and that I enjoyed cleaning up. When I had finished, the party was still in full swing. Convinced it would be a long time before people would leave and I could get any sleep on the sofa bed in the living room, I gathered up my clothes, quietly and quickly said good-bye, and drove home, content in all my choices. I had looked at the situation and my options, and I'd made a choice to do something other than eat.

Feeling sorry for yourself or feeling isolated is not a good enough excuse to overeat when you've made a commitment to change old habits that work against you. One option is to feel whatever you feel—sad, lonely, angry—and recognize that you've felt this a lot in the past and have covered it up with food. Perhaps by staying with your uncomfortable feelings you will be able to look at other alternatives to overeating, such as going for a walk or leaving a celebration a little early.

TAKING ACTION

1. **Feel first, eat second:** When you want to eat out of loneliness, first feel your feelings. Don't rush to cover them up with food. When did they begin? Did you eat when you felt lonely and out of place as a child? Did you feel any better after you ate, any more a part of things, or did you still feel like an outsider? Write a few paragraphs about this in your notebook.

2. **What are your options?** Look for other solutions to loneliness besides food and overeating. Initiate a conversation by asking someone about himself or herself. When there is a lull in the conversation, ask another question. People love to talk about themselves. Look for something that needs to be done, and pitch in. Most people appreciate this kind of help, and it will give you something to do that might even make you feel more at ease.

3. **Scram!** If there are no other alternatives, leave as soon as you comfortably can. Just knowing that you won't be staying for a

long time can make the remaining time more bearable. If you're leaving soon, you don't have to cover up your discomfort with food.

4. **Pass on these tips.** Teach your children these options, and let them know that you feel uncomfortable in some situations. Often, we believe we are unique in feeling out of place or lonely at social functions. Children, especially, feel they are unique in their feelings of isolation.

BE YOURSELF

Eleanor had been invited to attend a large dinner party for several hundred people at a fancy hotel. She was seated at a table for twelve, and the meal was beautifully served by a staff of highly professional waiters. Eleanor accepted the roasted potatoes and broccoli, but when the waiter came around with the roast beef, she knew it could be an awkward moment. She hadn't eaten red meat in nearly twenty years, and she didn't intend to begin now.

"Would you like the end cut or the center cut, madam?" the waiter asked.

"I'll just have the parsley," she replied, trying to sound sophisticated. The waiter looked surprised. "I don't eat meat," Eleanor explained, not wanting to make a fuss.

"Would you like a fruit plate?" he offered, eager to please. Of course she would. A few minutes later he presented her with the most beautiful plate of tropical fruit she could imagine. Some of the other women at the table eyed her plate jealously.

"I should have ordered that," one commented. "The roast beef isn't that good." Eleanor passed strawberries and slices of kiwi to a few of the people at the table, and she thoroughly enjoyed her meal.

If you happen to eat differently from the people you're with, you may feel uncomfortable at first. You could use this as an opportunity to overeat and cover up your feelings of discomfort, or you could ask for what you want.

When you separate yourself by saying, "Oh, no, I don't eat meat. I'm a vegetarian" or "No, I can't have that—it's filled with chemicals!" you are creating a distance between you and others that causes everyone discomfort. Instead, simply ask for what you want or eat around the food you're avoiding. There's no need to create a scene or draw attention to yourself or your food choices. Simply explore the options and do the best you can.

TAKING ACTION

1. **Speak up:** Don't be reluctant to ask for what you want. You may be able to get it. Most hosts and restaurants want to be helpful and please you. They can't always read your mind or know your preferences unless you tell them. When it's appropriate, check ahead with friends or restaurants to be sure that there will be foods you can eat comfortably.

2. **Be unobtrusive:** There are a number of simple, quiet ways you can handle eating differently without having to draw a lot of attention to you or your food. If you are on a low-fat diet for your health or weight and everyone else is eating pasta with cream sauce, garlic bread slathered with butter, and rich desserts, just ask for marinara sauce for your pasta, and have extra salad.

   Don't make a fuss when you are handed a plate containing food you don't or can't eat. Simply say, "No, thanks, maybe I'll have some a little later," or pass the plate on to the next person without saying anything. You may find that no one even notices that you eat differently.

3. **Don't arrive hungry:** Eat a little bit before you go out. If you're on a restricted diet or don't want to overeat, eating before you go can take the edge off your hunger. Then you can choose small amounts of the foods you want or can have, even if there's not much to choose from. When you're hungry, you're more apt to eat everything in sight and pay for it the next day.

4. **Teach your child how to order in restaurants:** Take your child with you to restaurants on several occasions when you ask to have food prepared in a certain way, so she can see how easy it is to ask for what she needs. Share your initial feelings of discomfort with her, and tell her how they changed over time. Give her suggestions for handling similar situations.

26

SUPPORTING YOURSELF

I t's time to stop your denial, lay aside your blame and guilt, get the support you need, and learn new positive eating patterns. If your mother had taught you other responses, you may have used food differently, but she didn't. Caught in her own negative patterns, and possibly less aware during her entire life than you are now, she did the very best she could. She was unable to identify and solve either her own emotional problems or yours. She did not know that there may be physiological reasons for eating disorders. Neither did you.

Now that you have this awareness of the connection between mind and body, it's time to discard the old myths and misunderstandings. You can begin to stop using food as a form of punishment, and you can pass your new habits along to your children. You do not need to be punished; you need understanding and love. You've punished yourself enough throughout your life.

You need to replace your self-hatred with a loving understanding. The child inside you may have grown up in a dysfunctional family where she was unable to get all the love she needed. She was not always treated with understanding and respect. You are not alone, and your family was not unlike many others. Few of us have led storybook lives.

The child inside you was not emotionally damaged or physically hurt with food because she was bad. She was hurt because of her mother's ignorance or family cultural patterns. You can never undo the experiences of your childhood, but you *can* give yourself some of what you need now and get support from people around you.

Your mother may not have cooked complete meals for you when you were young or taught you how to cook, but the mother inside you can learn to prepare simple, healthy meals and care for you. There is a feeling of satisfaction that comes from giving to someone out of love. You can feel the pleasure of being both giver and receiver, a gift you can pass on to your own children, breaking the chain of eating disorders that has been in your family for generations. At the same time, you will be addressing both the physical and emotional reasons for your overeating.

As you reach outside yourself for additional help, encourage your children to do the same. It may be much easier for them to attend a support group if they are older, or to see a therapist with you than for her to do it on their own. Since many of your issues surrounding food are similar, you are all likely to benefit by doing some of this outreach together. Remember as you reach out for support the necessity of looking at both the emotional and physiological reasons for changing your negative eating patterns.

YOU ARE YOUR BEST FRIEND

The person in your life you think of as being your best friend is perceptive. She knows you aren't perfect, and she doesn't care. She stands by you when you are at your worst, offering comfort and understanding. She values you and loves you no matter what you do or say, even when she is upset or angry with you. She is not blind or stupid; her perceptions are not worthless or false. She looks inside you and sees what's there. If your best friend can see who you truly are and still accept you with unconditional love, why is it so difficult for you to do the same?

Look through the eyes of your best friend to see your lovable qualities. Recognize them, accept them as being part of you, and use them to move forward. The ability to love yourself and to take small steps to free yourself from your eating patterns is something you will teach your children. The way out of any problem is always the way through; there's no way around it.

TAKING ACTION

1. **Ask a friend:** Invite your best friend to tell you which qualities she values in you and why, so you can look at them and see what you have been overlooking. Write them down in your notebook and look at them one at a time. When was the last time you thought about your *positive* qualities? When have you shown these qualities to your friend? To someone else? When did you offer the gift of these qualities to yourself?

   Start consciously by giving the best of you to yourself. If your friend sees you as being generous because you give your time to other people, start giving time to yourself. If she sees you as being a caring person, give yourself some of this gentle caring. If she values your sense of humor, lighten up with yourself.

2. **Cook for a friend:** Make a dinner for yourself that you would usually only prepare for a very special friend. It can be simple or elaborate, but do everything you would ordinarily do for someone else. This could mean shopping for unusual spices to make a dish that requires a little more preparation than usual. It could also mean buying flowers for the table, lighting candles, and using good dishes, even for a take-out meal.

   As you prepare the meal or the setting, realize you are doing this for the most important person in your life—you. Be aware of how you feel inside as you accept this gift of love. If you feel uneasy, repeat this exercise once a week until you feel more comfortable.

3. **Plan ahead; cook ahead:** Take time to think about the foods you need to eat throughout the week to feel light, vital, and content. Cook one large dish each week, and freeze the extra portions for those times when you're too busy to cook. Do a little extra for yourself, just as you would for someone else you love.

   When you fix a meal for yourself, remind yourself that the meal is being made with love for your best friend. Allow yourself to feel the warmth and contentment that comes from being given this gift. Enjoy how it feels to make food for someone you love as an expression of your caring.

4. **Your child's special qualities:** Talk with your daughter about her most positive qualities and elaborate on each of them, giving her an example that she can use as a focal point for her own growth. You might begin by saying, "What I love about you is _____, like the time when . . ." Help her to see the best friend inside herself, who may have been buried under piles of self-doubt and criticism. Help her to gain the ability to love herself by letting her see herself more clearly through your love for her.

OTHER FRIENDS AND FAMILY

Your habits began in childhood as you observed or reacted to the people around you. Your friends have accepted your habits, and they may even share a few. If close friends or family members can give you any emotional support for your program of recovery from negative eating patterns, accept it as a miracle in your life. But, as I noted earlier in this book, don't *expect* them to be able to give it to you, and don't be disappointed if they can't.

Some of your eating habits are cultural patterns that have been in your family for centuries. Some of them involve eating foods that don't work for members of your family any more than they do for you—yet they're eaten over and over again. Biochemical deficiencies are often passed along from generation to generation. You have the ability to correct yours and by doing so, being a role model for others in your family who are ready and willing to look at themselves. But they are not the issue; you are.

This is *your* program, *your* journey, and you are becoming aware of it because you're ready. You can encourage your children to take this journey for themselves, but if they are not ready to take it now, let them be. Show them through your example what it is like to love yourself and take care of yourself. All you can ever do is offer your example and your support.

OVEREATERS ANONYMOUS AND OTHER SUPPORT PROGRAMS: THE FRIENDS YOU HAVEN'T MET YET

When you think that no one else can possibly understand what you've been through and how you feel, when you feel stuck, when you need someone who will take the time to talk with you at any time of the day or night, turn to people who are working with the same problem. You can find them in Overeaters Anonymous and a number of other Twelve-Step programs, all based on Alcoholics Anonymous. You can find them, too, in support groups for people with eating disorders and addictions in communities throughout the country.

Georgia was miserable. She had just passed the bar exam and joined a law firm, but instead of feeling wonderful she cried herself to sleep each night. After years of abandoning her exercise regime to study and overeating to calm her anxieties over school, she didn't even recognize her own body anymore. She had never been this heavy. Once a slender 130 pounds, she now weighed almost 200 pounds.

Each time she looked in the mirror she felt helpless and depressed. Every day she promised herself that she'd stay on her diet, and every day she failed. To add to her problems, Georgia was in a relationship that had become as full of anger and arguments as once it had been with love. She had a good job, but nothing else in her life was working, and she felt completely out of control around food. "I'll do anything," she vowed one morning. "Anything at all, as long as I can stop destroying myself."

Not knowing where to turn, Georgia opened the phone book and called Overeaters Anonymous. A shy person and a loner all her life, she had been trying to avoid OA. The last thing she wanted to do was talk about her problems in a roomful of strangers. But doing "anything" meant giving OA a try, and that night Georgia went to her first meeting.

She walked into the large room filled with women chatting with one another, and looked around. There was not one person in the room with whom she could identify. She was dressed in a business suit from her day in court, and her looks contrasted sharply with those of the women here, most of whom were wearing housedresses or work shirts and slacks. Georgia started to walk out, but then advised herself, "Don't jump to conclusions, counselor! Get more information—things aren't always what they seem."

No one greeted her or looked up as she took a seat at the back of the room and waited for the meeting to begin. When people new to the group were asked to stand up and introduce themselves, Georgia gathered her courage and said briefly that she was out of control and needed help. As the evening progressed, some of the women in the room complained that the program didn't seem to be working for them. They spoke about feeling deprived and about failing to stay on their diets. There were no words of encouragement, no solutions offered. It was one big gripe session. The women who came over to speak with Georgia sounded discouraged and defeated, and she left the meeting feeling let down. The next night she went to a different OA group.

Whereas the first group had been moderate in size, this one was huge, and Georgia was able to completely avoid participating. She hid at the back of the room once more and didn't speak to anyone. After the meeting, women banded together in clusters and talked. They seemed like friends and made no overtures for her to join them.

Georgia began to attend this group's meetings regularly. But each night, she left without having spoken and drove home feeling empty inside. "This isn't working," she said to herself as she left her tenth meeting. "But this time I can't give up. I'm going to go to a different group every night of the week if I have to until I find what I'm looking for."

It took several months to find a small, structured OA group of dedicated, supportive people with whom she could share her feelings and feel comfortable. Within this support group, she was able to begin working the Twelve Steps to recovery. The people in her support group were not on any specific nutritional program. In fact, Georgia was the only person who was addressing both the emotional and physiological aspects of her problem. The group accepted that Georgia was there just for emotional support—and gave it to her. After nearly a year in her group, Georgia is within five pounds of her normal weight. More important, she has friends who listen to her and offer encouragement. She refused to give up until she found a group that felt comfortable, and she worked the steps of the program.

There are a number of Twelve-Step programs within reach of almost everyone. They are all designed to help people with problems that arise out of addictions and dysfunctional families. You can begin by going to any one of them if you can't find an OA group near you. You may find that the first group you attend will meet your needs. If it doesn't, don't give up. Like Georgia, keep looking until you find the supportive group you need.

Twelve-Step programs include Adult Children of Alcoholics (ACA), which deals with issues of having grown up in any kind of dysfunctional family; Al-Anon, for family members of alcoholics; Codependents Anonymous (CoDA), for people whose lives have been seriously affected by being in dysfunctional relationships and for anyone who has been in relationships with compulsive or addictive people; and Incest Survivors Anonymous (ISA), where you will find a surprisingly large number of people with negative eating patterns. When you find a group to attend, remember that you may be one of the only participants looking at more than the emotional issues involved. That's fine. Work your physiological steps on your own—with the help of a nutritionist if you need one—and use the group for the emotional support for which it was designed.

If you can't find one of these groups, call Alcoholics Anonymous, which is listed in the phone book. Just get plugged into *any* Twelve-Step program. If you have issues concerning food, chances are that someone else there will have them, too. Members of one group are also often able to direct you to other meetings if you are looking for a different focus.

One of the precepts many people in OA believe is that you are powerless over food forever and cannot ever become a normal eater. Laura Eldridge and Tricia Hadden, who were involved in OA and other Twelve-Step programs for years, disagree. "When I tap the higher power, I am no longer powerless over food. I am responsible for what I eat," Laura explains. As for full recovery and considering oneself to be a normal eater, she has observed that "lots of normal eaters get cravings at times." For the strength to resist them, Laura returns to the teachings of OA and to her own experience of feeling better when she does not eat problem foods.

Laura and Tricia used to speak about permanent recovery through OA at many groups. They referred to its "bible," the *Big Book*, for support that this recovery is possible. Their talks were inspiring. Since a number of negative eating patterns are caused by physiological imbalances that can be restored, they recognized that full recovery *is* possible for many people. If you attend OA meetings and disagree with some of what you hear, use whatever works for you and let the rest go. Laura and Tricia have, as far as I have been able to discover, moved beyond their concept of permanent recovery groups into their own lives. They found a solution, worked it, passed it on to others, and began lives without a focus on food.

In addition to Twelve-Step programs, you may find eating-disorder support groups run by therapists where you can find people who will listen and help you see that you are not alone. Look in your newspaper or call a local therapist for information about support groups that might fit your needs. When you reach out and persist, you will find such a group. Remember that their focus may not include balancing the body with proper nutrients. You can always introduce them to the mind–body concept by sharing this book with them.

TAKING ACTION

1. **Find a *supportive* support group:** Look for a group that concentrates on recovery instead of dwelling on the negative. In some support groups, the participants talk about their struggles and what is working for them. In some others, unfortunately, the emphasis is on complaining. You want to walk away from a meeting feeling understood, inspired, and hopeful. If a group leaves you feeling depressed or discouraged after several meetings, find another group.

2. **Jump in and participate:** As hard as it might be at first, share as much as you can about yourself. Just as you identify with what other people say, others will identify with your problems and will be understanding. You cannot deal with a hidden problem; you cannot be supported if you retreat. Most people in Twelve-Step programs and other support groups are committed to helping not only themselves but others as well, out of gratitude for the support they've received. These groups work because people participate. Be one of the success stories by doing everything you can to help yourself and others.

    Not everyone in each group will reach out or support you. Some people are stuck. Whenever you can, show your caring to someone who looks isolated and shut down, and help them to lift themselves. That may be what they need to move into recovery. Give others the love and understanding you want.

3. **Work every step:** If you are in a Twelve-Step or other organized program, work each of the steps suggested by the group. They are designed to help you, just as they have helped others. Just being around supportive people is not enough. Awareness is not enough. If you are having difficulties, talk about them. As you realize you are not alone and your problem is not unique, you will be able to progress by taking action.

4. **The mind–body connection:** Don't forget to include balancing your body with the proper nutrients. This means eating a healthy diet based on plenty of whole grains, beans, and vegetables. It

often means adding nutritional supplements. A nutritionist or a doctor who uses nutrition in his or her practice can provide you with information on the nutrients you need. Remember that both your mind and your body's needs must be addressed before you can be forever free from your negative eating patterns.

FINDING A NUTRITIONIST

Some of your eating disorders may be caused by biochemical imbalances. In fact, it would be unusual if they did not exist. If after reading this book you feel you want professional support in this area, you may want to consult with a nutritionist. This person may be a medical doctor with a strong emphasis on nutrition, a credentialed nutritional counselor (M.S., Ph.D.), or a registered dietician (R.D.). It may take some searching to find the right person. Good nutritionists are hard to find, but are well worth the effort.

To locate a good nutritionist, ask for referrals from friends, from your medical doctor, or another health-care professional, such as a nurse practitioner or a psychotherapist.

Whom to Look For

A good nutritionist should be someone who:

1. Has thorough training in nutrition and experience working with people who have eating disorders, and whose primary practice is nutritional counseling.

2. Understands that everyone is biochemically individual, and has methods for determining your particular needs (taking a thorough health history, doing blood tests, and using other accepted means).

3. Will explain your nutritional imbalances to you in a way you can understand, and will teach you how to restore your body to balance using foods first and nutritional supplements second. This person should be able to back up any recommendations with references from scientific studies.

4. Takes your life-style and food preferences into consideration and uses your input in planning your nutritional program.

5. Listens to you and answers all your questions to your satisfaction.

Whom to Avoid

Avoid any nutritionist who:

1. Uses one program for everyone. We are all biochemically individual, and you want your particular needs evaluated and addressed.

2. Cannot answer any of your questions to your satisfaction or does not give you the time and support you need.

3. Says you have to have expensive tests before he or she can work with you.

4. Uses testing methods you do not understand or do not feel comfortable with, even after they are explained to you. Most nutritionally oriented doctors and well-trained nutritionists do not consider hair analysis, saliva analysis, or live-cell analysis to be reliable tests to show nutrient deficiencies.

5. Says you have to take vitamin or mineral supplements but does not explain why to your satisfaction. Blood tests, like those done by SpectraCell (see Resources) are one reliable method for determining the need for supplements.

6. Says you have to buy the foods or vitamins he or she sells.

FINDING A THERAPIST

You may want to work with a trained therapist even though you have the support of yourself and friends. Asking for additional support and professional guidance is a sign of strength, not weakness. You are not here to make your way through life alone, but to share and benefit from your interactions with others. The objective support and clinical expertise of a professional therapist experienced in eating disorders can be very valuable in helping you to work through your issues. Not everyone will choose to include individual or group therapy in her program. If you do, you may not know how to find a therapist.

Where to Look

Begin by asking for personal referrals from friends or from health-care professionals whom you trust. When asking for referrals, you don't have to talk in any detail about why you want a therapist; you can just say that you would like someone to talk to. If you cannot find a therapist through the people you know, call an agency such as the Family Services Association of America, listed in your phone book. They have a number of therapists from which you can choose.

Next, check with any hospitals that provide treatment for eating disorders. They will have a referral list of therapists who work in this area. You can also ask people in any Twelve-Step program you attend.

What Questions to Ask

In deciding whether a particular therapist will be right for you, it's important that you ask the following two questions:

1. **Do you have the experience to deal with my particular problem?** If at all possible, you want someone who has experience working with people who have eating disorders. If not, look for someone with experience with other compulsive behavior, such as substance abuse and other addictive behavior. A therapist who is familiar with eating disorders can usually help you to cut through the key issues surrounding your negative eating patterns more quickly than one who is not.

2. **What are your credentials?** Look for a licensed therapist. This category includes psychiatrists, psychologists, social workers, and marriage and family counselors. Some R.N.s, especially those working in eating-disorder clinics and hospitals, have also been trained to do therapy.

While not all licensed therapists are necessarily good, any more than are all doctors, dentists, or other professionals, their training provides them with skills that most untrained counselors lack. Furthermore, they are governed by the ethics of their profession.

If you have severe problems and believe you may need medication, a medical doctor must evaluate you, prescribe medication, and monitor your progress. You can work with a psychiatrist, or you can seek out a therapist who works closely with a medical doctor. Any good therapist will have a connection with a doctor who can medicate, so you don't necessarily need a psychiatrist. However, a psychiatrist specializes in psychological evaluation and treatment using medications and so may be your best choice. Orthomolecular psychiatrists are doctors who use nutrition in their practice.

Is It a Mesh or a Miss?

The way you work with a therapist is more important than any questions you might ask, and you will know after one or two sessions if this is the therapist for you—at least for now. Be willing to invest a little time and money in a few sessions.

Some therapists may be willing to give an initial free or low-fee visit, or talk with you for a short time on the phone so you can get a sense of them and their work. Some are not willing to do this. If necessary, shop around. Explore all referrals thoroughly, especially those given by people whose opinions you value. Don't base your decision on whether or not an initial visit is free. Ask questions, and pay attention to your feelings.

You need to feel safe with the therapist and secure in his or her knowledge. A good therapist knows how to listen, hears what you say, and knows how to answer any questions. You have a right to ask anything that's on your mind, and you should get straightforward answers to your questions.

"How long will my treatment last?" is a difficult question for any therapist to answer accurately, but a therapist should be able to give you some kind of an idea, no matter how rough. Some therapists do long-term work, while others do short-term crisis intervention; many fall in between. At the end of one or two sessions you should have a sense of whether or not you feel comfortable with the therapist professionally and personally.

Feeling Comfortable— but Not *Too* Comfortable

You need to feel safe all the time, but you don't need to feel comfortable in therapy all the time. In fact, you shouldn't. You have used or misused food to feel comfortable in the past, and as you change your habits and look at your issues you will feel discomfort at times. Your therapist can explain this discomfort and give you suggestions for experiencing or transforming it without resorting to food.

If you are in a supportive therapeutic situation that feels very good *all* of the time, you may not be making progress. Take a close look at what is going on to make sure you are using your valuable time well by discussing your progress with your therapist. You may want to take stock at intervals that you and your therapist agree upon.

If you don't feel good about the way your therapist handles any issue, bring this up with him or her. The way a therapist deals with an issue will help give you the information you need to make decisions. Don't just walk away from therapy or ignore your issues because you feel uncomfortable or dissatisfied. Confront the issues that arise. If you are uncomfortable at any time during your therapy, talk about it. There may be a number of reasons for your discomfort. A good therapist is always willing to explore them with you.

You may feel very uncomfortable confronting someone, especially an authority figure like a therapist, but you need to know that a good therapist feels comfortable being confronted. If yours gets repeatedly defensive or attacks you in any way, get a different therapist. Report any sexual advances immediately to the appropriate professional organization.

Therapy is not forever. It can help you to become more aware of your obstacles and of why they are in your life, and it can give you the tools you need to move on. The goal of a good therapist is to make himself or herself obsolete. You are responsible for your own life, and you are also responsible for guiding your daughter until she is able to take on the responsibility for hers.

The support you need is around and within you. Use all the resources available to you to leave your pain behind and move into your loving heart, creating health and happiness for yourself. Never give up until you get where you are going and have the support to stay there. Teach your children—first through your own example, and then with words—to do the same. As you take each step toward freedom from overeating, ask yourself if you're looking at both the emotional and physiological aspects. Always remember the mind–body connection and always work to balance each part of yourself. This is what will work to move you past your negative eating patterns permanently and allow you to get on with your life.

RESOURCES

The books, tapes, and nutritional supplements in this section are among the best of those currently available. Where there are no popular books on any topic, technical books and articles are cited. Those most highly recommended are indicated by an asterisk (*).

You should be able to locate high-quality nutritional supplements at your local health food stores and some pharmacies. If you cannot, the resources listed will ship good quality nutritional supplements to you quickly. Audiocassette tapes can be found in numerous book and record stores, or ordered from the addresses included here. When you are writing for catalogs or more information, be aware that a self-addressed, stamped envelope will get you the quickest reply.

AFFIRMATIONS (A), VISUALIZATION (V), MEDITATION (M):

Benson, Herbert, *The Relaxation Response*, New York: Avon, 1975. A pioneer book in relaxation and meditation. (M)

Frankhauser, Jerry, M.S.W., *The Power of Affirmations*, Farmingdale, N.Y.: Coleman Publishing, 1980. (A)

Gawain, Shakti, *Creative Visualization*, New York: New World Library, 1995. An excellent handbook on creating health through visualization. (V)*

Hart, William, *The Art of Living: Vipassana Meditation*, San Francisco: Harper & Row, 1987. Practical everyday applications of meditation with clear information and examples. (M)*

Hay, Louise L., *I Love My Body*, Santa Monica, Calif.: Hay House, 1985. A 30-day affirmation guide to a healthier body. (A) *

————, *Meditations to Heal Your Life*, Santa Monica, Calif.: Hay House, 1994. (A,M)*

Lazarus, Arnold, *In the Mind's Eye*, New York: Guilford Press, 1977 (V).

LeShan, Lawrence, Ph.D., *How to Meditate*, New York: Bantam Books, 1974. One of the best, most comprehensive books on a variety of simple meditation techniques. (M)*

Levine, Stephen, *A Gradual Awakening*, New York: Anchor Books, 1979. A simple, gentle meditation guide. (M)*

————, *Healing Into Life and Death*, New York: Anchor Press, 1987. How to heal yourself from emotional and sexual abuse and bring forgiveness into your life. Meditations for those in physical and emotional pain. (M)*

Naparstek, Belleruth, *Staying Well with Guided Imagery*, New York: Warner Books, 1994. (V)

Wilson, Paul, *The Calm Technique: Meditation Without Magic or Mysticism*, New York: Bantam Books, 1989. A slim but comprehensive guide to no-frills meditation. (M)

COOKBOOKS, GENERAL:

Beasley, Joseph D., M.D., and Susan Knightly, *Food for Recovery: The Complete Companion for Recovering from Alcoholism, Drug Addiction, and Eating Disorders*, New York: Crown, 1994.

Brody, Jane E., *Jane Brody's Good Food Book: Living the High Carbohydrate Way*, New York: Bantam Books, 1985. Half nutrition book, half cookbook, this single volume can provide you with months of low-fat, high carbohydrate meals.*

Casale, Anne, *Lean Italian Meatless Meals*, New York: Fawcett Columbine, 1995.

Diamond, Marilyn, *The American Vegetarian Cookbook from the Fit for Life Kitchen*, New York: Warner Books, 1990.*

Goldbeck, Nikki and David, *American Wholefoods Cuisine*, New York: Penguin Books, 1984. Information on whole foods plus recipes.*

Manners, Ruth Ann and William, *The Quick and Easy Vegetarian Cookbook*, M. Evans and Company, Inc., 1993.

Roth, Harriet, *Deliciously Simple: Quick-and-easy low-sodium, low-fat, low-cholesterol, low-sugar meals*, New York: New American Library, 1986.

Simmons, Marie, *The Light Touch Cookbook: All-time favorite recipes made healthful and delicious*, Vt.: Chapters Publishing, Ltd., 1992.

EXERCISE:

Bailey, Covert, *The New Fit or Fat?*, Boston: Houghton Mifflin, 1991.*

Fenton, Mark and Seth Bauer, *The 90-Day Fitness Walking Program*, New York: Perigee, The Berkley Publishing Group, 1995. By the editors of *Walking* magazine.

Iknoian, Therese, *Fitness Walking*, Human Kinetics Publishing, 1995. Takes you step-by-step to help you create a walking program tailored to your needs.*

EATING DISORDERS:

Bruch, Hilde, *Eating Disorders*, Basic Books, 1973. The first authoritative book on eating disorders.

Hollis, Judi, Ph.D., *Fat and Furious*, New York: Ballantine Books, 1994. More good information on the emotional side of overeating.*

Orbach, Susie, *Fat is a Feminist Issue*, New York: Berkley Publishing Group, 1979. How compulsive overeating is a woman's response to social pressures that begin in childhood and permeate our lives.

Tribole, Evelyn, M.S., R.D., and Elyse Resch, M.S., R.D., *Intuitive Eating: A Recovery Book for the Chronic Dieter*, New York: St. Martin's Press, 1995. Learning about hunger and how to trust your body's messages.*

NUTRITION, GENERAL:

Barnard, Neal, M.D., *Food for Life: How the new four food groups can save your life*, New York: Crown, 1993. How to concentrate on eating more whole grains, beans and vegetables.*

Goldbeck, Nikki and David, *The Goldbecks' Guide to Good Food*, New York: New American Library, 1987. A complete shopping guide to the best, most healthful foods available in supermarkets, natural food stores, and by mail.*

Kirschmann, John D., *Nutrition Almanac, Third Edition*, New York: McGraw-Hill, 1990. Good reference book with comprehensive food composition tables to show you how much fat, calcium, magnesium, etc. is in various foods.*

McDougall, John A., M.D., and Mary A. McDougall, *The McDougall Plan*, N.J.: New Century Publishers, 1983. How to gradually move into a more healthful diet and lifestyle. Contains some recipes as well. The information is better than the recipes are tasty.

Null, Gary, Ph.D., *Nutrition and the Mind*, Four Walls Eight Windows, 1995. Information on nutrient deficiencies as they apply to eating disorders, allergies, candida and more.*

Nutrition Action Healthletter. CSPI (Center for Science in the Public Interest), 1501 16th St., NW, Washington, D.C. 20036-1499. $19.95/year. A membership includes ten newsletters with recipes and interesting articles to educate you and your children, two posters, and a ten percent discount on all CSPI publications.*

Pennington, Jean A.T., *Food Values of Portions Commonly Used*, New York: Harper & Row, 1989. Contains amounts of specific amino acids, vitamins and minerals in commonly-eaten foods.

Pfeiffer, Carl C., *Mental and Elemental Nutrients*, New Canaan, Conn.: Keats Publishing, Inc., 1975.

Werbach, Melvyn, M.D., *Healing With Food*, New York: HarperCollins, 1995. Diets and nutrients for specific health problems from the leading authority on nutritional medicine.*

Williams, Roger J. and Dwight K. Kalita, eds., *A Physician's Handbook on Orthomolecular Medicine*, New York: Pergamon Press, Inc. 1977.

NUTRITION, SPECIFIC:

Allergies, Food—and the Rotation Diet Information

Appleton, Nancy, Ph.D., *Secrets of Natural Healing With Food*, Rudra Press, 1995. Understanding your body's biochemistry and the role of food allergies, as well as other health concerns.*

Coca, Arthur F., M.D., *The Pulse Test*, Secaucus, N.J.: Lyle Stuart, Inc., 1982. A simple technique for determining food allergies at home.*

Jones, Marjorie Hurt, *The Allergy Self-Help Cookbook*, Emmaus, Penn.: Rodale Press, 1984.

Mandell, Marshall, M.D. and Lynne Waller Scanlon, *Dr. Mandell's 5-Day Allergy Relief System*, New York: Pocket Books, 1979.

Nonken, Pamela P., and S. Rodger Hirsch, *The Allergy Cookbook and Food-Buying Guide*, New York: Warner Books, 1982.

Philpott, William H. and Dwight K. Kalita, *Brain Allergies: The Psycho-Nutrient Connection*, New Canaan, Conn.: Keats Publishing, Inc., 1980.*

Amino Acid Therapy

Blackburn, George, et al, editors, *Amino Acids: metabolism and medical applications*, John Wright, PSG, Inc.,1983. A highly technical book giving the biochemical reasons for using amino acids for various health problems including carbohydrate craving. For doctors and medically-minded patients.

Chaitow, Leon, N.D., D.O., *The Healing Power of Amino Acids*, Thorson's Publishing, 1989.

Erdmann, Robert, Ph.D., *The Amino Revolution*, New York: Fireside Books, Simon & Schuster, 1987. Includes information on amino acids and depression.

Kaye, Walter H., et al., "Bingeing Behavior and Plasma Amino Acids: A Possible Involvement of Brain Serotonin in Bulimia Nervosa," *Psychiatry Research*, 23:31–43.*

Slagle, Priscilla, M.D., *The Way Up From Down*, New York: St. Martin's Press, 1992. A thorough discussion of amino acids and depression from a medical doctor with years of experience.*

Candida

Connolly, Pat, *The Candida Albicans Yeast-Free Cookbook*, New Canaan, Conn.: Keats Publishing, Inc., 1985.

Crook, William G., M.D., *The Yeast Connection*, New York: Vintage Books, 1986. Everything you wanted to know about Candida, and maybe a lot more, from one of its pioneer doctors.

Trowbridge, John Parks, M.D., and Morton Walker, D.P.M., *The Yeast Syndrome*, New York: Bantam Books, 1986.*

Blood Sugar Imbalances

Anderson, R.A., et al., "Effects of supplemental chromium on patients with symptoms of reactive hypoglycemia," *Metabolism*, 36:351–355, April 1987.

Appleton, Nancy, Ph.D., *Lick The Sugar Habit*, Avery, 1996. How to free yourself from sugar.*

Bland, Jeffrey, Ph.D., *Your Health Under Siege: Using Nutrition to Fight Back*, Brattleboro, Vt.: Stephen Greene Press, 1981.*

Mertz, Walter, "Chromium and Its Relation to Carbohydrate Metabolism," *Medical Clinics of North America*, Vol. 60, No. 21.

Depression

Baumel, Syd, *Dealing with Depression Naturally*, Keats Publishing, 1995. A thorough compilation of drug-free treatments for a number of types of depression, including a chapter on amino acids.*

Breggin, Peter R., M.D., *Toxic Psychiatry*, St. Martin's Press, 1991. 400 plus pages of information about the harmful effects of drugs commonly prescribed by psychiatrists for anxiety and depression.

Caston, J. Christopher, M.D., "Clinical Applications of L-Tryptophan in the Treatment of Obesity and Depression," *Advances in Therapy*, Vol. 4, No. 2, March/April 1987.

Gold, Mark S., *The Good News About Depression*, New York: Bantam Books, 1995. Medical and nutritional information on solutions to depression.

Slagle, Priscilla, M.D., *The Way Up From Down*, New York: St. Martin's Press, Inc., 1992. A book on depression with information on amino acids and serotonin included.*

Magnesium, PMS, and Osteoporosis

Abraham, Guy E., M.D., "The Calcium Controversy," *Journal of Applied Nutrition*, Vol. 34, No. 2. Available at no charge from the author. P.O. Box 3378, Torrance, CA 90510-3378.*

————, "Nutrition and the Premenstrual Syndrome," *Journal of Applied Nutrition*, Sept. 1984.

————, "The Importance of Magnesium in the Management of Primary Postmenopausal Osteoporosis", *Journal of Nutritional Medicine*, 1991, Vol. 2, 165–178. *

Briscoe, Anne M., Ph.D., and Charles Ragan, M.D., "Effects of Magnesium on Calcium Metabolism in Man," *The American Journal of Clinical Nutrition*, Vol. 19, No. 5.

Facchinetti, F. et al, "Oral magnesium sucessfully relieves premenstrual mood changes," *Obstetrics and Gynecology*, 1991, Aug., 78 (2): 177–81.

Piecsse, John W., "Nutrition Factors in the Premenstrual Syndrome," *International Clinical Nutrition Review*, Vol. 4, No. 2.*

HEALTH CARE PRACTITIONERS, SUPPLEMENTS, AND LABORATORY TESTS

Health Care Practitioners

ACAM (The American College for the Advancement of Medicine) 1-800-532-3688. Call for information on receiving a free listing of medical doctors in your area who use alternative and complementary medicine in their practice. Some will undoubtedly be familiar with amino acid therapy as well as how to assess any of your nutritional deficiencies and how to treat them with nutritional supplements.

American Holistic Medical Association: An organization for medical doctors, osteopaths and naturopaths who use nutrition in their practice. 4101 Lake Boone Trail, Suite 201, Raleigh, NC 26707. (919) 787-5146.

EMDR (Eye Movement Desensitization and Reprocessing): a new non-invasive method of rapidly healing trauma or other emotional road-blocks. Used by psychotherapists and psychiatrists across the country. EMDR practitioners have been sent to earthquake areas and to Bosnia, to teach local people how to use this technique for those in dire need. For information on someone near you who uses EMDR, call (408) 372-3900.

MedSearch:You can now access more than 12,000 holistic health care practitioners across the country coded by city, state, zip code, name, or medical specialty using the Internet. For more information call (703) 471-4734, or E-mail: abrecher@arxc.com. The WebSite for the service is: http://arxc.com.

OHM (Society for Orthomolecular Health Medicine): the only medical group centered on nutrition, this small organization can give you names of doctors whose use of nutrition is central to their practice, many of whom use amino acid therapy. (415) 922-6462.
2698 Pacific Avenue, San Francisco, CA 94115.*

Well Mind Association: a lay organization for the greater Washington, D.C. area, that can supply you with a list of practitioners in that area of the country. (301) 949-8282. 11141 Georgia Avenue, #326, Wheaton, MD 20902.

Supplements

AMNI (Advanced Medical Nutrition, Inc.) 1-800-356-4791. This company has a free catalog on high-quality vitamins, minerals, amino acids and herbs. Some may be less expensive than those of similar quality available in health food stores. They are particularly useful if you want to shop by phone. An extremely ethical company.

Optimox, Inc. 1-800-223-1601. This company sells an excellent nutritional formula for PMS which is high in magnesium and B6 (Optivite), and one designed for postmenopausal women (Gynovite). Both were developed by Dr. Guy E. Abraham, an M.D. who has had extensive research done on his formulas through impartial doctors and medical schools. I have used Optivite for men with depression who were taking amino acid therapy, since they also need additional B6 and magnesium.

Laboratory Tests

ImmunoDiagnostic Laboratories 1-800-883-1113. This laboratory has one of the most accurate blood tests I've seen which shows the presence of *Candida albicans* antibodies in the bloodstream. Your doctor can call them for more information. When many other laboratory tests for *Candida* failed to show a suspected overgrowth, IDL found it in my patients. As with all tests, sometimes an overgrowth was not present.

SpectraCell Laboratories, Inc. 1-800-227-5227. This laboratory has patented vitamin blood tests designed to identify hidden nutrient deficiencies in your cells. They also have a blood test that assesses your cell's ability to resist damage from free radicals. Have your doctor or health care professional call for more information. One of their tests shows your body's ability to utilize fruit sugars as well as other sugars—an invaluable test for someone with low blood sugar or carbohydrate cravings.

SUPPORTING YOURSELF
Loving Yourself

Ball, Carolyn M., *Claiming Your Self-Esteem*, Berkeley, Calif.: Celestial Arts, 1990.

Ellsworth, Barry A., *Living in Love With Yourself*, Salt Lake City, Utah: Breakthrough Publishing, Inc. 1988.*

Huxley, Laura Archera, *You Are Not the Target*, Los Angeles: Jeremy P. Tarcher, Inc., 1986.

All Stephen Levine books (see Meditation books).*

Patent, Arnold, M., *You Can Have it All*, Beyond Words Publishing., 1995.

Pelletier, Dr. Kenneth R., *Sound Mind, Sound Body*, New York: Simon & Schuster, 1994. The importance of a positive outlook for good health and achieving your goals.*

Pollard, John K. III, *Self-Parenting*, Malibu, Calif.: Generic Human Studies Publishing, 1987. Learning to love, support, and nurture your "inner" child.*

St. James, Elaine, *Inner Simplicity: 100 Ways to Regain Peace and Nourish Your Soul*, New York: Hyperion, 1995.*

Sexual Abuse

Ainscough, Carolyn and Kay Toon, *Breaking Free: A self-help guide for adults who were sexually abused as children*, Fisher Books, 1993.

Bass, Ellen and Laura Davis, *The Courage to Heal: A guide for women survivors of child sexual abuse*, New York: HarperPerennial, 1994.*

Engel, Beverly, MFCC, *The Right to Innocense: Healing the trauma of childhood sexual abuse*, New York: Ivy Books, 1989. Includes choosing a therapist, finding support groups, and many additional resources.*

Twelve-Step Programs

Look in the telephone book for listings for Overeaters Anonymous, Adult Children of Alcoholics, Codependents Anonymous, and other Twelve-Step programs, or send a self-addressed, stamped envelope to Overeaters Anonymous, 4025 Spencer St., Suite 203, Torrance, CA 90503.*

L., Elisabeth, *Twelve Steps for Overeaters: An Interpretation of the Twelve Steps of Overeaters Anonymous*, San Francisco: Harper & Row Publishers, Inc., 1982.

McFarland, Barbara, and Tyeis Baker-Baumann, *Feeding the Empty Heart: Adult Children and Compulsive Eating*, San Francisco: Harper & Row Publishers, Inc., 1988. Information for adult children of alcoholics, as well as compulsive overeaters, with an emphasis on Twelve-Step Programs.*

Tapes: Catalogs available

Hay, Louise, Hay House, Inc., P.O. Box 6204, Carson, CA 90749-6204. 1-800-654-5126. Affirmations and visualizations by the author of *You Can Heal Your Life*.

Martin, Kathleen, Ph.D. Excellent tapes for self-esteem, weight control, and other areas (Less Stress, Body Image, Slimming Thoughts, etc.) from an exceptionally knowledgeable practitioner and teacher. Write or call for more information. (619) 751-8788. P.O. Box 1773, San Marcos, CA 92079. *

INDEX